I would like to thank Elizabeth Claman for editing this manuscript. I would also like to thank everyone who helped me along the way while I did research on Sir Francis Drake, excavated for the treasure, and battled with those who tried to impede my progress.

Drake's Plate of Brass

BEE IT KNOWNE VNTO ALL MEN BY THESE PRESENTS

JVNE.17.1579

BY THE GRACE OF GOD AND IN THE NAME OF HERR

MAJESTY QVEEN ELIZABETH OF ENGLAND AND HERR

SVCCESSORS FOREVER, I TAKE POSSESSION OF THIS

KINGDOME WHOSE KING AND PEOPLE FREELY RESIGNE

THEIR RIGHT AND TITLE IN THE WHOLE LAND VNTO HERR

MAIESTIEES KEEPEING. NOW NAMED BY ME AND TO BEE

KNOWNE VNTO ALL MEN AS NOVA ALBION

CG. FRANCIS DRAKE   (Hole for sixpence)

Table of Contents

List of Images

Prologue

I moved to San Francisco from New York when I was in my late-twenties and soon embarked on a new and very lucrative career as an Institutional Fixed Income Salesman. In my second year at Morgan Witter, I earned over $100,000, and was feeling pretty proud of myself. When it became clear I'd earn significantly more the following year, the Managing Partner of the office pulled me aside and said, "Now that you've got some money, don't put it up your nose, or blow it on a fancy car. Buy a house in Marin County."

In 1986, I did buy a house in Marin with a splendid view of the bay for $292,000. It was a one-story, four bedrooms at 35 Via Corona on Greenbrae Ridge, a graded stretch above Highway 101, not far from Sir Francis Drake Boulevard. The following year, I spent $25,000 putting in a large two-tiered deck, a hot tub, a barbecue pit and pathways filled with river-rock. It was a sight to behold! I got married three years later and my wife and I held many, "Bring Your Most Interesting Friend" parties that were attended by more than one-hundred people.

The house turned out to be one of the most amazing things that ever happened to me, the marriage, not so much. When it ended in a messy divorce, my ex got the house for a while, and I rented an apartment in San Francisco, taking full advantage of the club scene there, especially Club Galaxy and The Bottom Out, my two favorite nightspots. At both, I met a lot of interesting characters and some deliciously free-spirited women. But in the mid '90s I got my house back, and the friends I made along my street were happy that I returned.

One Saturday morning, I was chatting with my friend and neighbor Steven Stern. He lived just three houses away in his mother-in-law's house along with his wife and children. I mentioned how the water that always trickled out alongside my driveway developed an oily sheen, and jokingly added, "I'll bet when Sir Francis Drake was here one of his men died and they dumped them in a pit with an oil lamp that's starting to leak 400 years later."

Steve surprised me by saying, "Nope. But you're closer than you think. The treasure of Sir Francis Drake is buried along this ridge."

"Treasure?" I said, grinning. There are 7 billion people on this planet, and I imagine that every one of them would love to find a buried treasure. In a way that's what we stockbrokers feed on every day.

He explained how in the mid-1970s his mother-in-law Mary was visited repeatedly by a UC Berkeley professor, who told her that in 1936, <u>Drakes famous, "Plate of Brass was found right where her house was built in the mid-1950s.</u> The professor pestered Mary repeatedly, asking if he could go under the house with a metal detector to see what else he could find, but she wouldn't let him. "Grandma" Mary was one of the few original owners who still lived in the neighborhood.

Hearing this story piqued my curiosity, so I talked to other neighbors to see what they could tell me about Drake and the alleged treasure. The sum of their various stories made clear to me why Drake was such a big deal in Marin County, where so many places are named for him.

Over the course of the next year, I found myself thinking more and more about Drake and his treasure, until finally in the spring of 2000, through some unexpected twists and turns I became obsessed with it and with him to the point that I saw everything in my life related in some way to his. My initial research into the differences between the Julian and Gregorian calendar systems showed that there was some cosmic connection between our lives. When I pursued this theory and undertook the process of converting the calendars from one system to the other, there was mathematical evidence of a link between his death in 1596 and my birth in 1956.

For over 400 years, there has been speculation about the possible location of Drake's landing site and the contents of the greatest buried treasure of all time. What follows is an account of my twenty-two year quest to provide definitive answers to these questions and the extreme measures and measurements that were undertaken to prove that Sir Francis Drake landed along the San Quentin Peninsula of Marin County in 1579 and claimed the land he called Nova Albion, for Queen Elizabeth I of England.

CHAPTER 1

My Quest Begins

Once I moved back into my house on Via Corona, on a typical Saturday morning, I'd mow the lawn and do whatever gardening was needed to keep my property in top shape. My girlfriend Carol did the same thing on the inside of the house, recruiting her two daughters and my daughter Susan to help her with the work.

One Saturday in June 2000, there was a brief, heavy morning shower. As soon as it ended, I went outside, and was wheeling the lawnmower   from the garage to the backyard when I noticed a large, bright green rock I never saw before protruding from the ground. When I knelt to look at it more closely, I saw that there were arrowhead-like shapes cut out of it. I owned 35 Via Corona for fourteen years by this time and always thought Greenbrae Ridge would have been the perfect place for a Coast Miwok Indian village because its vantage point would have let them keep an eye on everything that happened on the bay, the marshland, and along the surrounding hillsides.

Later that day, after I finished gardening, I began to look around my backyard more closely to see if there were other signs that this might have been a Miwok site. I spotted several large triangular rocks that seemed to be pointing upward toward the water tank at the top of the hill, so I climbed over the fence that separated my yard from my neighbor Rod Cooper and walked about halfway up the hill. Standing on a rock above his yard, I turned and looked back down. I saw that the triangular stones in my yard and the one I was standing on formed a very tall, skinny triangle. I found it odd that I never noticed any of this before. I walked back down the hill, climbed over the fence, and began scouring the ground in search of anything else that struck me as a possible Miwok artifact. Before long, I turned up numerous small, flat triangular stones that might be arrowheads. I picked up several stones and took them inside to show Carol and the kids. We all felt sure they were proof that the Miwok lived here.

On Monday morning, full of excitement, I called Jim Dietz of the Miwok Museum in Novato to ask him to see what I found. I also called William Denton, a Registered Professional Archaeologist who lived in Mill Valley. They were both interested. Between the time I called them and when they came to my house the following weekend, I found over 250 more "arrowheads" on the surface of the ground, as well as two more large triangular rocks, I did not notice on Saturday. I also spotted some small old- looking metal pieces when I used a stick to loosen the dirt around the large triangular rocks.

On Saturday, June 24, Dietz, and Denton came to my house, and we were joined by my next-door neighbor, Rod, who was curious too. They took their time looking around my yard, but they told me emphatically that I did not discover a Miwok site. Denton said the metal pieces were probably just flashing, and the "arrowheads" resulted from natural fracturing. Dietz also said that nothing he saw revealed evidence of a Miwok village. But both said I'd done the right thing by contacting them.

Denton added, "Believe me. You don't want a Miwok site in your yard." He proceeded to tell me about the nightmare an unfortunate property owner in San Rafael experienced when a Miwok site was discovered in his yard. Archaeologists, local tribes, and the state and federal government wanted to take control of the site, essentially forcing the man off his property.

Somewhat disappointed after they left, I walked around my yard more, still feeling there was more to what I found than just "natural rock fracturing" and "old flashing." I paid particular attention to the three places in my yard where nothing would grow, thinking they could be significant. Then, I recalled the morning when David Stern told me about the Berkeley professor wanting to go under his mother-in-law's house because Sir Francis Drake's "Plate of Brass" was found there. I sat on top of one of the triangular rocks and gazed around my yard, wondering if Drake might have buried some of that treasure on my property.

Regardless of whether the Miwok lived on Greenbrae Ridge, I still believed that they had been here, maybe even with Sir Francis.

It was nearly dark outside when Carol called me in for dinner. I told her that before we sat down to eat, I wanted to see what I could find online about the Miwok, so I turned on my computer.

The first image I found was painted in 1816 by Ludvik Choris. It depicted two hunters standing side-by-side, one holding a bow, the other a stick that carried an animal they'd just killed. They were high up on a hillside; below them was a marshland adjacent to a large body of water. Behind them, in the distance, there were distinctive land formations that I recognized all too well. I shouted for Carol to come in and look. <u>The scene in the painting was the exact view from my backyard. I'd been looking at that scene every day for fourteen years, and there was no way I was mistaken!</u>

Instead of going out dancing or getting together with our friends as we usually did on Saturday nights; as soon as we finished eating, I sat back down at the computer and began reading articles and stories about Sir Francis Drake. As I did, I kept having the strangest sensation, as though this was not my first time learning the things I was reading about his challenging childhood, his brilliance as a navigator, his fearlessness in battle, his daring as a pirate, his successes as a leader of men, the rage he provoked his Spanish enemies, who called him El Draque, "the dragon," and about his fascination with ancient wisdom from various parts of the world. Some people praised him as an honorable man of deep faith; others berated him as a self-serving scoundrel. But everyone seemed to agree that he was a brilliant and powerful person.

One article talked about Drake's obsession with the number 72, which seemed yet another connection, as that was one of my lucky numbers, too. That gave me an exciting idea. Even though it was dark out, I grabbed a flashlight and a measuring tape and ran out to measure the distance between the points of the triangular rocks in my yard. They turned out to be precisely 72 inches apart! It was too dark to measure the distance to the one up the hill, but I knew it would be 72 feet without doing so. The hair on the back of my neck stood on end because, at that point, I knew I was onto something!

I took the next three days off work and spent them 24/7, learning everything I could about Sir Francis. I read excerpts from his own writings, compiled by his nephew in The World Encompassed, which chronicled his circumnavigation voyage (1577-1580). I read about the "Plate of Brass" that David Stern told me about. I read numerous theories about possible locations where Drake landed, where his treasure was buried, and articles that discussed the concept of "Six Houses on a Square," referring to the cabins drawn on an inset on something called the Hondius Broadside Map, created by a famous Dutch mapmaker.

I printed out an image of the Plate of Brass I found, then blew it up using a photocopier, and immediately ordered a copy of a magazine that contained a reproduction of the inset of the Hondius map, but when it arrived, I was unimpressed. The inset was nothing more than an ink drawing of a piece of land in the shape of a peninsula shaped like Florida with what appeared to be an island next to it. On the water in the middle, there was a tri-masted ship and the words " Portus Nova Albion," which was translated as "The New World." On the peninsula was the image of a man who looked like an Indian beside a smoking fireplace. Above the ship, on what would be the far side of the body of water, there were cabins with stick figures that could have been men or birds standing nearby. As recently as the 1970s, the inset of this map was a hot topic for treasure hunters hungry for Drake's treasure, but nobody ever figured out its secrets.

As I began putting all these bits of information together with what I found in my yard, I wondered if this might be my opportunity to strike it rich. After all, I had a distinct advantage over all those others who'd hunted for Drake's treasure in the past because nobody would bother me in my backyard nor question my right to the treasure if that's where it turned up. On Monday morning, I went to my job at Morgan Witter. I told my supervisor I needed to take an extended leave of absence. I could tell he thought it was for some kind of medical reason, and I didn't dissuade him from that misconception. It was better if no one knew the real reason except Carol. She was the only person I felt comfortable trusting with my grand scheme. She was as excited by the idea as I was.

It soon became apparent that I also needed to tell my neighbor Rod Cooper. Greenbrae Ridge was not divided into suburban lots in the sixteenth century. If the treasure was buried under my yard, there could also be treasure under his. At first, he was skeptical, but as I produced more evidence, he began to get excited, too. We drew up a "Treasure Sharing Agreement" and signed it. Under its terms, I would bear any costs associated with the search; if I found anything on his side of the fence, I would share it with him. However, if I only found treasure on my side, it would be all mine. He was still a bit dubious, but that was a good thing. He'd be less likely to try to take the lead and dig up anything on his own. I spray-painted the outline of the area where Rod agreed I could excavate if working on his side of the fence became necessary.

Among many things, I read that Drake was an

expert in geometry who calculated the best headings to overtake, and intercept ships he wanted to attack. The stones I found were triangular, so I did a quick refresher about the geometric principles of triangles. Then armed with my enlarged copy of the Hondius Map inset, I used colored markers to map my backyard, showing the property lines, decks, walkways, plantings, the places where nothing would grow and the positions of the triangular rocks. When I completed that step, I drew several isosceles triangles onto the map using various natural features as critical points. When I was finished, <u>the result showed a zone where enough points came together that there was a good chance the treasure might be buried there.</u> It crossed into Rod's yard, but within the part on my side were the three places where nothing would grow. One of them might be the spot.

It was now July 1, and I was ready to begin my search in earnest. My friend in San Francisco named Joshua Davis, was in excellent physical shape from rock climbing. I asked him if he and his rock-climbing buddies would like to come over on Saturday to help me dig for treasure. He thought it sounded like fun and agreed. Before they arrived, <u>I marked one of the places where nothing would grow with spray paint, so they'd know exactly where to dig</u>. Late Saturday morning, he and four other guys showed up, and we all went to work, but the ground turned out to be so hard that progress was slow. After eight hours, we'd only dug down two and a half feet and were exhausted. But they agreed to return on Sunday.

I softened the dirt overnight by letting a hose run on it, so our work on Sunday went faster. By mid-afternoon, the hole was about six feet deep. At that point, we were all tired and had blisters on our hands. When I asked Joshua and his friends when they'd be back, they said they were finished since we didn't find anything. But I was far from discouraged. I bandaged my blisters, put on a pair of work gloves, and continued digging. The hole was eight feet deep at sunset. The following day, the soil dried out, and I noticed that the color changed from a muddy brown to a very light yellow.

The hole I dug was cylindrical, and now that it was dry, I could see indentations in the walls that I wanted to examine more closely. When I climbed down to look, I saw they were shaped like bota bags. I read that Drake, and his men stole bota bags filled with gold dust from the Incas, which further excited my imagination.

As I continued working, it became clear I needed to dig in Rod's yard too. Since he often worked from home and I didn't want him peering over my shoulder, I waited until I knew he'd be gone the whole day. Finally, early one morning, I saw him leave, wearing a suit. As soon as he'd walked down the hill to the bus stop, I jumped into my car and drove to Big 4 Rentals in Corte Madera for a mini backhoe. I never operated one before, but they didn't ask about that at the rental counter and just said it would be delivered to my door. About an hour and a half later, it was sitting on the street in front of my house. The Big 4 driver who'd delivered it was gone, and it didn't come with an operator's manual. Still, I climbed aboard and spent the next 20 minutes figuring out how to maneuver it. Once I did, my first big challenge was driving it through the narrow space between my house and the fence to get it into my backyard. Luckily, I made it without damaging anything. Then, I maneuvered it up a slight incline to the area I wanted to excavate. Several hours of work didn't produce any treasure, so I decided to go ahead and dig in Rod's yard, feeling glad we'd signed that Agreement.

I cut the wire fence separating our yards and drove the backhoe to the edge of the spray-painted area. By sunset, I created a 20-foot-long trench within the marked area in Rod's yard. When I knocked off work, I left the mini backhoe facing downhill with the shovel positioned over the trench. mini backhoe facing downhill with the shovel over the trench. Fortunately, Rod arrived home after dark and had no idea I started excavating in his yard. I wasn't surprised to hear him pounding on my front door the following day. He told me that if I didn't stop digging, fill in the hole, repair the fence, and get "that damned machine" out of his yard, he'd take legal action against me. Since we'd signed the Agreement, we both knew he was only blowing hot air because he couldn't really sue me over something he'd agreed to in writing. I didn't find anything on his side of the fence, so it was no skin off my back to do as he asked. Then, I voided the Treasure Sharing Agreement, being reasonably sure there was nothing valuable in his yard yet still confident I'd find something of value.

I was curious about the composition of the massive heap of rocks generated by digging with the backhoe. To see if any were of value, I made a crude sluice box and placed it in the uppermost corner of my yard. Then, I power-washed the rocks in it, not realizing where the runoff would go. I'd been doing this for several days when the man from a house on the street below mine pounded loudly on my front door, hopping mad because the muddy runoff ended up in his swimming pool. He demanded that I pay for the cleanup and "stop whatever the hell" I was doing. I agreed to his demands, paid him what he asked, and there were no further problems.

After excavating two large areas and not finding anything significant, I kept going. I believed I created a reasonably accurate map. All I needed to do was patiently and methodically dig in each "treasure zone" section until I found something. The next place I chose was the second of the three places where nothing would grow. It was between my deck and the fence I shared with Rod. Its diameter was half the size of the prior excavation, and the clay was much softer, so I could return the backhoe for the time being and use a shovel to do the work. By the end of just one day working alone, I removed about four feet of clay. Since it was getting dark, I decided to call it a day. The next morning, when I approached the edge of the hole to start digging again, I couldn't believe my eyes. In the wall on one side, I saw the outline of a man's body with a spear running entirely through it. I ran back into the house and told Carol that there was something she needed to see. We stood there for a few minutes in total disbelief. At that point, I decided to take samples of the heavy gray clay from the hole and several other places around the yard. Then, as soon as I was finished, I pushed everything that came out of that hole back into it and filled it in. I surely didn't want anyone nosing around the dead guy down there.

I wanted to find out if the yellow-gold color I noted in the first hole might indicate the presence of gold, so I took samples from around the bota bag impressions. I had a sneaking suspicion that the fireplace could be a smelting furnace where Drake could have melted the gold and silver loot into an unrecognizable form. I found a company in Oakland called E & M Labs, Inc. that said they could analyze my samples, so I dropped them off on July 15 and then waited excitedly for the results.

While waiting for the results, I excavated the last of the three areas where nothing would grow. This spot was triangular. It wasn't long before I hit what appeared to be a piece of metal embedded in cement. There was no reason for cement or rebar to be in my yard. Stranger still, as I continued to dig, I realized it wasn't just one piece of cement, but a hollow cube made of cement open on two sides. At this point, I called Marin Municipal Water District to ask whether this could be an old storm drain. They sent a representative to my house to look around, and he told me that although there was a water line running through my yard, what I found was separate from anything they'd installed.

I felt sure this cement cube must somehow be related to the treasure, though I couldn't imagine how. Once I uncovered it completely, it looked like something the Romans would have constructed as part of an aqueduct. I wondered if it might be some elaborate portal to the treasure site, so I called the National Park Service before doing anything further. When the rangers came out to look, they told me they could do nothing about anything I found, even if it was related to Sir Francis Drake, because it was on private land. My boss called me about that time to say that my leave of absence lasted long enough, and I needed to return unless I could produce a doctor's statement. So, I reluctantly stopped my 24/7 investigation and began limiting my excavations to weekends and after office hours.

During the last days of July, my father came to visit me from Connecticut and was at my house when the results of the soil sample testing arrived in the mail. The timing couldn't have been better because part of the reason for his visit turned out to be "family concern" over my "crazy new obsession." Like me, he was amazed to see the high percentage of gold and silver in the samples, especially the ones taken from around the bota bag impressions. The percentage of gold was an exact match to what archaeologists found at another air-driven gold smelter used during the 1500s. <u>The report also showed that there were extremely high quantities of silver in the clay in my yard, with one sample assaying at 84.5% silver!</u>

My father, the doubter, thought we must be misreading the report or that there was some mistake, so he called E&M Labs. They verified that the information was both correct and accurate and told him that the samples from my yard contained 100 times more gold and silver than could typically be expected from soil in Marin County. By the end of his visit, my dad was still skeptical, but at least now he didn't think I was crazy. He gave me his blessing to continue digging.

Then, a new challenge emerged. At the start of the Labor Day weekend, I began feeling severely exhausted and dizzy. The afternoon heat made me feel so debilitated that I was forced to lay down. Despite the over-90° temperature readings, I couldn't stop shivering. By Monday, I was so nauseous I couldn't keep anything down. The worst part was not having a clue what was wrong with me. On Tuesday morning, I called in sick to work, and as soon as my doctor's office opened, Carol drove me to my Physician in San

Francisco. Dr. Goldman checked my vital signs, looked me over, checked my skin, palpated my glands, then handed me a cup and sent me to the bathroom for a urine specimen. The following week he called to inform me that it was Boron poisoning.

I didn't know about Boron, so I read everything I could find online. The most exciting detail was that Boron was essential in ancient metal smelting processes. This, plus the gold in the soil samples, gave me all the evidence I needed to confirm that I discovered Sir Francis Drake's primitive gold smelter in my backyard. Sick as I was, I felt elated that the man by the "smoking fireplace" on the Hondius' map inset was a credible clue about the location of Drake's treasure; I hoped it would prove the first of many.

The results of my medical research were not favorable. There was no "cure" for over-exposure to Boron; I could only avoid future exposure. Over time, my body would eventually reduce the Boron to a manageable level through urination, and the symptoms would gradually subside. Although I didn't feel strong enough to resume my excavations or even go to work, I did continue my online research. With proof of Drake's smelting operation, I contacted Edward Von der Porten, President of the Drake Navigator's Guild. He might be intrigued by my project and interested in exchanging ideas and strategies.

I knew that Navigators Guild met regularly to discuss the techniques used by Sir Francis Drake to pursue clues regarding the location where he perhaps landed and buried his treasure. At the time, I was ignorant of the conflicts between various groups or the lengths to which any of them went or would go to control Drake's legacy.

Mr. Rosenthal and I talked on the phone about my claims, so he agreed to see me, and we met at a San Francisco diner after I got off work one afternoon. I told him what I found and showed him some photos I'd taken. As I talked, I could see that he was becoming increasingly agitated. He spilled his water and was almost stammering as he told me that I should not tell anybody about what I discovered and should not continue my work because people would think I was crazy.

His reaction was so extreme that I couldn't figure out what to make of it for the life of me. Rather than motivating me to stop my research, it made me even more determined to continue. Clearly, the man knew things he wasn't revealing, and I was now determined to find out what they were. I researched him online and found that he held a well-publicized meeting in 1970 where he claimed to have new information about the origin of Drake's Plate of Brass. Nevertheless, his reaction to my revelations told me something was up. I decided my best bet was to maintain my focus and continue my excavations once I was well enough. I felt more confident than ever that whatever Mr. Rosenthal said, I would be a fool to stop my endeavor.

CHAPTER 2

The Peninsula and The Island

By mid-October, the symptoms of my Boron poisoning subsided enough for me to return to my job at Morgan Witter full-time and resume my excavation schedule. I spent most weekends digging from dawn to dusk and, during the week, left the office around 2:00 and drove straight home to dig until dark. Now, I faithfully wore gloves and a dust mask.

This time around, <u>I started digging small exploratory holes at random around the yard</u> in hopes of turning up something interesting. Every time I filled a bucket full of stones, I sprayed them off so the runoff would not end up in a neighbor's backyard.

Every night, when I finished, I'd bring the stones inside to look at them through a magnifying glass to match them with pictures of various precious gems "in the rough." Many seemed promising. Drake's treasure was often referred to as "The Emerald Treasure," and there were many green stones to examine every night.

Steve Stern's wife Sally, grew up on my street, and told me about "Drake's Rock." When she was in high school, this was a place where many of the local kids went to get stoned and drink beer. In the '70s there was a cement staircase that started in the backyard of 39 Via Corona that all the kids used to walk downhill to the small meadow next to the freeway where Drake's Rock was located. After hearing her story, I decided to check out the spot.

The old cement staircase was now gone and the only way to get there was to park in the "Park and Ride" lot where the on-ramp for US 101 intersected Sir Francis Drake Blvd. The next day after work, I parked there, then crossed several medians that divided the on and off ramps and then along the shoulder of the freeway for half a mile with cars whizzing by. Along the way, I noticed many large stones lodged on the hillside that must have come to rest when the area above was bulldozed before construction began in the 1950s. I was intrigued by one huge stone that looked like the head of a giant sea turtle. It reminded me of something I read about primitive peoples who believed the sea turtle was the "Mother of All Creatures".

I managed to reach the meadow Sally described without getting struck by a car during rush-hour traffic. Then, I walked over to the massive blue-green stone known as Drake's Rock, walked around it, and wondered how Drake moved it into the meadow where it was sitting for 400 years.

On the way back to my car, I stopped a couple of times to look at some of those enormous stones, noticing several that looked like other parts of a sea turtle. I also stopped to look closer at the turtle head I'd seen on my walk to the meadow. It was perched about six feet above the roadway, and I guessed it weighed close to 300 pounds. I stood and gazed up at it for a bit and knew I needed to bring it home because it seemed like an essential piece of the puzzle I was trying to solve.

The following Saturday morning, I drove over to Kerner Boulevard in San Rafael, where day laborers wait to be hired, and picked up a team to help me move the massive turtle head back to my house. This was the first of many stones I brought home to solve the riddles that Drake and the Miwok left. It didn't take long before my entire living room floor was covered with orderly columns of stones, with the largest of each shape placed at the top of the column, and the smaller stones placed in descending order. By doing this, I saw that nine distinctive stone shapes were too similar to have resulted from natural fracturing or coincidence. When I held each of the different shape stones in my hand, I soon realized that each stone was a tool with specific functions, such as hammering, sawing, chiseling, etc.

Even more surprising was that they formed a sea turtle when I took all nine shapes and positioned them correctly! Each turtle had a head, two large front flippers, two small back flippers, a tail, the top of the shell, and two pieces for the underside of the body. The turtle in its entirety must have been like today's Swiss Army knife for its stone-age fabricators. Because there were so many stones of each shape that ranged from very small to very large, I deduced that children were taught from the time they were young how to flint stones in these specific shapes to produce a complete set of tools. Logically, this makes a lot of sense. If a child or young adult separated from the rest of the tribe, they could make a new set of tools and, thus, have what they needed to survive.

Carol had an early commitment on a Sunday morning the weekend after Thanksgiving, so I went out dancing alone that Saturday night at Club Galaxy. After spending many of my Saturday nights there for the past ten years, I knew enough people that I never felt alone. I was dancing on the stage with at least twenty-five other people when I started a conversation with a woman named Nancy, from Oakland whose passion in life was dancing. She was a great, improvisational dancer with a zany sense of humor, and we spent the evening drinking, dancing, talking, and laughing a lot. I felt comfortable sharing my story about the search for Drake's treasure with her. She was intrigued and offered to help, so we exchanged phone numbers before leaving the club.

When she came over a few days later to check out what I was doing, she had some exciting ideas about the Hondius Map, suggesting that since all precious stones are crystals of one form or another, if I drew lines following crystal patterns to connect essential points on the map, I might find other clues to the treasure's location. I gave her an extra copy of the map. The next time we got together; she showed me what she meant. The lines she'd drawn revealed the image of <u>a diamond-like shape superimposed on the map's inset. I would soon learn that this is called a rhombic dodecahedron.</u>

Throughout the winter, I explored many of the hillsides visible from my backyard to see if they might provide clues that would help me decipher the Hondius Map's secrets. When it rained or was too cold outside, I spent the time at home in front of my computer or at the County Library researching.

Directly across the freeway in Larkspur Landing, there used to be an old rock quarry and a brick factory that later became the site of a large apartment complex. On a hillside above it, I found a long piece of rusted heavy gauge metal wire that looked old enough to have been used by Drake's men to haul the treasure over the hills, after it was unloaded, I decided to excavate there to see what else might turn up. I devised an elaborate plan to avoid detection, as I wanted to avoid being hassled by the authorities. One Friday night, under the cover of darkness with nothing more than the light from a full moon, I loaded my car with a hand truck and 20 large plastic storage containers. I drove to the parking near the excavation site. Then, I tied the containers to the hand truck and hauled everything uphill to where I planned to do the work. I hid everything to avoid being disturbed or stolen and then drove home. All I needed to do now was wait for an opportunity when I could dig without being caught.

A strong winter storm blew in two weeks later, and I implemented my plan. I headed to the site with a tarp to put over me and another one to sit on. I sat there digging for two days in the torrential rain and howling wind but found nothing interesting. I wasn't discouraged because if I was ever going to locate Drake's treasure, I was willing to explore every possibility and follow up on every hunch and potential clue. If it was easy, somebody would have already succeeded.

A month later, I was walking on the steep hillside between my house and US 101 when my eye was drawn to a large, odd-shaped white object on the ground. My heart began racing because I sensed it was worth adding to my collection. When I got close enough, I saw that it was made of some kind of stone, but it seemed too fragile to safely pick up and move. I quickly drove home, grabbed a piece of plywood, and headed back to the hillside. Then, I gently eased the object onto the board and brought it home. I saw its features more clearly after letting it dry out for a week. <u>Though broken, it was a powerful sculpture of a man's head wearing an earring and a headdress</u>, that looked like reproductions I'd seen in Mexico of stone carvings of Aztec warriors, except I was sure this was no cheap replica. But how in the world did it get here? Could Drake have brought it to Nova Albion from Mexico? After several days of research, I located a San Francisco art dealer specializing in South and Central American artifacts. The following Saturday morning, I put my prize in a box and drove to Union Square. Once again, my heart was racing as I entered the Mesoamerican Gallery. The owner politely asked if I needed any help.

I replied, "You tell me." I set the box on a table and lifted off the cover.

He looked at the sculpture inside, and his eyes grew large. He immediately identified it as part of a stone relief from an Aztec Temple that was built between 1500-1550. The material was alabaster, which only came from western Mexico.

That was just the encouragement I needed to continue my quest. I knew that the treasure was close to where I found the sculpture, and I was ready to do whatever was necessary, no matter how extreme, to locate and recover it!

By spring, I was optimistic that the black markings

on the Hondius map inset contained the code that would allow me to find where Drake hid the treasure. Jodocus Hondius did not accidentally allow arbitrary ink spots to mar such an important document. With the aid of a photocopier, I enlarged the inset multiple times. As I looked at the magnified version, I realized there was a pattern to those marks. I was already sure that the fireplace on the peninsula represented the ancient smelter I discovered.

Using that as my reference point, I planned to dig holes of the same size and shape and in the same position as the black marks on the map. But before starting, I needed to determine what scale Hondius used to create the inset before I could reproduce them correctly.

I went to the City of Larkspur Building Department. I was fortunate to find the original topographic map of my street before it was graded and leveled and the "plat" map showing where the houses were built. By placing an overlay of the plat map on top of the topographic map and comparing that to the measurements I made of the distances between the key features in my yard, I determined that one inch on the Hondius Map was equal to 33.33 feet. My calculations were correct because when I applied that scale to the rest of the features on the inset, I found that all the actual distances were divisible by the number 72. With this information, I could dig holes of the right shape and size to correspond to the black marks shown on the Hondius Map.

If seen from above, the maze of excavations would replicate the images on that part of the inset.

The next day, as I was standing in my backyard, looking up towards the water tank, the image of the "peninsula" on the inset flashed through my mind, prompting me to rush to my computer and try out a new online program called "Google Earth" to look at my property. As soon as I zoomed in on my house, I could see that my neighborhood was built on land that looked like the Peninsula on the map" This was the most important discovery about the Hondius Map in 425 years. Hondius drew the map "flat," so its images could not be easily identified unless one understood that a "flat" view simply used outlines to represent actual landforms. At that moment, I realized that the shape of "The Island" on his map was identical to the contour lines of the highest elevation shown on the topographic map I picked up from the City of Larkspur. The Peninsula and The Island on the Hondius map were views of Greenbrae Ridge from two different distances.

As employed in drawings and paintings, perspective is used to create the perception of distance. Although it was invented in the mid-fifteenth century, for the next 100 years or so, it was only used by artists willing to experiment with this "new" technique. All others rejected it as an irrelevant distraction. Hondius didn't use it in the renderings on his map. Now, having determined the scale of the inset and knowing that it was drawn "flat," I tried to match up other features on the map to their "flat" image. It turned out that the water on the map wasn't really water at all, it was the outline of the land known today as Larkspur Landing. Only the outline of the shape was of importance. This insight into using the map meant implementing my plan would take much more time.

A few days later, after the stock markets closed, I sat down with my Branch Manager, Ben Catalanatti, and told him about my project and what I discovered. Ben was a great guy and responded by saying, "If this could happen to anyone, it could happen to you. Take as much time as you need to pursue it but cover your accounts. You only need to come into the office half of the time." I practically skipped out to my car and grinned all the way home. Catalanatti gave me the green light to pick up my work pace.

While excavating numerous holes around my yard, according to the marks on the map, I noticed that the ground was made of distinctive layers of different colors. I referred to these as the green, red, and gold paths. My gut told me that if there was a treasure buried down below, it would be hidden in some sort of cavern, so I needed to dig down 6-8 feet and stamp my foot hard against the heavily clayed soil to see if I heard a "hollow sound," that might signal the presence of a cavern.

One of the articles I read about Drake during the rainy season was written by Harold Archibald, who lived less than a mile from my house in San Rafael. I called him and asked if he would meet me to discuss his article. He invited me to his house on a Saturday afternoon and showed me his garage filled with large pieces of wood and metal from excavations he'd done at Drake's Bay. During the 1970s, he'd been involved in the debate over Drake's landing site. He had yet to decide where the treasure was buried. However, he did find one of only three Spanish Real coins from the 1500s ever discovered in Marin County.

I told him what I was doing and invited him to visit my house. After he finished looking around, he told me another treasure attributed to Drake was discovered on an island in the Caribbean. Drake had buried an enormous pile of gold and silver and two "magical" stones deep inside a grotto on the Isla Cueva. At the bottom of that treasure, Drake placed a cannon barrel so that he would know that he recovered everything he had buried once the cannon barrel was exposed. Harold also warned me that booby traps were common practice among pirates hiding treasure.

One afternoon, not long after I learned this, I was excavating one of the black marks from the map when I found what appeared to be a cannon barrel! Luckily, I didn't damage or puncture it because I found a warning tag from PG& E on my front door the following day. What I thought could be a cannon barrel was the utility's main north/south gas pipeline, and the tag demanded that I stop digging in that area. A few days later, representatives from PG&E returned to verify that I stopped working near the pipeline and to replace some missing government-required pipeline identification markers. While we were talking, they told me that PG&E flew planes and helicopters over their pipelines daily to ensure that nothing was happening to them.

Several black marks on the Hondius Map inset corresponded to places beneath my two-level deck and hot tub. At first, I worried I'd need to destroy the whole thing to proceed with my search. But after some brainstorming, I saw that I could dig in the narrow space between the two decks. I started this new excavation exactly where the map indicated. As soon as I got a foot below the surface, the dirt was replaced by thousands of white stones. While removing the stones and placing them into five-gallon buckets, I heard voices that sounded like a conversation between a man and a woman. The man said, "All white stones are good." I shook my head and groaned aloud, wondering if this was some kind of auditory hallucination. The voice sounded perfectly conversational with no trace of a foreign accent. It was so odd that I didn't want to tell anyone about it, not even Carol. The layer of white stones was three feet deep, and they filled ten buckets, but after removal, there was only dirt below them.

Less than two weeks later, it happened again. I was digging at the other end of the narrow space between the upper and lower decks when I heard another conversation between a man and a woman. This time, I heard the man say, "Birds and bird heads are good." What could the correlation between the two comments be? If "all white stones are good" and "birds and bird heads are good," what good was I being pointed toward, and by whom? I had no idea, but I repeated those phrases like a mantra as I continued working.

Guided by the voices, I took special care to wash off the white stones and tried to figure out what might be "good" about them. In my garage, I smashed several buckets of white stones with a sledgehammer to see what, if anything, was inside them. When I finished, my garage floor was covered with broken stones. I knew that most gemstones would fluoresce when exposed to ultraviolet light, so I used lights for my old black-light posters to test them, and I was excited to see my garage floor twinkling with bright blue, red, white, and yellow specks. Unfortunately, everything that fluoresced was so small that there was no economic value. I swept everything up and put it back into the buckets. I never disposed of any rocks from my excavations and stored them in buckets in the garage. At this point, the garage was filling up with stacks of buckets, and Carol was starting to get a bit stressed by my mess.

As I continued digging every day, <u>my yard took on the appearance of a war zone where land mines left deep craters</u>. I was intrigued by the well-defined layers of different colored soil. <u>My next task was to find out from a geologist if those striations were a natural occurrence or might have something to do with the treasure.</u>

I was still in touch with a friend from college named Dr. Paul White, who was a Geologist living in San Diego. When I called him and told him what I had in mind, he said he was coming to the Bay Area on business and would be glad to look at what I was talking about. It was too late for him to see anything the night he arrived, so we sat around drinking beer, smoking weed, and rehashing old times. He told me that on two occasions after we'd graduated from Penn State, he'd been hired to investigate possible treasure sites in Mexico, so I knew he was the right guy to help me.

In the morning, we walked outside and climbed into some holes so he could look closely at the striations. His professional opinion was that they were not natural features but had been created. He warned me that treasure hunting was a dangerous business. He advised me to avoid filing any excavation plan with the City of Larkspur. Doing so would create a public record that anybody could use to monitor my progress. If I found anything valuable, filing a plan could result in criminals showing up to steal anything I found.

He also told me that my excavations needed to be deeper since, to the best of his knowledge, buried treasures were generally much deeper, more like 20 to

30 feet or more below the surface. He referred to Oak Island, where, for centuries, people attempted to dig up a buried treasure left by either Captain Kidd or Blackbeard with no success. He said there could be a cavern below my excavations. He warned me about booby traps and the danger of getting stuck below ground if a tunnel collapsed, adding, "There's a good reason that every movie about pirates and buried treasure contains a scene showing skeletons of men who died trying to get the treasure." I thanked him profusely for his help before he returned to San Diego that evening.

When children are involved in a divorce, the parents must talk occasionally to make various arrangements. This was true for me and my ex, Melanie. It was also true for Carol and her ex-husband. Occasionally, he would call her, and she'd always be upset at the end of those conversations. He was an extremely successful surgeon with much money and severe control issues. The Doctor constantly complained about paying "too much in child support" and wanting his daughters to spend more time living with him so he could pay less. At that time, my own arrangement with Melanie was stable. My daughter Susan spent every other weekend with me and got along well with Carol's girls.

Carol's dispute with the Doctor over visitation continued for such a long time that I grew exasperated with the tensions he was causing in my household. Finally, I called him and said we needed to talk face-to-face in his office. Several days later, when we met, I told him his threats about re-opening the custody case must stop because Carol agreed not to ask for additional money even though their daughter Nancy would now be with us full-time. He agreed to stop harassing Carol, so I thanked him and said, "If you do decide to pursue this matter further, you owe me the courtesy of a phone call beforehand." The Doctor agreed to honor my request.

After that, things settled down for a while. Carol was grateful that I stepped in, and so were her kids. Our day-to-day life together as a family ran very smoothly. Susan must have said something to Melanie about what I was doing in the backyard because one day, she told me, "Mommy thinks you're crazy."

I spoke to my father often, and during a conversation, he informed me that Melanie called him and my sister to tell them about my "crazy excavations." At that point, I called Melanie and clarified that nothing she or anyone else said could deter me from continuing my project.

At the start of the July 4 weekend, I was digging near the end of the lower deck when my shovel struck metal. This location was 36 feet downhill from the gold smelter I discovered a year earlier. I already knew that neither the Water District nor PG&E owned pipelines near this location, so <u>I wondered if this could be a cannon barrel. I proceeded to unearth it very carefully</u>. When I removed it from the ground and measured, it was 12 feet long.

To determine if this was a cannon barrel, I conducted my research in the stacks of UC Berkeley's Bancroft Library. There, I found a book that contained dimensions and sketches of cannons used during the 1500s. My find matched one of the examples in the book, and I wondered if Drake left the cannon barrel at the top of the treasure instead of beneath it.

If so, I needed to begin digging downward directly below it. I worked cautiously. When I dug down five or six feet, I suddenly saw <u>a multicolored image of a large parrot wearing a golden crown. in the tunnel wall.</u> I took a photograph and dug carefully around it, sensing it might be important, not wanting to damage it.

By now, between everything I'd seen and the reports from various experts, I had no doubt that Drake's treasure would soon be mine. But to continue digging in that tight space, I needed different tools, for starters, a mini jackhammer. I bought one, hoping my progress would be smoother, but I quickly realized I was facing new problems as my excavation deepened: the darkness, the lack of fresh air, and the high humidity. To continue, I needed lights, fans, and power cords long enough to extend from an outlet in my house down the tunnel to wherever I was working. I purchased several portable work lights and fans but kept getting shocks when crawling over places where two power cords connected when the connection was hidden by mud. To solve this problem, I placed thick black plastic sheeting on the tunnel's floor and ran the power cords underneath it. A ceiling collapse was a constant danger because I would be trapped below ground with no fresh air. For safety's sake, I learned to control my breathing and heart rate to decrease water produced through respiration and sweating.

I continued digging and believed everything was in place for a real breakthrough.

CHAPTER 3

Slave-Trader, Privateer, and Marauder

Before continuing with my own adventure, I need to share some of what I was learning about Drake. From the start, as I read about his life, I often felt that I was inside some elaborate video simulation with the events unfolding around me, as though I'd been present, a participant, in some of his life's most intense moments. I also found odd parallels between his life and my own, most striking that we were both born during total lunar eclipses of the Saros cycle 120, and that Drake died during one as well. Since the time of the Babylonians, the term "Saros Cycle" has been used to explain the cyclical and serial nature of solar and lunar eclipses.

Francis Drake was born in Tavistock, Devon, England, on September 5, 1541, and died on October 18, 1595, off the coast of Panama. Virtually all accounts of Drake's life state that he was born around 1540 and died on January 28, 1596. I will explain why the actual dates of his birth and death were not disclosed toward the end of this book. That discovery deepened my kinship with him, and I felt he was guiding me on my quest.

Our early lives had nothing in common. I grew up in a comfortable middle-class family on Long Island, he was in a devout Protestant family during a time when Catholics under Queen Mary I were rampaging through the English countryside, forcing Protestants to recant, or be burned at the stake as heretics. As a Protestant preacher, Francis' father Edmund was a target, so he took his family first to Plymouth, where many Protestants were seeking refuge, then to the County of Kent, where the whole family lived in the hull of an abandoned ship.

Francis played on the deck of their ship, standing at the tiller, imagining that he was captaining the vessel through menacing seas with his eleven younger brothers as his crew. The tiller was nothing more than a piece of wood used to support the clothesline where his family's laundry was hung to dry. At other times, he would climb out on the bowsprit and imagine himself busy with the foresail sheets while the bow dipped in and out of the crests of the passing waves. I had no trouble picturing this because, as a teenager, my family owned a small motorboat. After taking a course and earning a Captain's License, I was allowed to take the boat out by myself. I spent many hours with my friends cruising the waters off the south shore of Long Island.

At age 14, Drake was apprenticed to Jacob Smith, the bachelor shipmaster of a sailing barque that transported merchandise up and down the east coast of England and across the Channel to France. Smith was a tough man with a hot temper and a sharp tongue. He was quick to punish Francis but also recognized his excellent work. Smith liked his apprentice and bequeathed ownership of the sailing barque to Francis upon his death.

After Smith's death, young Francis continued the barque's routes and business, putting into practice all he'd learned. He grew into manhood, confident in his abilities on the sea and business matters. Drake was a spiritual man who believed he was in God's hands and doing His work.

In his early twenties, Francis worked as first mate in the slave trade for his cousin John Hawkins. Hawkins was employed by Queen Elizabeth I. The Queen needed money from the lucrative slave trading business to finance and build a Navy for England that could rival the Spanish Armada.

In 1564, the Queen gave Hawkins a ship called the Jesus of Lubeck. After filling the vessel with slaves in Guinea, they headed across the Atlantic to Borburata, Venezuela, and from there, to many other sites. Hawkins and Drake employed whatever it took to close the sale in each place: clever arguments, bravado, and even violence. Drake paid careful attention to his cousin and learned to trade slaves, Captain a ship, and lead men! When they returned to England, there was a celebration in their honor because the slave trading business returned profits far beyond the expectations of their financiers.

On the next slave trading venture to West Africa, Hawkins captained the Jesus of Lubeck, another of Hawkins' cousins, John Lovell, captained the Minion, and Francis Drake went with them as Captain of the Judith.

When they arrived at the "hunting ground" of the Guinea coast, Hawkins ordered 150 men to go ashore to hunt for slaves. The Africans fought back and shot many of Hawkins' men with arrows containing such potent poison that even minor wounds resulted in death. Few slaves were captured on this first attempt, but Hawkins did not give up. At a port along the African coast, the King of a native tribe asked Hawkins to help him fight against a rival tribe. The King agreed to give Hawkins all the men they captured in return for his help.

Hawkins' crew and the King's men attacked and defeated the other tribe, burned their village to the ground, and captured 850 prisoners. However, the King reneged on his deal with Hawkins and kept almost half of the prisoners for himself.

Hawkins' fleet was forced to head across the Atlantic with just under 500 slaves. They stopped at Dominica, Margarita, and other ports, selling approximately half of the slaves on board.

Their next stop was Río de la Hacha in Colombia, where Drake showed his mettle in battle. Drake threatened the Spanish Governor of the region to purchase what the English were selling or face violent consequences. A show of force was necessary, and when the battle was over, the Governor purchased every slave on the ship.

After the fleet set sail back to England, a storm came up, damaging the Jesus so severely that they needed to repair it. Hawkins ordered the ships to anchor outside the harbor at the Mexican island of San Juan de Ulloa. The Port Officials questioned Hawkins about his need to enter the harbor. Hawkins pointed out that he'd made no attempt to assault the treasure ships that entered the harbor and claimed he was only there to make repairs and pay for provisions they needed. He convinced the Port Officials and the Harbor

Master to allow the five ships to enter. The following day, thirteen armed Spanish vessels arrived to serve as escorts for the treasure ships. Hawkins sent a contingent to repeat what he'd said to the Port Officials. He added that he would only allow the escort vessels to enter the harbor if they guaranteed not to attack his ships. After ten hostages from both sides were exchanged as surety for the deal, the Spanish fleet entered the narrow harbor and moored right alongside the English ships.

Hawkins' men were busy with the repairs despite a pounding storm when they noticed suspicious activity on the Spanish ships.

Hawkins was about to send a Spanish-speaking crewman to see what happened when the Spaniards attacked. All the Englishmen on shore were killed, and a gaping hole was blasted in the hull of the Jesus, and the Minion was fired upon. The Jesus was carrying the proceeds from the slave trading business, and it was severely damaged. The injured men on the Jesus needed to be moved under fire to the Minion.

The Angel and the Swallow were soon sunk, and very few crewmen were rescued. As the storm winds howled and gunfire flew, Hawkins ordered Drake to pull the Judith alongside the Minion to pick up some surviving crewmen from the Jesus and then leave the harbor. When Hawkins fled the port on the Minion, he left the ten Spanish hostages from the exchange unharmed on the floundering Jesus. Unfortunately, the ten English hostages in the hands of the Spanish were not as lucky. Considered prisoners of war, they were brutally tortured and killed.

This account was the first I read about Drake's adult life. It triggered one of my "you-are-there" trances. One moment, I was sitting outside on the upper deck in my backyard on a Saturday afternoon, reading. The next, I was surrounded by cannon fire, shrieks of pain, exploding wooden ships, torn sails, and the throes of battle.

Many men who'd come aboard from the Minion were severely wounded. As they died, they were laid on wooden planks on the main deck in preparation for their watery burial. The storm raged while Francis said a brief prayer and the bodies were pushed overboard into the sea.

Drake obeyed Hawkins' orders and sailed out into the Caribbean. With the storm still raging, he could not see the Minion. He worried that if he lay too long in wait for Hawkins, the Judith would be vulnerable to attack. As his primary responsibility was the safety of his ship and crew, Drake decided to sail back to England. He arrived without further incident and hid the gold and silver carried onboard the Judith until things played out.

When Drake reported to the Queen that Hawkins' ship had been lost, he was taken to the Tower of London and held prisoner as a deserter. However, when Hawkins and the Minion arrived back in England five days later, Hawkins cleared Drake of wrongdoing.

Shortly after Drake's release from prison, he officially joined the Royal Navy, just as the political conflicts between England and Spain grew even more contentious.

Elizabeth thought that she deserved to be compensated for the ships that were destroyed by the Spanish during Drake's and Hawkins' bloody battle in the Caribbean. She ordered Drake and Hawkins to address the Queens' Council regarding the attack so the Queen could use their testimony to justify the seizure of the gold bullion from a Spanish vessel docked in Plymouth. After they testified, Elizabeth met with the Spanish Ambassador. She postulated that the fastest way to get her money back would be to seize gold bullion that was to be delivered to the Spanish Governor of the Netherlands. The Ambassador was outraged by her veiled threat and convinced the Governor to embargo all English property in the Netherlands until this situation was resolved. As soon as that embargo was in effect, the Queen seized the gold bullion and steadfastly refused to discuss the issue further. Political tensions reached a boiling point when the English Ambassador in Madrid was asked by the Spanish government to leave the country, and the Queen retaliated in turn by placing the Ambassador under house arrest.

A period of protracted political tensions ensued. All the while the Queen was having ships built as quickly as possible, using the bullion from the Spanish vessel to fund the construction projects.

To steer the Spanish away from her real goals, the Queen initiated a rumor that John Hawkins set sail with twenty-five ships, intending to attack and capture Spanish treasure ships. This sent the Spanish on a wild goose chase on the high seas and kept them from closely monitoring traffic in and out of English harbors.

While the Spanish ships were on high alert for any signs of sea attack by the English fleet in the Atlantic and Caribbean, Drake slipped out of Plymouth in 1570 with two small ships named the Dragon and the Swan. The goal of this mission was to explore the Spanish Main, scouting out vulnerable spots along the Spaniards' route for transporting New World treasure. Drake searched for a location to hide and attack on land or by sea. By the time he returned to England, he formulated a clever plan to implement on a future voyage. He decided to attack the town of Nombre de Dios in Panama, where the Spanish hoarded treasure before it was loaded aboard ships that would transport it back across the Atlantic.

CHAPTER 4

The Cimaroons

In early 1571, Drake sailed the Swan back to the Caribbean to carry out the Queen's orders to steal the Spanish gold for England. During his last voyage, he identified the site where he would set up a base camp for this mission. It had a small, natural harbor well hidden by trees growing to the water's edge. There was a narrow entrance protected from the wind. There was also fresh water, fresh fruit, and pheasants to hunt. His crew's first task was to widen the freshwater stream that led into the jungle in case they needed to move the ships further inland to avoid detection.

While this work was going on, Drake took the Swan back out to sea to discover how the gold was being moved to Nombre de Dios. He found that it was being gathered and stored. In Panama's port city on the Pacific side of the Isthmus, then carted overland by mule trains to the Caribbean side. The mule trains did not operate during the rainy season between

December and April. During these reconnaissance missions, when a slow-moving Spanish ship was sighted heading in his direction, Drake would sail the Swan back through the narrow opening into his hiding place and simply vanish. After Drake and his men finished all the preparatory work on the Swan's "nesting place," he returned to England and reported to the Queen.

Then, in mid-1573, he sailed back to the Caribbean with two ships, the Swan and the Pasha. This time, his younger brother Joseph sailed with him. Drake wanted to mentor Joseph as his cousin John Hawkins mentored him. On arriving back at the Swan's nest, Drake and his men established friendly relations with several settlements of "Cimaroons," former slaves who escaped the tyranny of their Spanish masters and run away to live in remote areas, often high in the mountains. With these men to guide Drake and his men through the jungle, he felt confident that he could attack and capture a Spanish mule train and bring its gold and silver home to England.

Diego, Drake's staunchest ally in the Cimaroon community, helped his men construct living quarters in the style of a clandestine Cimaroon village. The sweltering heat and humidity of the jungle made for harsh working conditions, so Drake only required that his men work every other day. For their hard labor, he rewarded them by clearing an area of jungle where they could amuse themselves by playing croquet or bowling on their days off. The men also set up a blacksmith's forge that could be used to repair broken iron fittings for the ships. It took several months to do this work. While these activities were underway, Drake set off on a series of small raids on ships sailing by netting hogs, corn, and vegetables to supplement the plentiful fish and fowl at the Swan's nest.

It was now the rainy season, and the Cimaroons told Drake the treasure convoys did not cross the Isthmus at this time because the mule tracks became impassable. During this time, Drake took pleasure in creating diversions to fool the Spanish regularly sailed near Nombre de Dios to make them think he would attack by sea. In response, the Spanish set numerous traps to catch him but never succeeded.

By the end of the rainy season, intense storms and continuous jungle heat took a toll on Drake's crew, as did a yellow fever outbreak that spread through the camp. Within three days, six men died, and thirty more were stricken. When Drake's younger brother Joseph died in his arms, he ordered the ship's doctor to dissect the body to hopefully discover a remedy. When nothing was found that could suggest a cure, the doctor created a potion that he hoped might work, but rather than try it on the ailing crew members, he tested it himself and died from it. Fortunately, Drake remained healthy throughout the epidemic, but twenty-eight of his fever-stricken crew died.

By the time Drake and his remaining crewmembers were ready to begin their raid, thirty Cimaroons decided to join forces with them, guide him through the jungle, and fight alongside them against their common enemy, the Spanish. The Spanish Treasure Galleons just arrived at Nombre de Dios in preparation for loading and transporting the season's first shipment of gold back to Spain. In preparation for his attack, Drake divided his men into two groups. One group would stay to guard the Swan's nest and care for the crewmen who were still sick, and the other, made up of his eighteen strongest, boldest men plus the thirty Cimaroons would go with him to steal the treasure.

They set out along the mule-train route with two Cimaroons ahead as scouts. At any hint of trouble, Drake's men were prepared to vanish into the forest that bordered the trail. They needed to consider every person they might encounter along the way as potential spies for the Spanish. Hence, his men were prepared to kill anyone they met. They marched through the jungle for two days until they came to the town of Venta de Las Cruces (literally "warehouse at the crossroads"), which was halfway between Nombre de Dios and the City of Panama. To avoid detection, they decided to pass around the town. However, they carefully noted where it was and the size of its warehouses. They began moving uphill until they finally broke out of the jungle's humidity and into a pine forest's cooler, dryer air. Drake knew that the mule trains moved at night, so while most of his men slept, sentries stood guard and listened for the sound of the bells. The mules wore harnesses adorned with bells that could be heard from far away when the mule train was moving along the trail.

They continued onward until Pedro, the Cimaroon at the head of the party, suddenly stopped and pointed to the open rocky field ahead of them. At this point, they would have to leave the cover of the forest and travel out in the open. It already took them six days to reach the highest point of their journey, and from that vantage point, Drake and his crew saw the Pacific Ocean for the first time. They stood and stared for quite some time before beginning their descent. The prospects of what lay ahead fueled their pace downhill through the forest, over some rolling hills, and onto the grass-covered plain from which they could now see the City of Panama. The Cimaroons told them to be prepared to hide in the tall grass at a moment's notice because, on this plain, they could be spotted from a great distance away.

Two Cimaroon scouts went ahead of the party and stopped at a village to find out when the mule train might be heading in their direction, and they returned with good news. Two mule-trains were about to leave Panama City that very night. The instant he heard this news, Drake ordered an about-face, and the entire raiding party retraced their steps for twelve miles, stopping about six miles from Venta de las Cruces. From there, it would be much easier to retreat downhill with their booty and back to the harbor where the Pasha and the Swan awaited their return.

As nightfall approached, Drake gathered his men around the fire to share a meal and a few shots of Brandy as they discussed their plan. Since the attack would occur at night, all the men were to take off their shirts and put them on over their coats so that they could tell each other from the enemy when the skirmish began in the dark. Men were to be positioned on both sides of the trail so they could pop out at the front and rear of the mule train the moment Drake blew his whistle. Until then, they were to maintain complete silence. The men took their positions in the forest and waited as they could hear bells in the distance.

Then, unexpectedly, they heard a horse's footsteps from the opposite direction. Drake had warned his men to remain still and quiet if anybody happened to come along the trail while they were hiding, but one man, Robert Pike, drank a bit too much earlier and jumped up because he thought it was time to attack. One of the

Cimaroons pulled him back down immediately, but it was too late. The man on the horse saw the glimmer of his shirt in the light of the moon and took off along the path toward Panama and the approaching mule train. Fifteen or twenty more minutes passed, and the sound of the bells was growing louder by the minute. As soon as Drake blew his whistle, the men rushed out and stopped the mule train in its tracks, but this was only the first of the two trains, and it carried nothing but provisions.

The muleteers were rounded up and brought as captives to Drake. He demanded to know where the gold, silver, and jewels were. Shaking with fear, one of the muleteers told Drake that the man on the horse reported seeing a man who'd stood up and warned the mule train. The Treasurer of Lima, who was traveling with the second mule train, was taken by his bodyguard back down the trail toward Panama. At the same time, this first mule train carrying the provisions was told to continue to Venta de Las Cruces to find out if the horseback rider's suspicions were correct. The muleteers told Drake that the entire group would be wise to leave before the Spanish sent troops to hunt them down. Without hesitation and without saying a word, Drake walked over to Pike, drew his sword, and executed him on the spot. He then calmly walked over to Pedro and the two men discussed their next course of action.

There were only two choices: they could go back into the forest and once again circle around Venta de las Cruces on the way back to their ships or cut hours off their trip by staying on the trail and dash through the center of the town. Drake thought for a moment. He ordered his men to ride the mules down the path until they were about a mile outside the city. There, they were confronted by an armed Spanish guard. Drake shouted that they were English and demanded passage in the name of the Queen of England, but this was met with a hail of gunfire, which killed one of his men and wounded Drake. Then suddenly, there was a war cry, and all thirty Cimaroons rushed out from behind the mules and ran toward the startled Spanish patrol, all of whom quickly scattered into the forest and fled for their lives. Drake and his men now moved quickly down the trail with the Cimaroons and entered Venta de Las Cruces together. The mere sight of Cimaroons inside the town caused the civilians and soldiers to panic, and they all began running toward the monastery to seek refuge. Drake barricaded them inside; his men pillaged the town, and they were on their way back to the ships by daybreak.

When they arrived at the Swan's Nest, Drake was pleased to see that the sick men he'd left behind had recovered. The entire crew gathered to offer their thoughts about whether to proceed with the mission by land or sea. Drake paid close attention to what each man said and thought carefully before responding. After listening to them all, he decided they would attack by sea rather than attempt another raid along the route of the mule-trains.

The following day, he took one group of men and sailed aboard the Swan, leaving the Pasha in the harbor under guard. The remaining men were ordered to leave the sanctuary and search for a passing ship carrying provisions. The first one they came upon was loaded with turkeys and pigs. Rather than move the animals to their own boat, Drake's men offloaded the frigate's crew onto a dingy and cast them off as Drake's men sailed the Frigate and its bounty back to the harbor. Drake's trip also netted a frigate with a small quantity of gold. Now, all New Spain was abuzz with Drake's exploits. No one knew where he was hiding or when he would strike next, so troop ships were ordered to remain on high alert.

As soon as the newly commandeered Frigate was tallowed and readied for action, Drake took it on a trial run. While at sea, he came upon a large ship flying under the flag of France, commanded by Captain Tetu, who shared the news that the Catholics massacred the Protestant Huguenots in France some months before. Drake, therefore, saw him as an ally, remembering his own family's treatment at the hands of the Catholics. Captain Tetu wanted to partner with Drake on his next venture, and Drake agreed. The French crew was starving and severely dehydrated, so it took nearly a week of rest before they were ready for action. This raid would involve twenty Cimaroons, twenty men from the French ship, and fifteen of his own men.

The Cimaroons reported that the mule-trains were moving again from Panama City to Nombre de Dios, and that the Spanish was no longer on high alert since Drake was not sighted on land for several months. Every one of Drake's plans relied on the element of surprise and some kind of twist in the method of attack that never failed to catch the Spanish off guard. This time, Drake's raiding party sailed one of the frigates and two small boats to the mouth of the Rio Francisco and left the frigate tucked behind a spit of land. The two small ships tethered up the river to aid in their return trip. From there, they once again hiked westward through the intense jungle heat. In two days, they bypassed the town of Venta de Las Cruces. The heat and humidity were so unbearable that the Spanish worked at night and slept during the day throughout the region. When he sent out his Cimaroon scouts, they discovered that a long mule train with 190 mules carrying nothing, but silver and gold would arrive just before dawn. All fifty-five men waited silently in the forest alongside the mule trail.

As soon as the mule train moved into the correct position, Drake blew his whistle, and his men sprang out to attack. The first and last mules were commanded to halt and lie down, and all 188 other obedient animals followed suit. Guarding the train, forty-five soldiers drew their swords to put up a fight, but when Drake's raiders fired their guns, they turned and fled. It didn't last long, but after the melee, One Cimaroon was dead, Captain Tetu was severely wounded in the stomach, and most of the mules were killed.

As the sun rose, it was painfully apparent that Drake's men could not carry as much gold and silver as 190 mules, so they dragged most of the silver to a nearby stream and buried it in the sand and gravel.

The sound of men and horses approaching could now be heard in the distance, so they headed immediately back into the forest and began the nearly twenty-five-mile trek back to the mouth of the Rio Francisco. The men staggered under the weight of the gold bars they were carrying. Their painfully slow pace and Captain Tetu's grave injuries led Drake to leave Captain Tetu behind with a few men to hide in the forest for a few days so that he could recuperate before the long hike back to the ship. After that, Drake's group only traveled a few minutes when two of the Cimaroons reported that one of the Frenchmen wandered off carrying gold because he did not want to wait for the group. Drake knew that this man would be captured and tortured by the Spanish until he revealed where they buried the silver. However, there was no time to waste, so the group began moving again, traveling all night through a terrible storm. They stopped the following afternoon when they broke out of the jungle at the point of the river where the two small boats were supposed to be waiting to take them to the ship, but there were no boats.

The only vessels they could see offshore were seven Spanish ships coming from the direction of the Swan's nest, where the Pasha the Swan and the other larger ships were waiting. At that moment, every man had the exact same fear that the two pickup boats were captured by the Spanish and the crewmen were tortured until they gave up the location of the Swan's nest and the spot where the Frigate had been. Drake told his men that he'd go alone to search for the boats while they waited in hiding. Six hours later, they found the two boats with the Frigate. When he asked why the men moved the ships, they reported that a gale-force wind made them retreat to the Frigate. Drake led the small boats back up the river to join the rest of his men. All of them gave a shout of joyful relief on seeing him.

By dawn, they were back at the Swan's nest, unloading the treasure and dividing it between the French, English, and Cimaroons. But before he could rest, Drake needed to go back to see if Captain Tetu and the other two men escaped the jungle. He discovered sadly that the Spanish took Captain Tetu and the other Frenchmen captive and recovered the silver Drake and his men buried in the sandy stream bed. Nevertheless, when they tallied up all the gold bullion, Drake saw they made an impressive haul.

When it was time for Drake to return to England, after loading the treasure in the Swan's and Pasha's cargo holds, he returned control of the fully provisioned Frigate to the French crew. He invited the Cimaroons to take anything they wanted from among the spoils. The Cimaroons carried their hand-picked prizes back into the jungle as he sailed off. Drake was pleased with the bullion he was bringing home and knew the Queen would be too. His only sorrow as he headed back across the Atlantic was the weight of losing his younger brother and knowing how heartbroken their parents would be.

With the help of the Gulf Stream and favorable winds, the Swan and Pasha arrived in Plymouth on August 4, 1573.

CHAPTER 5

The Hollow Sound

At the beginning of August 2001, the tunnel under my deck was about 20 feet long, and at its far end, I dug out a "room," which was almost large enough to stand upright. I hadn't yet found the opening to the hollow space I expected to find. However, I continued my practice of periodically banging on the floor and walls. The hollow sound now seemed loudest at one end of the "room," so I continued to dig in that direction. After a few more feet, I found myself at the entrance of another room, though this one was not of my own making. It was different from any place I'd come across in that it was partially filled with silt so fine that as I dug, it simply refilled any excavation I attempted. After wasting almost an hour repeatedly trying to contain the silt, I decided to take a break to regroup.

By that point in the project, every muscle in my body ached from jackhammering, shoveling, loading the buckets with dirt, and dragging them along the tunnel to the opening. I finally acknowledged that if I was to keep going, I needed help, and I knew just where to find it: Kerner Boulevard in San Rafael. Close to a hundred men stood there hoping for work that Saturday morning. I picked several to help me, one of them named Jaime, who'd come here from Guatemala by way of Mexico, walking across the desert and eventually north to San Rafael. He told me San Rafael was a favorite spot for a lot of migrants because there are towns by that name throughout Central America. After that, whenever I needed help, Jaime became my go-to guy. He was always willing to come over, day or night.

Fortunately, I speak Spanish reasonably well and could explain what I needed them to do. For their effort, I paid them $15 an hour with the understanding that they were not to tell anybody what I was doing. I trusted them partly because they were here illegally and didn't want confrontations with the authorities any more than I did. I was happy to discover that none of them were afraid of working below ground, especially the Guatemalans, because back home, it was common to create deep hand-dug water wells. I felt a special bond with the Guatemalans because I knew they were the descendants of the Maya, whose culture I studied and admired. After the workers' first trip through the tunnel, I asked them if they'd noticed the image of the crowned parrot in the wall. The answer was a resounding "yes," so I asked them if they thought I was crazy for pursuing this project, and the answer was a unanimous "no." They said that images like this were commonplace in the Mayan culture, and they knew that I was on to something.

With their help, I was able to step up the pace. I often worked most of the night, got a few hours of sleep, picked up helpers in the morning, worked alongside them for a couple of hours, and then lay down and rested while they worked. Then, I'd drive them back to San Rafael when we were done for the day. They came three or four days a week and were great. Often, I'd buy us all burritos for lunch, and we'd sit on my deck and eat together. I always provided them with a case of bottled drinking water and let them use the bathroom in my house. Most important, I made sure to pay them in cash every day. I knew the job would have been impossible without them, especially with Jaime as a foreman. During that time, thanks to my boss, I continued working at Morgan Witter only two days a week.

The next time I returned to the room with all that silt, I noticed twelve stones stacked in the shape of an altar. The more I looked at them, the more I thought that somewhere in this room, there could be a secret door allowing me to enter another room where the real treasure was stored. I suspected such a room to lie right behind the 12-stone altar. However, given all the warnings I'd gotten and the Indiana Jones movies I'd seen, I suspected this could also be a booby trap. The stones were large and seemed somehow unstable. To the left and 10 feet above them, there was a massive, rounded stone the size of a Volkswagen that also seemed precariously perched.

Working alone over the next two days, I carefully removed each stone and kept a close eye on the killer stone above me. The last of the twelve stones was shaped like a gargoyle. Even though it was 8:00 p.m., I didn't want to stop working, so I gingerly removed it.

Suddenly, the entire underground cavern started to shake and move. I returned to the tunnel and braced myself against its more solid walls. The shaking continued for as much as ten seconds as rocks tumbled down all around my head, but when the shaking stopped, I was unscathed. I ran back into the house and got my video camera to see if I could record anything, but by the time I got back with it, most of the action was over. I listened to the news to hear if an earthquake occurred, but none was reported. This was the first of many deadly tricks perpetrated by Sir Francis Drake.

Whoever compiled the research for the Indiana Jones films did a great job because they prepared me better than anything for Drake's deadly tricks, of which there were many over the months to come. Aside from being very cautious, I discovered that the best way to proceed was to follow the lines of white clay embedded in the walls. I dug down another five feet, where the soil changed back to clay with many rocks mixed in. I created another cavern-like space by following the white clay lines and digging outward. On one wall, a stone sticking out made a hollow sound when I tapped on it. I thought that the treasure cavern was just on the other side. Foolishly, I got excited and pulled it out without stopping to think. The moment I did, all the dirt, silt, and rocks behind that entire wall began to pour through the hole left by the stone. I scrambled away on my hands and knees back into the tunnel from where I watched in horror as so many stones started pouring through the hole that the entire wall collapsed, which in turn caused the other walls to crumble as well. Within less than a minute, the whole space where I was working was reduced to a pile of rubble. I was lucky to get out alive for the second time in two days.

After that, Carol suggested that I not work alone anymore but only continue when Jaime and the other workers could help. "I don't want to lose you," she told me. I just laughed it off because her request was unrealistic.

One morning, I was at my desk in San Francisco for one of my rare days at work when I received a call from my brother-in-law, Mike. He told me he was in town on business and that my sister Beth insisted that he see me. When I asked why, he told me she was concerned because she "knew what I was doing." I started to say, "We've already been through this, Mike," but I knew that wouldn't get me anywhere, so I shrugged and invited him to come over to the house later that afternoon.

When he arrived, we drank a beer and exchanged pleasantries, and then I took him outside to show him my dig. Mike was usually calm and reserved, but seeing the extent of my backyard excavation, he reacted with furious intensity, "Jesus, Rob! You've got to stop this ASAP!" I looked at him and shook my head. Then he yelled. "What are you thinking? This is crazy!"

I was upset by his reaction and tried to explain in the calmest, most rational way I could, but he kept yelling. Finally, I told him I refused to listen to any more of his negative nonsense. Then I went outside to work while he fumed inside, dumping his anxiety on Carol and her kids.

When it was dark, I came back in and washed up. Mike seemed calmer; I took him to dinner at a Thai restaurant in San Rafael. I tried to keep things light while we ate but at the end of the meal, he began ragging on me again, so I told him in no uncertain terms that I didn't want him to stay overnight and that he should leave for Colorado as soon as we finished dinner.

He was upset but complied. He called my sister to let her know he'd be home late that night and headed to the airport as soon as I paid the check. At home, I talked with Carol about what happened with Mike. I thought she was still supportive of my quest, but I sensed something was wrong. Her words said she was still in my corner; her body language said something else. And that night, she said she was too tired for sex, which wasn't like her.

A week later, my father called to say he and his wife wanted to come out and visit me that weekend. I could tell from his voice that Beth and Mike were sounding the alarm about me. Hoping to get the conflict out of the way, I showed them around my yard as soon as they arrived. My father seemed skeptical, but he wanted to support me. His wife, always on the uptight side, was utterly hostile to my efforts. I tried to explain that now there was more evidence than there was at the time of his last visit. I made a mistake when I told him that I could see things that other people didn't necessarily see in the stones and about the patterns in the clay. My dad got a worried expression and told me I needed to stop what I was doing, go back to work full-time, and just concentrate on my job. His wife just frowned at me as he spoke. They left the next day.

After another week or so passed, I answered the doorbell early one morning. I found two Twin Cities policemen filling up my entryway. They pulled me outside and shoved me into the back of their squad car, saying I was being taken to the psych ward on a "51-50" charge. I screamed, "This is bullshit! You have no right to do this!" When I asked what a 51-50 charge meant, they said someone reported that I was a danger to myself and/or others.

I was furious! At Marin General Hospital, I was led into the psych ward, where the admitting nurse was my neighbor who lived immediately across the street. I was placed in a straitjacket and strapped to a table, face down. Then, a doctor came into the room and told me that I was there on a 72-hour hold that was requested by my father, and if needed, he told them that they could keep me there for up to two weeks. I was so angry that I spit in the Doctor's face.

Next, a nurse came in with a giant hypodermic needle to knock me out, but my anger kept me from going under. I just lay there, seething, so an hour later, the nurse returned and gave me a second dose, rendering me unconscious. When I came to, I found myself with another guy in a room with bars on the windows. He was pretty much catatonic, staring straight ahead and drooling. As it turned out, I was unconscious for 24 hours. During that time, they transported me by ambulance from Marin General to the psych ward at UC Medical Center in San Francisco, the same hospital where Carol's ex worked. The thought of him discovering I was in there made me sick with anxiety.

I was told once again that I was there on a 72-hour hold and that I'd be talking to a doctor soon. For those who've never been in a psych ward, I want to tell you it's a nightmare! People howling and moaning, crying, and yelling. And it smells like vomit and old piss. They take everything away from you that you could use to harm yourself, including your shoes, shoelaces, and belt, because they don't want anyone committing suicide.

Just as I was about to give up entirely and sink into the blues, much to my surprise, one of the nurses working in that hellhole turned out to be a woman who recognized me as a regular at one of my favorite clubs, The Bottom Out. She told me that if I behaved and could just chill out, I'd be out of there within 72 hours, maybe even less. So, I optimistically took her advice.

After coping with nearly two days in the looney bin, I was escorted into a room where I met with a staff psychiatrist who told me I was being released. That was the good news. The bad news was that when they let you out of the psych ward, they only gave you what you came in with, minus a few essential items! Since there was no money in my pockets when I was brought in, I had no money when they let me out. To make matters worse, they didn't give me back my shoelaces or the belt for my pants. Nice!

When I walked out the hospital door at 10:00 a.m., it took me a few minutes to get my bearings. I realized I wasn't far from my friends Tom and Sandy's place in Francisco's Haight-Ashbury district. I didn't have a cell phone or any money to call from a pay phone and check with them first, but luckily, Tom answered when I knocked on their door. He told me to come in, and after I told the two of them what happened to me, he was kind enough to drive me back to my house in Greenbrae. There was no sign of Carol when I got home around 11:30. Much to my surprise and dismay, there were two cops in my backyard, who ordered me to immediately fill in all the holes that I dug. That very afternoon I began doing so, though I only did so haphazardly since I had no intention of stopping my excavations.

That same day, around sunset, my doorbell rang.

When I answered it, a process server calmly handed me a large manila envelope. I opened it and found legal papers showing that my ex Melanie was now suing me to revoke our joint custody of Susan and grant me limited visitation rights. I slammed the door, furiously. After that, I walked through the house, noticing that most of Carol's and her daughters' things were gone, as were Susan's. I wondered if somehow Carol and Melanie were in cahoots and ganged up to have me taken to the psycho ward. Luckily, that turned out not to be the case. Carol called me around 8:00 p.m. to say that she and her kids just moved into a motel for a few days to escape the police and the nosy neighbors.

Sitting in my darkening living room with that process server's envelope in my lap, I was so distressed about everything that happened that I did not know what to do. But I knew that to begin undoing the mess, I needed to understand how it started. The following day, I visited the Twin Cities Police Department (TCPD), where I asked to speak with whoever was in charge. Captain White came out and ushered me into his office, then informed me that my father, my sister, and my ex-wife all submitted documents to the TCPD stating that I threatened to commit suicide and that I was a danger to myself and possibly to others, which was the basis for the 51-50.

I clearly and patiently explained that a man who believes he has found a priceless buried treasure would not contemplate suicide and that their claims were ridiculous. Captain White agreed with me and offered to provide me with copies of all the paperwork necessary to take legal action against my accusers and the County of Marin, if I agreed not to take any legal action against his department. After he gave me copies of the letters, I headed straight to Marin Civic Center. Being low on cash and without the advice of an attorney, I filed lawsuits on my own against all parties except the TCPD. Unfortunately, the response from the County stated that I'd be liable for all my opponents' legal fees, as there was a key document I neglected to file. With no other choice, I hired an attorney to cancel all the papers I filed. It would be nearly five years before I spoke to my father or sister again.

When Carol and her daughters got home, they tried to comfort me, but I was too hurt and upset. The events of the weeks to come didn't help. With so much drama and stress in such a short period, I knew I needed help. So I went to see a Crisis Counselor. The three sessions I spent with him helped me begin moving forward with my life, at least to take the next small step: going to Court to defend myself against Melanie's attempt to destroy my relationship with Susan. I didn't have enough money to hire an attorney to represent me. Unfortunately, Ben Franklin's quip, "He is a fool who represents himself," proved true. It was a short hearing during which Melanie's slime dog attorney chewed me up and spit me out. The Judge ordered me to undergo a County psychological exam at my own expense and informed me that I was only allowed to see my daughter once each week under the condition known as "Supervised Visitation." This meant that while I was with my daughter, a representative of the County or a person approved by Melanie needed to be present. It was hard to believe that anyone saw me as such a lowlife that I couldn't be trusted to visit my daughter without supervision.

The final blow came shortly after the hearing when I received a call from Carol's ex, who said, "I promised to let you know before I did anything. I'm filing papers tomorrow to reopen my custody case." When Carol met with her Attorney, he warned her that she'd lose her children if she didn't move out of my house immediately since I was a "bad influence," according to documents the Doctor obtained from a private investigator. What Private Investigator? I thought.

I soon found out that after I met with the Doctor, he called Melanie recruited her to build a case against Carol and me, and she was all too happy to tell him about my lifestyle. The Doctor suggested that if he could prove that Carol and I were unfit parents, there would be a financial benefit for both. She knew that I never let my recreational activities interfere with my daughter's needs. Still, she went along with it anyway because she always wanted more money! The Doctor hired a private investigator to follow us and gather evidence to improve his chances of having us declared unfit parents.

Considering our lifestyle, it was easy for the PI to get the evidence he needed. On Saturday nights, we went to Club Galaxy or the Bay Cities Socials events and partied most weekends. The 51-50 fiasco sealed the deal!

Carol knew that the Doctor wasn't the type to make idle threats so within a week, she followed her Attorney's advice and rented an apartment in Corte Madera for her and the girls, and they moved out. My heart was broken. I really thought she and I would be able to stick out any challenge.

During that horrible time, I found some strange solace in filling in the holes I dug, clearing away all the evidence of my futile obsession. After two months of working every afternoon, all of them were filled, except for one large one and the tunnel with the opening under my deck.

One day, while I was at work in the city, it began to rain heavily. It rained four or five inches when I left my job. I arrived home to find that one remaining hole was almost entirely filled with rainwater. Fearing the weight of all that water could collapse the hillside and cause a significant mudslide, I raced to a store, bought a pump, and emptied the water. The following day, I filled in the hole.

Just a few days after that, it rained again, and this time, I came home to find the tunnel under my deck starting to flood. I wanted to rescue the hundreds of dollars' worth of equipment from down there before the tunnel collapsed, so I changed my clothes, made sure that no cords were plugged in, and headed down. I knew it was dangerous to enter it when the clay was wet because the whole thing could collapse on me, but I needed to try. Luckily, I succeeded at least in that small endeavor.

Afterward, it seemed as though the flood signaled the end of a horrible chapter of my life. I labored like a medieval serf in a mine for months, been hauled away and thrown into the psycho ward, had my daughter taken away from me by the Court, and I lost Carol, the love of my life. Yet, through it all, I believed I'd been close to finding Drake's treasure. Despite all the naysayers, I remained sure there was a well-hidden portal somewhere down there and behind it, a cavern filled with gold and silver and countless precious gems! I knew that my quest for that treasure was not over. I believed that somehow, next spring when the ground was dry and the dust and chaos from my personal life settled down, I might be able to try again.

CHAPTER 6

Inca, Maya, and Aztec

On December 13, 1577, Drake began a new expedition, this one to disrupt the Spanish hold on the Pacific coast of South America. He set sail with one hundred and sixty-four men on five ships, the Elizabeth, the Marigold, the Swan, the Benedict, and Drake's own ship, the Pelican, which during the voyage was renamed the Golden Hind, the last of which with Drake aboard would be the only ship to complete the circumnavigation of the globe. Along on this voyage was Drake's longtime friend Thomas Doughty, who was also a well- known figure in the court of Queen Elizabeth. It was she who urged Drake to include Doughty as an officer on his fleet. The five ships proceeded to the Cape Verde Islands, where Drake captured a small Portuguese merchant ship piloted by Nunho da Silva. He confiscated the vessel and commandeered its maps as well as the services of da

Silva who led them across the Southern Atlantic and along the coast of Brazil. The maps recorded information gathered by Magellan and were extremely useful to Drake.

After barely surviving a harsh winter of rough sailing across the Atlantic, Drake's exhausted crewmen were growing restless, and were therefore receptive to Thomas Doughty's plot to mutiny against Drake. But before a serious challenge was mounted, Drake discovered and stopped it. Then as soon as they reached the coast of Brazil, he held a court-martial that sentenced Doughty to death for the crime of mutiny. Rather than executing him on the spot, Drake decided to wait until they returned to England to carry out the sentence. Doughty would be confined to his quarters for the remainder of the voyage.

Delayed by the court-martial, Drake and his men finally set course for St. Julian, the port in Patagonia where Magellan prepared his ships to round the Cape 58 years earlier. It was now June 19, 1578, winter in the Southern Hemisphere, so Drake remained there two months restocking the three main ships and burning the two supply ships that were not seaworthy enough for the dangerous trek through the Strait of Magellan. Their long wintering in Port St. Julian before attempting the trip around the tip of South America had a demoralizing effect on the crew. There was quarreling and enmity between the gentlemen and the mariners, and the long cold winter nights made the situation even worse. Drake knew he needed to act! One Sunday morning during religious services, Drake preached the sermon in place of the chaplain, Captain Fletcher. He spoke eloquently about harmony and survival and laid down new rules of conduct. Both

"Gentlemen" and "Mariners," he declared, were to work together as equals, apart from those who were officers. From this time on, everyone on all three ships was subject to Drake's sole command.

As he prepared to enter the Strait of Magellan, he was still troubled by what happened with Thomas Doughty. He remembered that it was Queen Elizabeth who urged him to take Doughty with him as an officer and couldn't help wondering if she had instructed Doughty to betray him. To show his new-found distrust for her, he changed his ship's name from the Pelican, a tribute to her majesty to the Golden Hind in honor of another of the voyage's patrons, Sir Christopher Hatton, whose family crest featured this mythical creature.

As the ships passed through the Strait, they ran into intense storms that battered them severely. The Golden Hind became separated from the other two vessels that were under the command of his vice-admiral Captain John Winter. When Captain Winter did not arrive at the rendezvous point, Drake assumed those ships were lost. It would be several years before he learned that when Winter could not find Drake, he thought that the Golden Hind sank, so he turned both ships around and headed back to England.

Gale force winds blew the Golden Hind so far to the south that their location was not shown on any of the maps on board. Magellan's map showed Tierra del Fuego as the northern point of a continent at the end of the chain of islands off the tip of South America, but Drake discovered that instead of land, there was a vast southern sea. This deep, 600-mile-wide sea would later become known as Drake's Passage. At the southernmost island, Drake went ashore with Captain

Fletcher on October 30 to set up a stone chiseled with the date and the name of Queen Elizabeth, claiming the land for England. Drake's journal makes mention of seeing penguins, which he described in his log as "large flightless birds," on that island, which he and his men killed for food.

Drake proceeded northward along the Pacific coast of South America, staying within sight of land, though he did not come ashore until he reached Mocha Island, off the coast of Chile on November 25. The Indians who inhabited Mocha experienced many years of cruelty at the hands of white-skinned, bearded Spaniards that arrived in sailing ships. Drake's men must have looked no different to them. During earlier voyages, Drake was warmly received by Indians, so he landed his ship quite openly, simply intending to stop for repairs and obtain needed provisions. He and his men were taken by surprise when an army of men with bows and arrows attacked them. Drake and many crew-members were wounded. Fortunately, these were not poison-tipped arrows.

Without restocking supplies or making repairs, the Golden Hind sailed onward. By this point in its journey, it was so battered by the wind and rough seas that the Spaniards were unable to identify it as an English "pirate ship." Since the English never ventured into Pacific waters, the Spaniards were unprepared for Drake's appearance there, even less for his attack. Drake used these facts to his advantage when on December 5 he sailed into the harbor at the small town of Valparaiso and came upon a fully loaded Spanish treasure ship, La Capitana, that stopped there on its way back toward Spain from Panama.

Naively, the Spaniards invited Drake and his

officers to come to their ship to drink a bottle of wine. As soon they were on board, the Spaniards realized their mistake. One of them jumped overboard and swam to shore leaving the others behind as Drake's captives. After securing the captive ship, Drake and his men entered the town, after the inhabitants fled. They raided several warehouses, put the La Capitana's crew ashore and took their ship out to sea. On it they discovered a significant quantity of gold in addition to over 1700 bottles of wine and a Greek pilot who could lead them to Lima.

On his way there, Drake sailed slowly along the coast of Chile stopping often to take whatever he and his men wanted. On several occasions, they headed inland to areas controlled by the Incas until the Spanish arrived and enslaved them. He raided some small Inca villages along the way and collected many leather "bota bags" filled with gold dust, and <u>at one site they took an Ica Stone, which was a religious artifact in the form of an elongated human skull decorated with elaborate markings</u>. There were several ancient civilizations from Egypt to South America where people of the upper echelon had their heads elongated as a sign of their high estate. Beginning at birth, a cloth was wrapped tightly around the head. Then as the child grew, the skull would elongate from the pressure. The best- known example of this practice is the Egyptian Queen Nefertiti, who died in 1396 BC.

As Drake and his men continued to explore the Pacific coast of <u>Peru, they came upon a shrine devoted to the goddess Umina, also known as The Emerald Goddess, as she took the form of a giant emerald the size of an ostrich egg.</u> She was honored in religious rituals during which people would bring other large emeralds to the shrine and place them around the Emerald Goddess in tribute. Long considered to be one of the great "lost emeralds," it disappeared during the period when the Spanish controlled South America. However, the truth is that it was not taken by the Spanish and subsequently lost at sea as some have presumed. Drake saw the giant stone, stole it, and took it back to the Golden Hind.

On February 15, 1579, Drake arrived at Callao, the harbor for Lima, the Peruvian capital. This portion of the Spanish Empire was nearly defenseless because, so few Europeans ever ventured this far from home. Drake worked under the cover of darkness, slipping into the harbor unnoticed, and quietly anchoring. His men went aboard all the ships in the harbor but found only one chest of gold bullion, which they immediately took back to the Golden Hind. When they encountered a watchman on one of the ships, they coerced him into telling them that twelve days earlier a treasure galleon filled with gold left Callao and was heading for Panama. Although no alarm was sounded, Drake spotted a small boat approaching the Golden Hind, so he forced one of his Spanish prisoners to shout out that this ship was under the control of Captain Miguel Angelo, a well-known figure among the Spanish. Instead of turning around, the small boat pulled up alongside the Golden Hind and the pilot climbed up to have a word with Captain Angelo. There, he found himself staring down the barrel of a gun, so he backed down onto his boat and shouted to the garrison on shore to sound the alarm. Drake and his men immediately disabled the other five ships so they could not pursue them as they sailed out of the harbor. His ship was much faster than the slow moving, heavily loaded galleon he was chasing. They hadn't sailed far from the port when suddenly the wind died completely and for the next two days the Golden Hind bobbed helplessly in the water. To make matters worse, the Viceroy of Peru heard of the raid and rushed soldiers to the port of Callao, where they boarded small boats and were beginning to close in on the Golden Hind when the wind finally picked up and Drake's ship sped out of their reach. As the wind speed increased the Golden Hind rapidly approached the galleon, La Nuestra Señora de la Concepción, nicknamed the Cacafuego (translation: roadrunner). The captain of the galleon could see a ship approaching but did not expect an enemy in those waters and mistook the Golden Hind for a friendly Spanish vessel. Drake commanded all sails to be fully deployed and on March 1, 1579, at roughly 6:00 PM, the Golden Hind attacked the Cacafuego with cannon fire until it was forced to surrender. The galleon's cargo included 80 pounds of gold, 26 tons of silver and 8 chests filled with pearls, and other gemstones. There was more gold and silver on board the Cacafuego than the Golden Hind could carry, so Drake decided to leave it on the Cacafuego and simply take the galleon with him.

Originally, he planned to return to England by passing back around the southern tip of South America, but that would be too dangerous now that the Spanish along the coast of Chile and Peru would be anticipating his return. He decided instead to find the rumored shortcut back to England known as the Northwest Passage.

Using the maps taken from the other ships they encountered, Drake sailed northward stopping along the coast of Nicaragua to clean and overhaul his ship and take on provisions. Along the way they captured a frigate near the island of Cano and outfitted it with cannons in case they came under attack. Two weeks later April 4, 1579, they captured another frigate carrying Chinese silks and porcelain. Its Captain Don Francisco Zarate was brought on board the Golden Hind and was received by Drake on deck. That night they dined together. When Drake admired several pieces of jewelry that Zarate was wearing, Zarate proposed a trade. In exchange for Zarate's emerald falcon pendant, Drake gave him an inlaid dagger and a silver chafing dish. Nine or ten officers including Drake's Portuguese pilot, Nunho da Silva joined them at table. Zarate wrote later how impressed he was by Drake's extremely intelligent and well- trained crewmembers who all seemed to adore Drake.

Drake left Nicaragua with four ships and decided as they sailed up the Pacific coast of Guatemala that they should stop briefly to see what they could of the Mayan culture, about which Drake heard interesting things. During their foray, he and his men saw evidence of the Spaniards' cruelty toward the Mayan people, and in part to even the score, they stole every golden object they could find from the Spanish, as well as a huge stone on which the image of a Mayan Warrior was carved, and then hauled all of it back to the ships.

On April 15, Drake arrived just outside of Huatulco in southern Mexico, the last Spanish port he visited. When they arrived, a trial of some natives was underway. Drake's men surrounded the courthouse and forced the Spaniards to leave the building. Then they helped the natives escape. Drake's men ransacked the town and desecrated the Catholic Church, whose artifacts reminded Drake and others of the Catholic purges they suffered. When Drake was ready to leave Huatulco, Nunho da Silva and Don Francisco Zarate requested to be freed and put ashore, and Drake agreed.

There was still one more place along the Mexican Coast Drake wanted to explore. For many years he heard of a great Aztec civilization that had been a fierce and powerful coalition of tribes with a rich cultural heritage, and, like the Maya and Inca, had advanced systems of learning. As each enemy tribe was conquered, the Aztecs assimilated the best features of those conquered cultures into their way of life. Military conquest and human sacrifice were closely inter-related for the Aztecs who believed that only by offering the gods human flesh could the human species go on living. It was said that their sprawling empire reached from the Gulf of Mexico to the Pacific Ocean and north south for hundreds of miles. All this, Drake was hungry to see.

Once again under the cover of darkness he and his men went ashore and made their way through the thick jungle hoping to discover an Aztec city. However, all they were able to find was the ruin of a temple, which was in some places streaked with brown swaths. "Blood from sacrifices," Drake said. The temple was constructed of hewn stones of different sizes and hues, some glowing under the light of the moon. Parts of it were decorated with bas-reliefs and sculptures, a few of which Drake and his men took back to their ship to add to their collection.

Drake would have loved to witness one of the Aztec ritual sacrifice ceremonies, but by the late sixteenth century, most of the vast Aztec empire was decimated by the Spanish conquistadors and their companions, the Franciscan Friars. The once noble race was by then no more, and their prior beliefs and complex understandings of the cosmos were supplanted by the teachings of the Catholic Church.

Drake's next goal was to find the Northwest Passage. He continued to sail northward, in search of that elusive way home. When he finally realized it did not exist, he turned the Golden Hind around and headed south again along the coast of Oregon and Upper California until he arrived at the mouth of San Francisco Bay in June 1579. Perhaps, the infamous famous summer fog drew him toward the mouth of the bay. It would certainly have provided cover and protected his ships and crew from being spotted by any Spanish pursuers. However, it was considered suicidal for a captain in those days to attempt sailing a ship no less a fleet of ships into an uncharted bay. If a ship loaded with men, provisions and tons of precious goods ran aground and the tide did not rise enough to free it, it might be stranded...forever!

He was certain that the Spanish were still looking for him, and from what he could see, the bay seemed able to provide him the safe refuge he needed to repair his ship, gather provisions, and prepare for his homeward journey.

The most important thing influencing his decision was that the Golden Hind was leaking so badly that it could not make the long journey back to England without repairs. He needed someplace where the ship could be "careened." If he attempted this anywhere along the coast, the Spanish could easily spot and attack them. It was a huge gamble, but Drake decided to take a chance and knew that his superior navigational skills would be put to a test if he wanted to bring all four of the ships far enough into the bay to hide

them. He knew that no Spanish Captain was likely to
take the same risk.

CHAPTER 7

Drake's Nova Albion

Having seen native villages in many locations along the coast of South and Central America, Drake realized that this area was probably inhabited, and since he and his men had been wounded by the natives on Mocha Island, they were somewhat wary as they sailed into this new bay.

Meanwhile, ten miles north of Drake's position, a group of men were watching the four large ships now moving in the direction of their village at Point San Quentin. They were a preliterate tribe who dressed in animal hides, lived in earthen huts, and never saw any vessel larger than their Tule reed canoes. They called themselves Miwok, meaning "people" in their language.

Drake guided his ships slowly into the bay and continued in a northerly direction for several miles until he'd passed the tip of the second spur of land. Then, he spotted a cove where he knew they could make landfall. It was well hidden, there was a marsh they could use to careen the ships, and a long shoreline where they could easily set up camp. The guns and cannons on board would be adequate to defend themselves unless they came under attack by hundreds of natives. They waited until the tide was high, brought three of the ships close to shore and established their basecamp. Drake chose the name, Nova Albion (New World), and claimed the land for England on June 17, 1579.

As soon as they landed, he dispatched scouts to find fresh water, and to see if there were natives in the surrounding hills who might attack their camp. Upon their return, they reported that there was a large native village just over the hill on the opposite side of the peninsula from where landed. Fearing an attack, Drake ordered his men to take over the Miwok village and to use force if necessary. After they took control, two crewmen with guns remained behind to prevent anyone from escaping to warn nearby villages about Drake's arrival. He ordered most of the crew to march from the landing site to the ocean and back.

Their mission was to capture anybody they found along the trail and to round-up all the men, women, and children from every village along the way. There were many villages along the route and when the crewmen returned, they brought thousands of Miwok to serve as laborers.

The Cacafuego was 50 feet longer than the other ships and needed twice as much draught. Even at high tide, the bay water was too shallow for the crew to bring her close enough to the shore to be unloaded. Scouts were again sent out to find a suitable place for the ship that carried tons of precious cargo in her hold. Less than two miles away they found a "convenient and faire" harbor where even at low tide, the water was deep enough to unload the Cacafuego. This location was impossible to see from any point south of the basecamp, so Drake aptly named it, "The Lost Harbor."

Drake knew that the Spanish would be relentless in their pursuit of him. His mind raced as he thought about every possible way to get back to England with the galleons' immense load of treasure. He summoned several of his most trusted men to his cabin where he listened to their ideas. One thing was clear, <u>if he left Nova Albion with all four ships; they could easily be spotted and overtaken on the high seas by the much faster Spanish ships.</u> Even if they transferred everything off the Cacafuego and then loaded it on the other three ships, they still risked being discovered and boarded, at which point Drake would be put to death as soon as any enemy saw the looted Spanish gold, silver, and jewels.

After weighing all the alternatives, Drake made the final decision. All the gold and much of the silver would be melted down and changed into unrecognizable ballast stones and then be blackened to disguise them. Only the Golden Hind would make the return trip to England, carrying these new metal "ballast stones" instead of the normal ballast stones made of rock. They would also carry some of the chests of gems and precious stones onboard. Under this plan, if the Spanish spotted the Golden Hind on the high seas and decided to board it, they would never suspect the real composition of the ballast. At most, the Spaniards would leave with a few gemstones and think they took everything of value. Anything that could not be carried back to England by the Golden Hind would have to be buried at Nova Albion, and Drake would return as soon as possible to collect it. This was an elaborate and labor-intensive plan, but Drake knew it would work, and the Miwok would provide the labor he needed.

Before they unloaded the ships, Drake needed to decide where to bury the treasure. He sat down and began to design the layout of the massive project he envisioned. For everything to work according to his plan, he needed wind and water. The scouts reported that there was a huge cavern filled with fresh water on a hill that was visible from the basecamp, so Drake hiked up to the ridge and determined that the location was perfect for what he had in mind. From there, he could see his camp, the Lost Harbor, the marsh, the surrounding hillsides, and the mouth of the bay. A strong breeze blew over the top of the ridge every afternoon which made it a perfect spot to operate a smelting furnace and at the top of the hill above the ridge was a natural spring which flowed year-round and was the source of the water in the cavern.

Having identified the three ships that would not sail back to England, Drake instructed his crew to use the extremely strong Miwok men to drag the two smaller ships into the nearby marsh where they were to be dismantled. Their wood and metal fixtures were to be used to construct crude but effective carts with wheels, which would then be loaded and pulled by the Miwok to pre-determined locations near Drake's camp. The Cacafuego underwent the same process in the marsh near the Lost Harbor. When the carts arrived at the camp, the Miwok women and children sorted the cargo into different piles. Everything that was made of silver or gold was set aside to be smelted and then loaded back into carts for the journey uphill to the smelting site. The gemstones that were not going back to England were loaded back into the carts and moved uphill to where they were going to be buried. The carts took different trails to go uphill depending on their contents. After they reached their destination, the empty carts were sent back downhill on different trails that would lead them back to the marsh where they would pick up another load and start the process over again. The carts were used repeatedly and there were hundreds of carts always moving.

<u>In the 1800's many discarded cards were found near San Quentin!</u>

While this was underway, the Golden Hind needed to be repaired as well as "careened and tallowed" before it could begin the long voyage back to England. Careening a ship was a dangerous but necessary process. It required a location where the ship would not be destroyed by wind and waves if there was a sudden change in weather and a storm blew in. It also required a location where the water was shallow enough so that when the tide went out, the ship could lie down on its side. Then, the crew smeared pig fat (tallow) in between all of the planks to make the ship watertight. As the tide began to rise the crew slowly pulled the ship up-right and when high tide was reached, the ship up-righted itself. This process was repeated to tallow the other side of the ship. After the work was finished, the Golden Hind sailed around Point San Quentin on its way to, "The Lost Harbor" where it would be loaded for the long voyage home.

On the high point of the ridge, Drake directed his men to build a natural draft coal-fire furnace that took full advantage of the afternoon wind to make it burn hot enough to melt the gold and silver. However, melting and casting metals under such primitive conditions was not a simple process. According to his research into the writings of Pliny the Elder, a Roman, zinc was required to absorb the lead that was present in the gold and silver when using a natural draught smelter. Lead was an impurity and Drake wanted to take as much pure gold and silver as he could carry back to England on the Golden Hind. However, the zinc he needed to remove the lead was not a naturally occurring element.

The largest single source of zinc is human bones! Through gestures and pantomime, Drake communicated his need for bones to the Chief of the Miwok people. Finally, the Chief understood, so he along with several of the tribe elders led Drake to a mound of shells piled outside their village. This was one of their sacred burial sites and when Drake's men handed shovels to some of the elders, the others stood arm in arm before the mound, looking quite menacing. Drake's men lifted their guns and fired, killing the Chief and many of the tribe elders.

Those who remained alive were given the shovels and forced to dig into the mound. Some of the women accompanying the group let out savage howls as the men extricated the first corpse. In response the men stopped digging, but Drake's men yelled, "Keep digging," and demonstrated in pantomime, so they continued until there was a stack of desiccated corpses on the ground. The women at that point turned in horror and ran away. Given the amount of gold that needed to be processed, Drake urged them to dig out more corpses, and they complied, until there was a large heap of them in various states of decomposition. This was enough to conduct the test, but Drake would need massive amounts of zinc to smelt so much metal.

He returned to the base camp and told the men he wanted to be left alone. Several hours passed, during which he contemplated every possible solution to the problem and by the time he rejoined the crew he reached a decision. He knew that the Aztecs sacrificed the men of every tribe they defeated, and Spanish enslaved every native man woman and child to labor in the mines. He rationalized that they defeated the Miwok as soon as they were rounded-up and held captive on the other side of the peninsula. The killing of the chief and tribe elders supported this rationalization. His plan was a blend of enslavement as practiced by the Spanish and human sacrifice as practiced by the Aztecs.

All the Miwok would be forced into some type of labor and their bones would be used as the supply of zinc to keep the smelter operating. Those who resisted would be killed immediately and brought to the smelter. Any laborer who dropped from exhaustion or stopped working for any reason would be killed and their body brought to the smelter. When there were not enough corpses in stock, groups of women and children would be marched to the ridge where they would be ritually executed. Those about to die could either jump into the smelter voluntarily and if they did not, Drake's men would force them to jump in or just pick them up and toss them in.

The smelting was not to stop for any reason. This procedure was to continue around the clock for as long as it took to melt all gold and silver, on the ships. If Drake was ever questioned by the Queen about this genocidal plan, he could justify his actions as being no worse than the Aztecs or the Spanish.

Drake ordered his artisans to create a brass plaque on which he himself wrote out the proclamation, claiming the area for England's Queen Elizabeth on June 17, 1579. He attached the plaque to a large, heavy wooden tree stump, and set it on the hillside near the spot where he would oversee that work his crew needed to accomplish before their journey home.

The smelter was in operation around the clock, and they poured the melted gold into earthen molds to create a fake "ballast stones." Once the metal cooled, they blackened the stones and then loaded them into carts for the trip downhill. From there, the Miwok pulled the carts along the edges of the marsh until they arrived at The Lost Harbor where it was loaded onto the Golden Hind.

The silver was another matter. There were so many tons of it that only a small percentage could be taken back as ballast stones. They would bury the rest of the silver on the ridge along with many chests of gemstones. To hide the silver, Drake applied his own brand of ingenuity. He created smectite clay from the naturally occurring minerals at the site. Then he mixed the melted silver into it, knowing it would remain moist if buried close enough to the spring. Even if it contracted during dry periods, it could be re-hydrated and expand again each time it rained. If the clay dried out, it would become hard as cement and could prove nearly impossible to take out of the ground. However, if the slurry remained moist, he anticipated that he could simply dig up the clay-silver bolus and take it back to England where the process would be reversed, and the silver would be separated from the smectite slurry.

Drake determined that some of the more fragile gemstones, and especially the emeralds, required a moist environment so they would not be destroyed. They buried these items close to the underground streams flowing downhill from the spring.

Having completed his plan for dealing with his valuable treasures, in a way, that seemed unassailable, Drake designed an intricate set of cascading tunnels and caverns that would be filled with either the silver-clay slurry or a different mixture of slurry for the gemstones he planned to bury. He prepared detailed drawings, and his men ordered to dig the pits to the specific dimensions he outlined, starting at the surface, and digging straight down until they reached the final depth for each pit.

Then, they worked their way up from the bottom digging out the areas that would become the tunnels that would contain the treasure.

Paper was easily destroyed by fire or water, so Drake made his maps for this labyrinth on indestructible stones. They placed a map rock inside every tunnel and pit and along the trails leading up to the ridge. To attain the desired shape, they chiseled rocks and added features to them with the same crude but effective adhesive the Miwok used to seal their dugout canoes. Drake made simple metallic oxide stains, formulated by combining the powders of two or more crushed mineral specimens that he collected during the expedition. He used these stains to "paint" indelible information on the rocks. Then he created a large "master rock map," and set it 72 feet away from the main excavation site and placed other marker rocks that would be used to pinpoint the entrance to the labyrinth of tunnels. The most important benefit to

Drake was that the "map rocks" and marker rocks would last indefinitely, as he was not sure how long it would be before he'd be able to return. Given the remoteness of the site, it was unlikely that anybody would come across the giant map rock and the marker rocks, even less likely that anybody could decipher them. He also placed a map rock at the start of every section of the entire tunnel and cave system. Each one displayed an exact but miniature replica of the completed tunnel, room, or cavern. The markings and patterns would be used to guide Drake and his men as they proceeded with the excavation or the eventual recovery of the treasure. Drake wanted the ability to verify that they were doing the work properly.

To assure that the moisture for this entire process would continue unabated, Drake's men redirected the course of the spring water as it approached the bottom of the hill. Instead of flowing through a natural series of streams and waterfalls formed over many centuries, they diverted the water into a set of cement channels that Drake designed, based on his studies of Roman aqueducts that moved water from one area to another. When the water entered the channels, they directed part of the total volume to the various underground tunnels, thus "watering" his treasure to keep it from drying out.

When they completed the excavations, the men began the more difficult process of filling the pits and tunnels one section at a time. This was the most crucial and complicated part of the process. At the top of the cascade there was a hole between the furnace and the aqueduct that functioned as a funnel. Pouring the silver slurry into the top of the cascade allowed it to flow down into the small branches that carried the water from the spring before they redirected it.

Drake ordered that Thomas Doughty be brought from the ship to the ridge so that he could see the entire operation in action. The Queen might not believe Drake when he told her that part of the treasure was buried, but she would have no doubt that it was true if Doughty reported it. When Doughty saw that the Miwok were being forced to jump into the smelter, he cried out to the crewmen stationed around the site. "Stop this man from killing innocent people." Filled with rage, Drake reached down and picked-up a spear left by a Miwok man before he jumped into the smelter. Drake ran the spear through Doughty's abdomen until it exited through his back. Impaled by the spear, Doughty slumped forward and began to speak, but only the word, "Why" came out of his mouth before he died. Drake ordered his men to place Doughty's body at the top of the hole that was funneling the silver slurry to into the stream bed and arroyos.

It took more than one year from the time they landed at Nova Albion to complete the massive project. When it was finished, Drake ordered his men to cover everything with the soil excavated from the pits. He knew that soon new plants would cover the area and it would look as if nothing ever happened.

CHAPTER 8

The Famous Artifact

Before the Golden Gate Bridge was completed in 1939, Northern California's Marin County was sparsely inhabited grassland used by local ranchers to graze their cattle. During the summer months, it was also a popular area for the citizens of San Francisco to escape the damp cold of the city's summer fog and enjoy warm weather amid unparalleled views of the Pacific Ocean and San Francisco Bay.

According to the transcript I read of a tape recorded in October 1956, it was just such a day in mid-1936, when a man named Beryl Shinn was driving on Highway 101 and got a flat tire. He decided that before changing it, he'd treat himself to a picnic, and headed uphill to Greenbrae Ridge where he could enjoy an unobstructed view of San Francisco Bay. After having some food and taking in the natural beauty of the area, he decided to look more closely at a large pile of rocks not far from the edge of the hillside. While he was examining them, sunlight reflecting off something caught his eye, so he reached down to retrieve an object trapped beneath the rocks. It was a small, odd-looking, flat, rectangular piece of metal, encrusted with grime and covered with some kind of markings, which he needed to clean to decipher. Curious what it might be, he took it home with him and scrubbed it clean. When friends came to visit, many admired it, finding it as unusual and intriguing as he did. Then one day, someone suggested that he show it to Dr. Herbert E. Bolton, a former President of the American Historical Association and director of the Bancroft Library. Dr. Bolton was also a professor at the University of California at Berkeley, a historian of international fame, and an expert at evaluating historical documents and artifacts.

In February 1937, Shinn took the item to Dr. Bolton, who felt that it warranted further investigation. He asked Shinn to leave it with him so he could figure out exactly what it was and what historical value it might have.

Two months later on April 5, Dr. Bolton called Beryl Shinn to share some great news. In his opinion the object appeared to be Sir Francis Drake's original "Plate of Brass." He called a meeting of the California Historical Society (CHS) for the following day, during which he formally announced the discovery and proudly proclaimed, "One of the world's long-lost historical treasures has apparently been found."

On April 7, 1937, both the San Francisco Chronicle and the Oakland Tribune carried full accounts of the meeting with pictures of the Plate. Shinn sold the artifact to the California Historical Society for $3,500, a considerable sum at that time. Then CHS presented it to the University of California and furnished a sum of money to be used "for such test or tests to determine the genuineness of the Plate as might seem desirable."

Within five days of the newspaper accounts of that announcement, a man named William Caldera contacted the President of the California Historical Society, stating that he found the same object several years before in 1939 near Drake's Bay while he was employed as a chauffeur for Bank of America's Board Chairman. Caldera also claimed to have disposed of the object a few weeks later by throwing it out of a car window while he was traveling by himself on the road between San Quentin and San Anselmo. Because he could not prove his story, it was ignored as something Caldera simply invented in hopes of gaining remuneration by piggybacking on Shinn's discovery.

The testing of the Plate was performed by three of America's top scientists: Dr. Colin G. Fink, Head of Electrochemistry at Columbia; Dr. E.P. Polushkin, a consulting metallurgical engineer for New York City; and Dr. Harold R. Harrison of MIT. The examination was conducted using the most advanced scientific tests available at the time and required more than seven months to complete.

Their full report and all of Professor Bolton's comments were fascinating to read. Bolton confirmed where the Plate was found by Beryl Shinn in 1936, and that the text of the inscription on the plate corresponded closely with the data cited in the book, The World Encompassed, compiled by Drake's nephew, based on his uncle's journal, the notes of Francis Fletcher. Instead of The World Encompassed, based from the logs of Sir Francis Drake and compiled by his nephew, published in London in 1628, with additional notes by chaplain Francis Fletcher, one of Drake's party on his voyage around the world from 1577-1580. Bolton stated, "In all probability, the plate submitted to us for authentication is the one that had been fastened to a post by Drake's order during his stay in California in 1579," and further added that a thorough examination of the Plate was nevertheless warranted because although the text of the inscription closely corresponded with Fletcher's data in The World Encompassed, anybody could have referred to that book and composed an inscription based on its contents then carved it onto a brass plate.

The report goes into detail regarding each of the tests the Plate was subjected to. For reasons you will discover as you read on, of particular interest to me was the following: "In regard to the lettering," the report stated, "it is also possible that, due to limited equipment on board Drake's ship, some unusual, homemade mechanical device was used in cutting the letters into the plate." Those who examined it also noted that the surface of the plate had many indentations, large and small, scattered over it seemingly at random. Their examination showed that these were not accidental markings but were made by a tool of some sort. It was their opinion that "practically all of the indentations were made after the letters had been engraved."

The last page of the 25-page report gave the following summary:

1. There is no doubt whatsoever that the dark coating on the surface of the plate is a natural patina formed slowly over a period of many years.

2. Numerous surface defects and imperfections usually associated with old brass were found on the

plate.

3. Particles of mineralized plant tissue are firmly embedded in the surface of the plate. This is likewise a very positive measure of the age of the plate.

4. Cross-sections of the brass plate show a lack of homogeneity, and significant amounts of chemical impurities as well as variations in the grain size. All three of these characteristics indicate an object of old origin.

5. Among the impurities found in the rest of the plate there is magnesium, which is present far more than the amount occurring in modern brass.

6. There are numerous indications that the plate was not made by rolling, but rather by hammering, as was the common practice in Drake's time.

On September 16, 1938, they submitted their report to the University of California and concluded: "It is our opinion that the brass plate examined by us is the genuine Drake Plate referred to in the book, The World Encompassed by Drake's nephew, from his uncle's journal and the notes of Francis Fletcher."

For decades the Plate was put on display all around the world and it was considered by many to be the most famous historical artifact ever discovered in the Western United States. In my mind, as I read through all the documentation regarding the Plate, there was never a question about its authenticity.

CHAPTER 9

How to Rewrite History

Late in 1955, some eighteen years after William Caldera claimed to have found and subsequently thrown away the Plate of Brass, he was interviewed along with William Bocqueraz about the incident. In 1936, Bocqueraz was the Chairman of the Board of Bank of America who employed Caldera as his chauffeur. This interview was recorded as part of the University of California's regional cultural history program to see if there was any merit to Caldera's story. Given the fact that his earlier story was utterly discredited, it seemed odd to me that the tape and transcript of this interview are in the Bancroft Library, labeled, "Finding the Drake Plate."

As part of the same cultural history program, Beryl Shinn was also interviewed on October 31, 1956, and here is what he said:

"In the summer of 1936 I was traveling south on Highway 101 from San Rafael toward the ferry to San Francisco, when coming down the ridge approaching Greenbrae one of my tires was punctured. Veering to the side of the road, I stopped my car. On the ridge above was a likely picnic spot. I climbed under a barbed wire fence and climbed to the top of the ridge. There an extensive view presented itself. To the east was Point San Quentin and Upper San Francisco Bay, bounded on the southwest by the Tiburon Peninsula. Below was the tidal estuary of Corte Madera Creek.

Approaching an outcrop of rock near the top of the ridge, I picked up rocks and rolled them down the hill. As I pulled one rock from the soil, I saw the edge of a metal plate, which was partly covered by the rock. When I pulled the plate free from the ground, I noticed that it was about the right size to repair the frame of my automobile. So when I returned to my car, I took it along and tossed it in.

Several months later I thought again of repairing the frame. While handling the plate, I noticed that it seemed to have some inscription on it. I scrubbed it with a brush and so noted a date, 1579, near the top of it. This interested me, so I showed it to a few of my friends, but none could make out what it was until one, a college student, deciphered the word "Drake" and suggested that the metal plate be shown to Dr. Herbert E. Bolton at the University of California. This was done and Dr. Bolton discovered that it was Sir Francis Drake's Plate of Brass."

This series of interviews marked the birth of a plan to steal the Plate of Brass and hide the theft by putting a replica in its place. The thieves believed that they could use the true artifact to locate and recover the great buried treasure of Sir Francis Drake. This complicated plan would involve several key players and take many years to complete. If executed properly,

NOBODY would ever suspect that a crime even occurred, and the perpetrators would be free and clear!

For this plan to succeed, it would be necessary to rewrite all history that related to the discovery of the Plate of Brass.

There is a proven method for changing the public's perception of historical facts. The steps in the process are as follows:

1. Take something regarded by the public as historical truth.

2. Create credible doubt about the truth by publicly quoting contradictory statements attributed to someone regarded as a credible expert in that field.

3. Create a credible alternative to the historical truth by publicly quoting statements by an expert in that field that affirm this possibility.

4. Publicly re-affirm the credible possibility whenever evidence is presented that could confirm the historical truth.

5. Repeat step four above until all individuals who possess actual knowledge of the historical truth have died.

6. Make a final public statement affirming the credible possibility. With nobody remaining alive to dispute the credible possibility history can be rewritten in the desired manner.

As you will soon learn, every step in the process was followed and the world now believes that Drake's Plate of Brass was a "fake." Nothing could be further from t he trut h!

CHAPTER 10

The Drake Navigators' Guild

On January 1, 1970, Dr James D Hart became the Director of UC Berkeley's Bancroft Library. Later that same year, and thirty-four years after Beryl Shinn discovered the Plate of Brass, there was a well-publicized announcement that on November 7, 1970, Mr. Edward Von der Porten, President of the Drake Navigators' Guild would host a luncheon during which new information would be revealed about the artifact. All who attended were presented with commemorative replicas of the Plate and a small brochure. Mr. Rosenthal informed the audience that The Drake Navigators' Guild recently heard that the Plate of Brass found by Beryl Shinn was not authentic after all but was created and presented as part of a hoax put on by the secretive fraternal organization of pranksters known as E Clampus Vitus. Even though Mr. Rosenthal's "new information" was completely unsubstantiated, it nevertheless raised serious doubts about the authenticity of the Plate.

In 1973, the State of California established "The Sir Francis Drake Commission" to investigate and adjudicate the merits of the various possible sites where Drake might have landed in 1579, and to prepare for the Quadra-centennial celebration of Drake's visit to the San Francisco Bay Area. On February 1, 1975, the list of members of the Commission was published, and they held a series of meetings and hearings and even struck a commemorative medal in Drake's honor. However, in 1978, after four years of investigation, they refused to endorse any theory about where Drake landed.

The Drake Navigators' Guild, led by Edward Von der Porten, was outraged, as they were strong proponents of Drake's Bay as the landing site, while many others believed it occurred along the San Quentin Peninsula. Mr. Rosenthal was quoted as saying this about the Commission: "We had major maritime authorities from all over the world here and where did they say [Drake] landed? Every one of them pointed to Drake's Bay, and what did [the Commission] do? Nothing!" The Guild's position was invalidated yet again, when in 1979 the State of California Historical Resources Commission rejected their petition to have Drake's Bay named as the official landing site.

In Nova Albion Research (1997) Oliver Seeler took a closer look at all these events, having spoken with Captain Harold Vancouver who was one of four Members of the Sir Francis Drake Commission that did not offer an opinion where Drake landed. Seeler states that Captain Vancouver made clear that Drake's Bay was not a fit anchorage to careen a ship, which would have been required to perform the needed repairs.

The debate over Drake's landing site combined with Mr. Rosenthal's assertions that the Plate of Brass was a fake enabled the Bancroft Library and the Drake Navigators' Guild to announce in 1974 that the Plate was to be re-examined to determine definitively whether it was the genuine artifact. The joint owners of the Plate; the California Historical Society was never consulted when Bancroft made this unilateral decision.

Bancroft commissioned Dr. Cyril Stanley Smith, from Oxford University to conduct the examination because he was the world's leading authority in the field of Metallurgy. At the completion of the examination, Dr. Smith issued a report that was sent directly to the Bancroft Library. However, the text of this report was never released to the public or to the California Historical Society!

Dr. Smith was not in attendance on April 14, 1976, when Kenneth Wagner addressed a luncheon of educators and representatives from various news media, who were anxious to hear the results. During Mr. Wagner's remarks, he stated that, "It was Dr. Smith's opinion that the Plate was a modern forgery." This statement was the top story on TV news reports and the front-page headline of most newspapers. By the next morning, people around the world believed that the Plate of Brass found by Beryl Shinn in 1936 was a worthless fake!

After reading the newspaper accounts of that luncheon, Dr. Smith felt it necessary to clarify his point of view and express it in writing because it was insufficiently represented in Mr. Wagner's remarks. On April 27, 1976, he wrote the following to Donald Hessen. I have bolded the more significant passages.

"...I was impressed by the close agreement

between the analysis reported by Dr Napoli's in Berkeley and those of Dr. Bridges in Oxford. Such agreement between analysts is by no means universal, but the present results are thoroughly convincing. Both the high zinc content (confirmed by the traces of beta phase observed in the microstructure by Fink in his 1939 examination and wisely commented on by Dr. Caley) as well as the low general impurity content are consistent with a piece of modern "common high brass" and are at least improbable for the sixteenth-century calamine product. I fully concur with Dr Napoli's comment that the analysis suggests the use of refined copper together with zinc made to conform with the maximum impurity specifications for 20th-century "brass spelter."

"....Some useful evidence might come from an examination of the details of the inscription in order to deduce the form of the tools used to make the letters. They were traced (impressed) not engraved or cut. Perhaps the tools were from a small arsenal of tracers, chasers and punches of the type used by silversmiths rather than the smaller set of more rugged chisels that would have been used by a ship's mechanic. Casts made of the impressions would help settle this point. I certainly had the feeling that only the spike notch and the coin hole were shaped with a mechanics rugged V-shaped cold chisel, and that most of the letters were impressed with a narrower tool with sides more nearly parallel. The punch used to make the periods was also too pointed a cone to be a mechanic's blunt center punch. Yet no curved punches were used—perhaps because the maker did not want to suggest such refinement.

In considering the form of the letters in relation

to those found in documents of the period, it should be borne in mind that the sailor who cut the plate was not necessarily literate and may simply have been copying something he could not read. Its style cannot properly be compared with that of formal documents or monumental inscriptions made in centers of civilization!

All of the features that I have noted make me inclined to the opinion that the plate is a modern forgery. However, I firmly believe that evidence from the viewpoint of a materials scientist is not in itself sufficient to form a historical conclusion. The opinion of an experienced curator taking into account the scientific evidence as well as all other factors is patently better than scientific evidence alone. The best of scientific measurements are historically significant only when related to comparable material—excepting only those measurements of age that depend upon invariable radioactive decay. None of my remarks should be taken as evidence of modernity of the plate unless and until the same criteria have been applied with negating results to ancient material of undoubted provenance.

It will disappoint many people if the new studies lead to the conclusion that the plate is a forgery, but the facts must be accepted. The incident is not, however, without educational interest, and it might be given positive educational value if the announcement were accompanied by some discussion of the techniques that are used today to establish authenticity... and a proper display would serve to bring science and the humanities closer together, not only in terms of the use of modern techniques but even more by showing that technology itself has a style and a history that interacts with broader human events.

Yours sincerely,
Cyril Stanley Smith

The lines that I have bolded in Dr. Smith's letter make quite clear that there was no genuine proof that the Plate was a modern forgery. Wagner's misquote of Dr. Smith's opinion aroused my suspicion of foul play. Furthermore, the "news" that it was a "fake" was so disappointing that the public became disenchanted with the entire Drake matter, exactly as the perpetrators wanted. This was part of the plan to rewrite history and freed the conspirators to engage in the next step of their perfidy. As I read through the documents that chronicled this sequence of events, I felt a surge of furious determination to find a way to set things right.

CHAPTER 11

The Disks and The Rod

In April 2002, I dug downward in a place that would not be visible to anyone who might still be interested in harassing me. I dug down ten feet before I began to move horizontally. I noticed the white lines in the tunnel walls just like those I saw the prior year. Again, I let those markings guide my excavation. After a month of work, I realized that this series of tunnels and rooms was quite different from those of my prior excavation. Rather than large caverns, I was excavating a series of much smaller rooms at different levels. At the 25-foot level, there was a lot of water. My research showed that water presented a major problem in ancient mining operations, so I was not surprised by what I was experiencing. This forced me to create a crude but effective pumping system. Each of the small pumps I purchased was only capable of moving water upward by 20 feet, but of course, I was down farther than that, so I improvised a solution. I set the first pump at the lowest point of my excavation and pumped the water about 20 feet up into a 32-gallon garbage can. When that garbage can was full, a second pump sent the water up to the surface and out onto the ground.

I remembered reading that Sir Francis Drake visited the Rio Tinto Mine in Spain, which was in operation since Roman times. When I turned on the computer to refresh my memory about Rio Tinto, I learned that the Romans devised a system to eliminate the water from the bottom of the mine via a series of water wheels that used the water from below to propel the water up from one level to the next. The same story contained a diagram of how the water wheels were arranged, and as I looked at them, I was shocked to see that the shapes and <u>positions of the little rooms that I created were almost in the same pattern as used in Rio Tinto.</u> The only difference was that Drake reversed the positions of several rooms when he re-created the Rio Tinto scenario to bury his treasure. I successfully pumped out the water and continued digging downward, setting up more pumps and 32-gallon garbage cans as I descended. My pumping system, however, was not as effective as I needed it to be. Removing the water from the excavation took at least two hours every day, and the area where I needed to work remained a muddy mess. Finally, I decided to abandon this route and start over at another location that looked promising on the Hondius map inset.

Since I focused my excavation on the black marks on the map the year before, this time I decided to start at the only place on the map represented by a white mark. It was the eye of the man standing next to the smoking fireplace. I determined where in my yard his eye would be located, and on June 15, commenced work, despite a rain shower. The dirt was extremely heavy from the rain, but I forged ahead. Two days later, I was about six feet below the surface when my shovel hit solid rock, so I moved a few feet over to try and dig around it, but I hit rock again. This seemed odd since I was in the correct location, so I decided to clear the dirt away from the rock to see what was going on. By early afternoon the dirt was cleared away and I found not one rock but two.

They were huge and together they formed a triangular arch. At that moment, I knew that this was the entrance I was looking for!

I immediately started digging below the arch, but the dirt was still too wet from the rain on the 15th. In a matter of minutes, my clothes were soaked through, and I was covered in mud. I certainly didn't need another round of toxic metal poisoning. So I got washed off, and although it was frustrating to stop, I decided to let the ground dry for a few days before continuing.

Throughout my quest, whenever I thought that I might find something of interest, I acted on it and was often rewarded. I had this feeling very intensely on the afternoon of June 17, 2002, exactly 423 years from the date on the Plate of Brass. I was taking a walk near the base of the old Hutchinson Quarry in Larkspur Landing. Behind a collection of upscale apartments, I climbed over a retaining wall at the back of a parking lot. Then, drawn on by that feeling, I started looking around on the ground. Almost immediately I spotted a round metal disk that looked like a very thick vending machine slug. I bent down and picked it up then saw a few others and picked them up too. On close inspection, I noticed that the whole circumference of each of these disks contained   ridges like those on a quarter, but the pattern on each one was different. Their ancient appearance made me feel sure they predated the quarry, probably by hundreds of years.

I was very excited when I brought home ten of them that afternoon, especially after I looked at them under my magnifying glass. Surely, they were old enough to have been associated with Drake's visit to Nova Albion. But what were used for? To see if the answer might have anything to do with the Plate of Brass, I needed to examine the patterns on their ridged edges, so I went to a local hobby supplies store and bought some modeling clay. The minute I <u>rolled the disks' edges in the clay,</u> I made my first legitimate discovery: by comparing their patterns with marks on my blown-up photo of Drake's Plate of Brass, I saw the disks' reeded edges were nearly identical to the variation of vertical lines in the inscription on Drake's Plate. I wasn't sure how those tools ended up where I found them, but I was very sure what they were.

The next morning at dawn, I climbed over the fence intended to prevent people from getting too close to the quarry's steep cliff, and spent an hour carefully searching, but found no more disks. However, I did see <u>a metal rod with very unusual features and markings on its end and sides.</u> As soon as I got it home, I used the clay once again and discovered beyond a doubt that this rod was the tool that made the horizontal marks on the inscription of the Plate of Brass. A few days later I returned to the base of the quarry, got down on my hands and knees and looked carefully at everything in the vicinity. I found several disks under a bush and more near the retaining wall, recovering eleven altogether, which I brought home and washed.

<u>I knew that these disks were the missing link in the controversy over the Plate of Brass!</u>

Nevertheless, to be certain about my find, I went through my files and pulled out Dr. Smith's letter, in which he'd said that without the tools used to create the Plate, he could not have made a final determination about its authenticity. Dr. Smith had long since died, but now that I found the tools, there was no doubt that the Plate Beryl Shinn found was genuine. But who could I share this information with to set everything right?

On the computer that night, I located a short report posted by Dr. Frank Asaro of the Berkeley National Laboratory that discussed the results of an X-Ray image of a replica of the Plate of Brass that was removed from the deck of a ship from the 1800s and brought to Berkeley for further study.

On June 18, I called Dr. Napoli and told him what I found. He said that it sounded quite interesting and recommended that I get in touch with Kenneth Wagner, Deputy Director at the Bancroft Library, who was very involved in every aspect of the Drake controversy. When I called Wagner's office, I was told he was out of town and would return on June 24th. The next day, I sent an email to Dr. Napoli, informing him that I found a few more and there were twenty-one "tools" in my possession, reiterating the key points made by Dr. Cyril Stanley Smith in his 1976 letter, and I asked him if he'd be willing to lead a scientific investigation to verify that these were indeed the tools used to produce the inscription on the Plate of Brass. Then I excitedly awaited his reply.

Now that I had the tools in my possession, I wanted the treasure more than ever! The ground was still wet below the stone arch in my backyard, so I purchased several 3' x 8' sheets of foil- coated insulation and sat on them as protection against the possibly toxic mud. Observing the patterns in the dirt, I started to excavate a new tunnel. The foil was quite slippery though, and I ended up sliding into the hole like a kid on a water slide, but I pulled myself out and kept digging.

By June 21, my new excavation consisted of a six-foot deep hole and a twelve-foot-long tunnel. At noon the sun was shining brightly when something remarkable happened that reminded me of the scene from Raiders of the Lost Ark, where Indiana Jones is in Egypt and discovers access to a mysterious burial chamber filled with treasure when he holds up a scepter through which a beam of sunlight shines, pinpointing the secret entrance. <u>At midday on the Summer Solstice the sun was at the perfect angle to shine down through the giant stone arch and onto the wall at the end of my twelve-foot tunnel</u>. It was so incredible that I ran to get my camera. The photograph I took looked like a still from the movie set, and the parallels with that scene were uncanny. I was sure beyond any doubt now that this tunnel was the passageway that led to the buried treasure.

On the morning of June 24, I called the Bancroft Library and made an appointment to see Mr. Wagner. Three days later when I arrived for the meeting, I saw the "Plate of Brass" prominently displayed in a case just inside the main doors to the building. Attached to the case was a two-paragraph recap of the story about Dr. Bolton and E. Clampus Vitus. I wondered why they would bother to display something that was discredited as a "fake". I paid little attention to it because I was excited to show Mr. Wagner and his staff what I found, hoping they'd agree it was significant.

We were not more than two minutes into our conversation when I said, "I have great news, your 'worthless fake' is a true artifact, and I can prove it." I told them what I discovered and mentioned that I spoke with Dr. Napoli just a few days before. I hoped my news would be met with whoops of excitement, but the faces around the table just looked blank and somewhat annoyed. The meeting only lasted about 20 minutes. As I was getting up to leave, I said to Mr. Wagner, "Let me know how you want to proceed," feeling sure what I presented would be a game changer despite the low effect of everyone's response.

<u>A few days later Mr. Wagner sent me an email in which he suggested that I take one of the disks to Metallurgical Laboratories in Concord to have it tested</u>. On July 9, I drove to the lab, and talked with the metallurgist who would do the work. He told me the Spectrographic Analysis required that he drill a small hole into one side of the disk to obtain a sample. I gave my consent and got back in the car for the 45-minute drive home.

I was at work in San Francisco the next day when the lab called and told me that the results were ready. When I arrived to pick up the disk and the report, the metallurgist said, "The metal doesn't match the composition for any specific alloy on any of the lists we have access to." Those results didn't disappoint me though; they made me think that the tools' metal must have been fabricated with alloys used four hundred years ago, but no longer in use today. Rather than suggesting the tools were irrelevant and the Plate a fake, they filled me with a sense of confidence and optimism that no one could shake.

The metallurgist also told me that earlier in the day he'd received a call from Mr. Wagner and provided him with my results as well. At the time, that didn't seem problematic. I fully expected a call from Wagner, congratulating me. But none was forthcoming. In fact, from that day forward Mr. Wagner would never take another phone call from me or respond to any of my emails. At first, I couldn't understand why, but as I thought about it, his response made me very suspicious about him despite his prestigious job. If the Plate of Brass were real, it would surely be worth at least $25 million by now. So why in the world would he turn down an opportunity to convert a "worthless fake" into a "priceless artifact," unless of course there was a deeper, darker secret that he needed to hide?

IMAGE 1
WHERE DRAKE'S PLATE OF BRASS WAS DISCOVERED

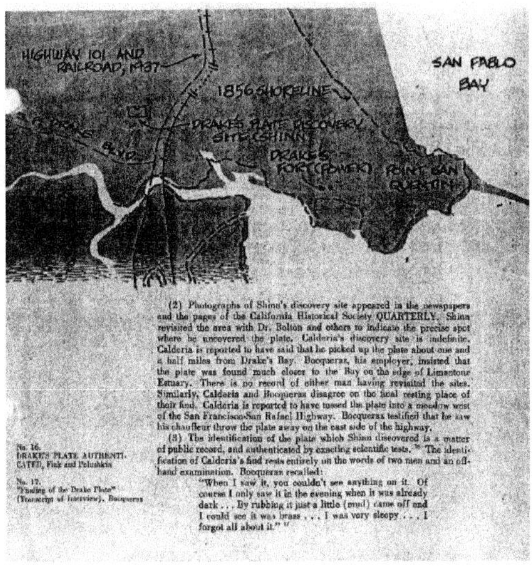

(2) Photographs of Shinn's discovery site appeared in the newspapers and the pages of the California Historical Society QUARTERLY. Shinn revisited the area with Dr. Bolton and others to indicate the precise spot where he uncovered the plate. Calderia's discovery site is indefinite. Calderia is reported to have said that he picked up the plate about one and a half miles from Drake's Bay. Bocqueraz, his employer, insisted that the plate was found much closer to the Bay on the edge of Limantour Estuary. There is no record of either man having revisited the sites. Similarly, Calderia and Bocqueraz disagree on the final resting place of their find. Calderia is reported to have tossed the plate into a meadow west of the San Francisco-San Rafael Highway. Bocqueraz testified that he saw his chauffeur throw the plate away on the east side of the highway.

(3) The identification of the plate which Shinn discovered is a matter of public record, and authenticated by exacting scientific tests. [16] The identification of Calderia's find rests entirely on the words of two men and an off-hand examination. Bocqueraz recalled:

> "When I saw it, you couldn't see anything on it. Of course I only saw it in the evening when it was already dark . . . By rubbing it just a little (mud) came off and I could see it was brass . . . I was very sleepy . . . I forgot all about it." [17]

No. 16.
DRAKE'S PLATE AUTHENTICATED, Fink and Polushkin

No. 17.
"Finding of the Drake Plate" (Transcript of Interview), Bocqueraz

Plate No. — Looking East over San Quentin Bay. Bocque Shinn found Drake's Plate of Brass below the far side of the outcrop embedded in the ground and partly covered by a rock, evidence that it had been where buried for a long time.

IMAGE 2
CHORIS PAINTING MATCHING VIEW FROM MY YARD

IMAGE 3
INSET FROM HONDIUS MAP – THE TREASURE MAP

IMAGE 4
HAND-DRAWN MAP OF POSSIBLE TREASURE ZONE

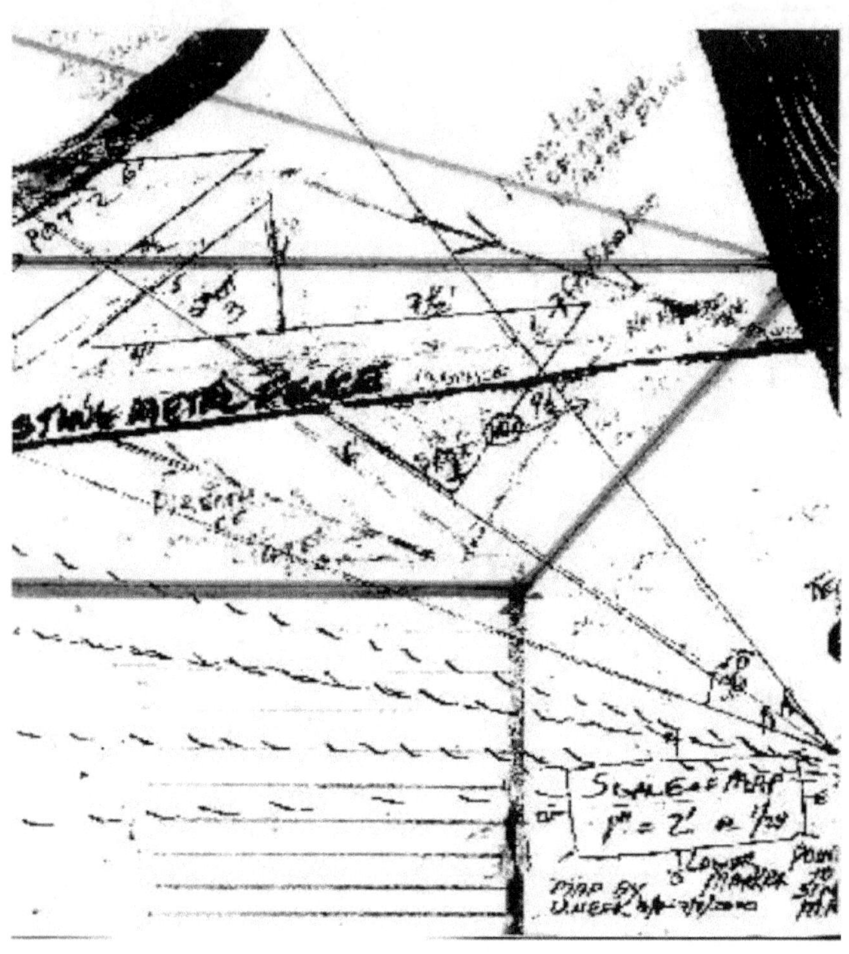

IMAGE 5
A SPOT WHERE NOTHING WOULD GROW

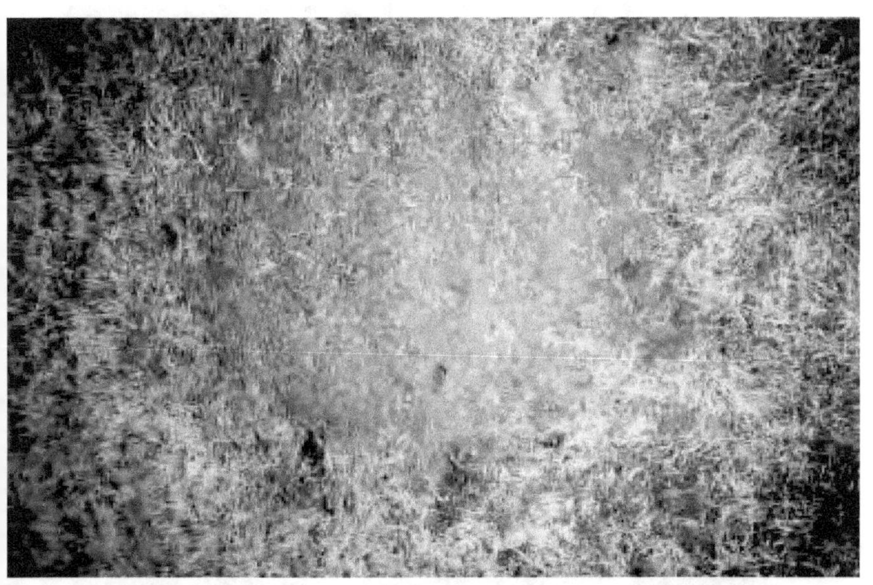

IMAGE 6
THE MINI BACKHOE

IMAGE 7
RESULTS OF SOIL ASSAY

Soil Samples Analyses Results, %

SAMPLE ID	GOLD	SILVER	COPPER	LEAD
1	<0.001	N/A	N/A	N/A
2	0.460	0.915	N/A	<0.001
3	N/A	1.870	N/A	N/A
4	0.060	N/A	N/A	N/A
5	0.065	84.515	0.005	N/A
6	0.085	0.345	N/A	N/A
7	N/A	1.240	N/A	N/A
8	N/A	2.685	N/A	N/A

SAMPLE 5 IS 84.515% SILVER

IMAGE 8
DIGGING SMALL EXPLORATORY HOLES

IMAGE 9
DRAKE'S ROCK

IMAGE 10
THE RHOMBIC DODECAHEDRON

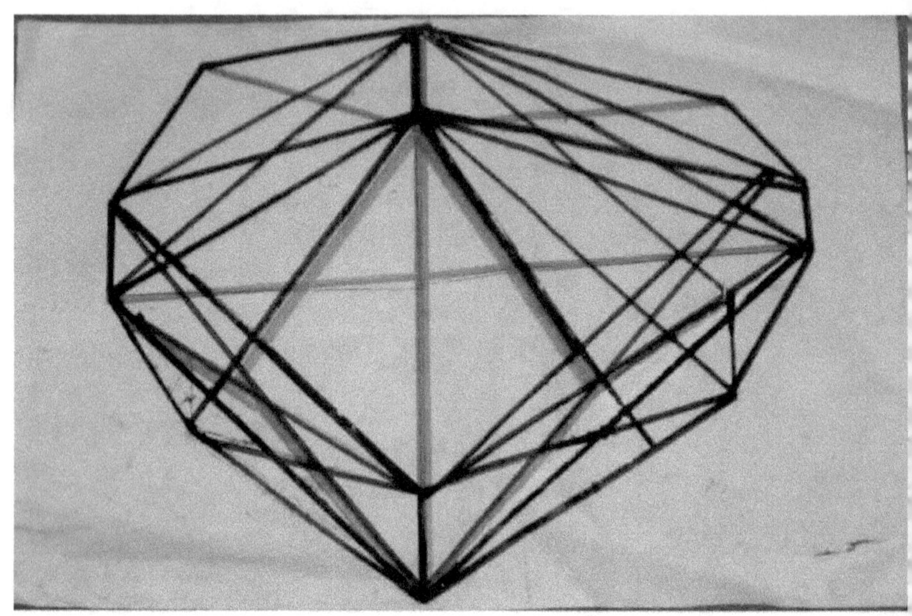

IMAGE 11
THE AZTEC STONE CARVING

IMAGE 12
ENLARGED INSET FROM THE HONDIUS MAP

IMAGE 13
THE PENINSULA

IMAGE 14
THE ISLAND

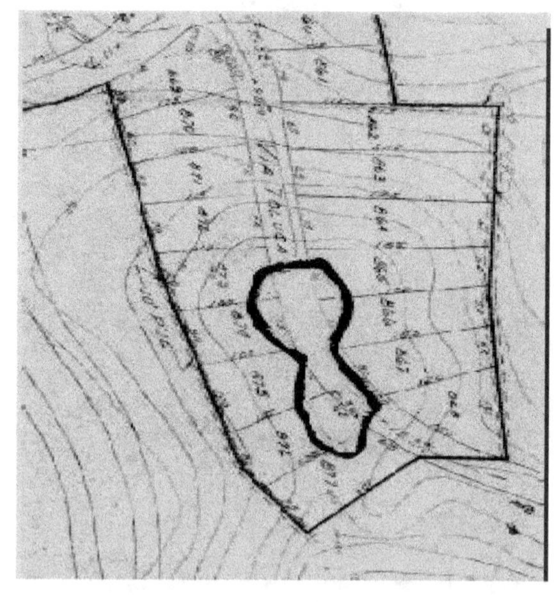

IMAGE 15
FLAT TREASURE MAP PERSPECTIVE
LARKSPUR LANDING

Hondius Broadside Map Inset compared to Google Earth image of Larkspur Landing

IMAGE 16
BACKYARD LOOKED LIKE A WAR ZONE

IMAGE 17
POISONOUS CAVERN CLAY IN COLORED LAYERS

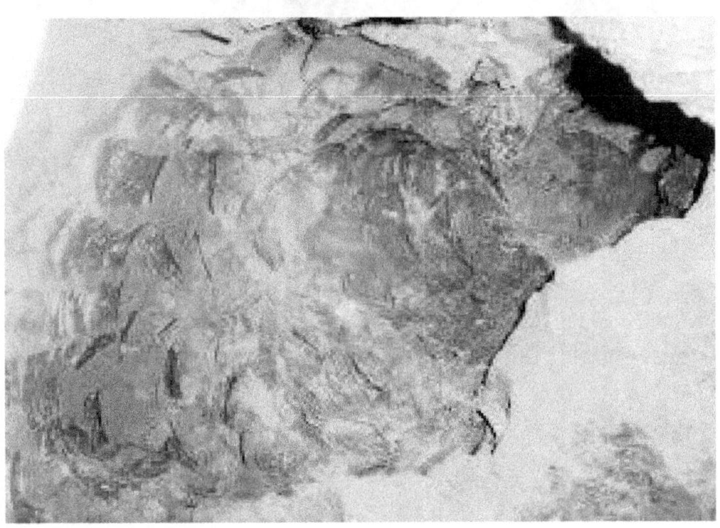

IMAGE 18
A 12 FOOT-LONG CANNON BARREL

IMAGE 19
CLAY IMAGE OF PARROT IN CAVERN WALL

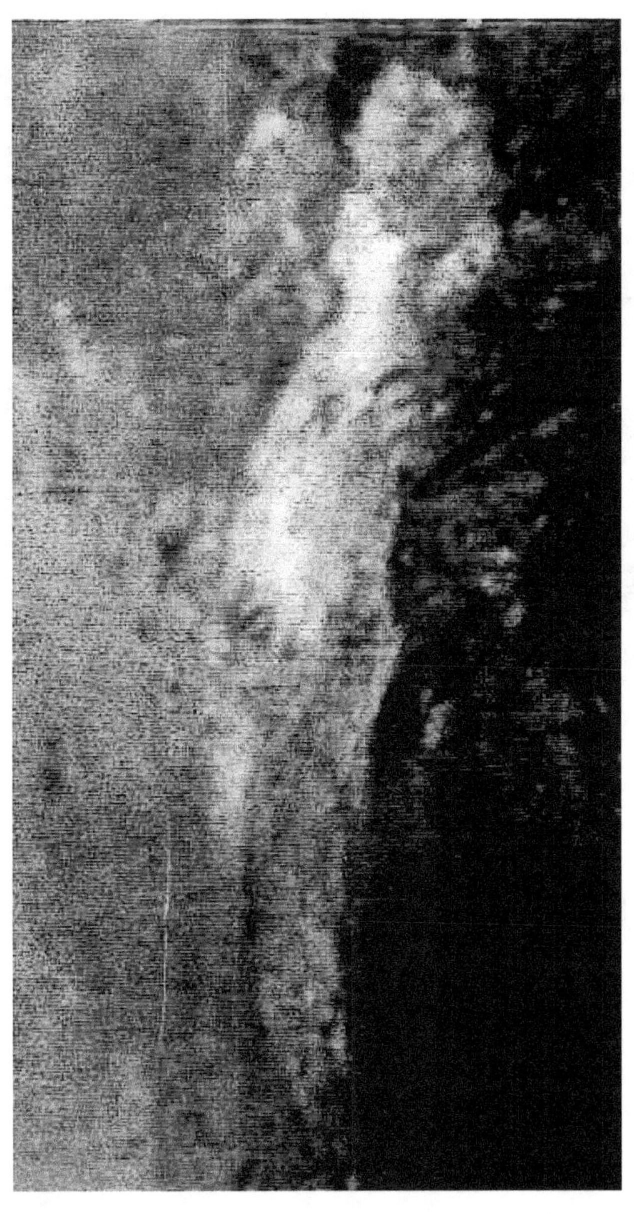

IMAGE 20
AN ICA STONE FROM PERU

IMAGE 21
THE EMERALD GODDESS OF PERU

IMAGE 22
HISTORICAL SKETCH SHOWING FOUR LARGE SHIPS

IMAGE 23
DISCARDED CARTS WERE FOUND
AT SAN QUENTIN

San Rafael, Marin County
November 14, 1857

D.D. Deub
Sheriff, Marin County

IMAGE 24
DRAKE'S RE-CREATION OF RIO TINTO MINE AT NOVA

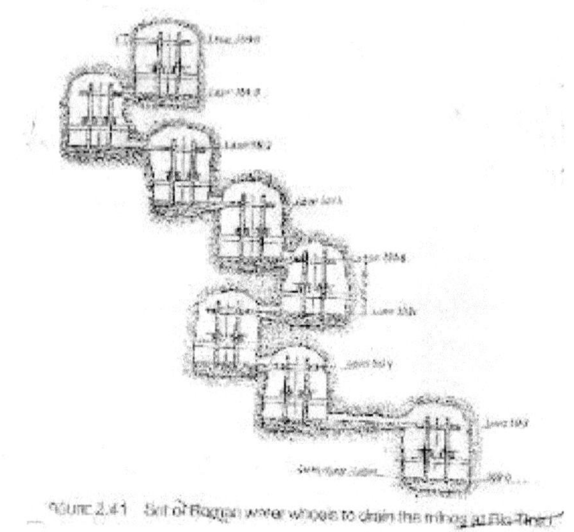

ALBION
ACTUAL ARRANGEMENT AT RIO TINTO (ABOVE)
RE-ARRANGEMENT AT NOVA ALBION(BELOW)

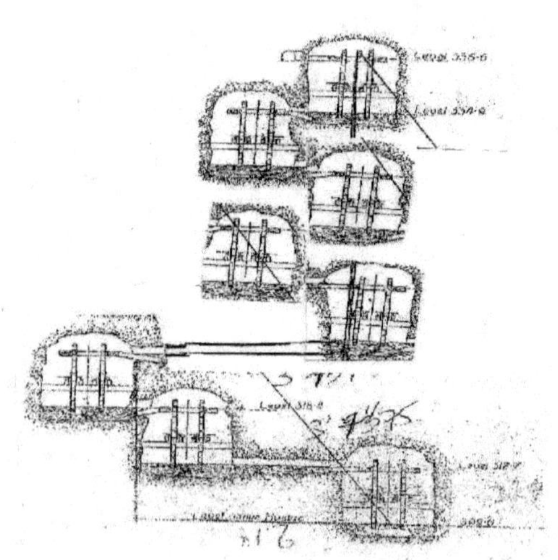

IMAGE 25
TRACING TOOLS ROLLED OUT ON CLAY

IMAGE 26
THE METAL ROD

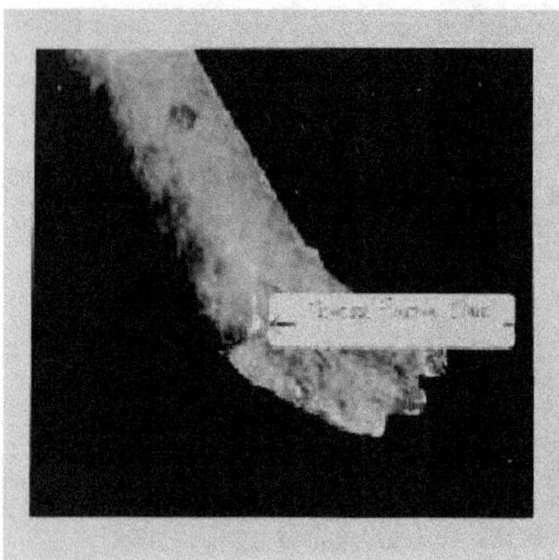

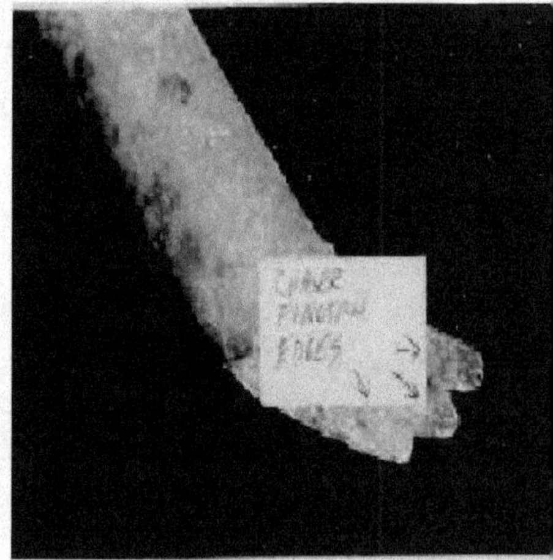

IMAGE 27
THE ENTIRE SET OF TRACING TOOLS

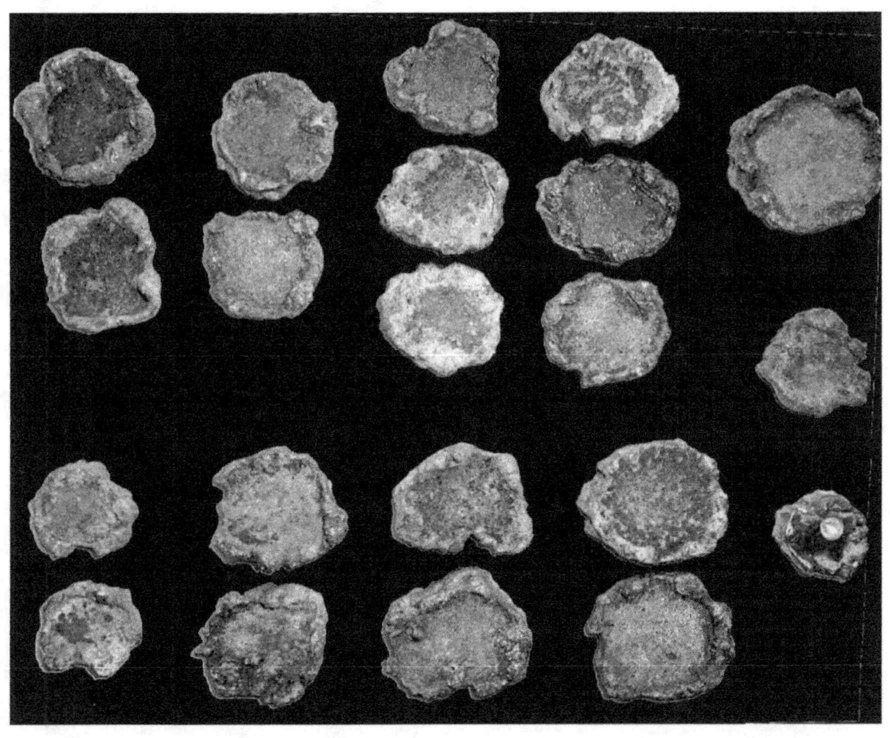

IMAGE 28
LIGHT AT THE END OF THE TUNNEL - SUMMER SOLSTICE

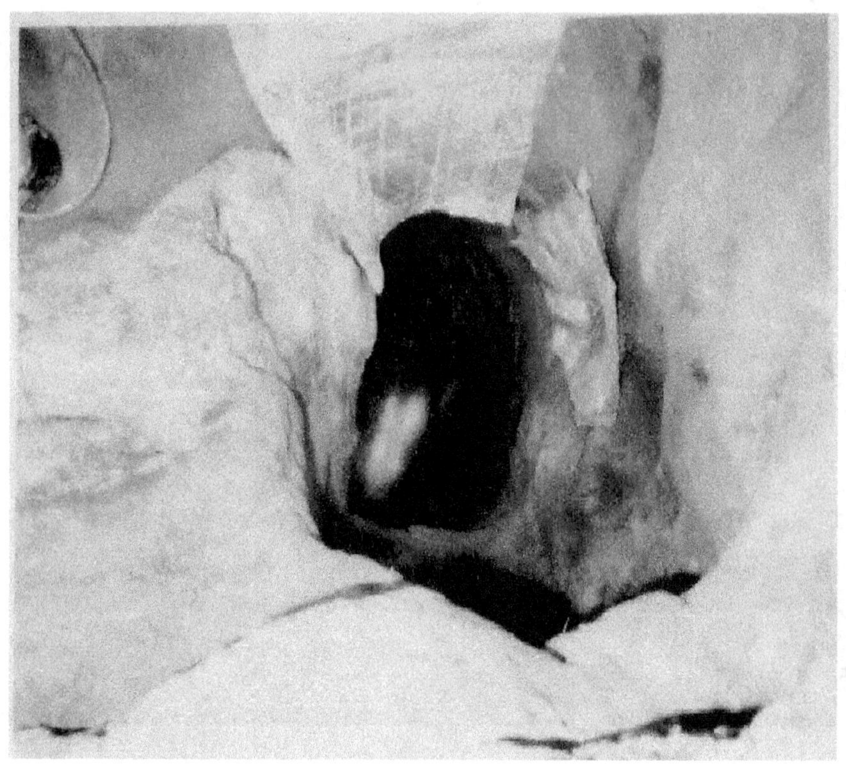

IMAGE 29
REQUEST BY WAGNER TO HAVE TOOLS ASSAYED

Page 1 of 1

u.neek

From:	████████@library.berkeley.edu>
To:	U.Neek <passaage@neteze.com>████████f@library.berkeley.edu>
Sent:	Tuesday, July 09, 2002 9:51 AM
Subject:	Re: From Robert Stupack

Rob,

I talked with ████████ after your visit and he's trying to think of any specialists he might know.

Meanwhile, it would behoove you, I feel, to have an assay done of the material in the dozen or so plugs you showed us. Their make-up and their hardness relative to a brass plate would have bearing on how well they might be used to trace into brass. Certainly the conventional chasing tools of the period were most typically in a form that we might call chisels.

I'll let you know if I can locate any specialists who might help us further.

████

At 04:48 PM 07/08/2002 -0700, U.Neek wrote:

████

>
>Just checking to see if there has been any progress in assembling the team
>of scientists and artisans necessary to study the "tools"?
>
>Please keep in mind that verifying the "tools" will have two immediate
>benefits:
>
>1. A meteoric rise in the overall value of Bancroft's Collection because
>the "Plate" will go from 'worthless fake' to 'priceless artifact'.
>
>2. An exalted position in the history of the Bancroft Library for the
>individual who creates this value!
>
>I eagerly await your reply.
>
>Rob
>
>
>

7/9/02

IMAGE 30
RADIOGRAPH OF THE PLATE OF BRASS

IMAGE 31
EVIDENCE OF COMPUTER HACKING

```
                          msxml4-KB8927978-enu
=== Verbose logging started: 1/30/2007  13:14:18  Build type: SHIP UNICODE
3.01.4000.2435  Calling process: C:\WINDOWS\system32\msiexec.exe ===
MSI (c) (84:F8) [13:14:18:859]: Resetting cached policy values
MSI (c) (84:F8) [13:14:18:859]: Machine policy value 'Debug' is 0
MSI (c) (84:F8) [13:14:18:859]: ******* RunEngine:
           ******* Product: c:\d772db47e9d1d0e0f12c5d04ab0205dd\msxml.msi
           ******* Action:
           ******* CommandLine: **********
MSI (c) (84:F8) [13:14:18:859]: Client-side and UI is none or basic: Running entire
install on the server.
MSI (c) (84:F8) [13:14:18:859]: Grabbed execution mutex.
MSI (c) (84:F8) [13:14:19:046]: Cloaking enabled.
MSI (c) (84:F8) [13:14:19:046]: Attempting to enable all disabled priveleges before
calling Install on Server
MSI (c) (84:F8) [13:14:19:062]: Incrementing counter to disable shutdown. Counter
after increment: 0
MSI (s) (D0:70) [13:14:19:250]: Grabbed execution mutex.
MSI (s) (D0:7C) [13:14:19:343]: Resetting cached policy values
MSI (s) (D0:7C) [13:14:19:343]: Machine policy value 'Debug' is 0
MSI (s) (D0:7C) [13:14:19:343]: ******* RunEngine:
           ******* Product: c:\d772db47e9d1d0e0f12c5d04ab0205dd\msxml.msi
           ******* Action:
           ******* CommandLine: **********
MSI (s) (D0:7C) [13:14:19:468]: Machine policy value 'DisableUserInstalls' is 0
MSI (s) (D0:7C) [13:14:19:671]: File will have security applied from OpCode.
MSI (s) (D0:7C) [13:14:19:765]: SOFTWARE RESTRICTION POLICY: Verifying package -->
'c:\d772db47e9d1d0e0f12c5d04ab0205dd\msxml.msi' against software restriction policy
MSI (s) (D0:7C) [13:14:19:765]: SOFTWARE RESTRICTION POLICY:
c:\d772db47e9d1d0e0f12c5d04ab0205dd\msxml.msi has a digital signature
MSI (s) (D0:7C) [13:14:26:593]: SOFTWARE RESTRICTION POLICY:
c:\d772db47e9d1d0e0f12c5d04ab0205dd\msxml.msi is permitted to run at the
'unrestricted' authorization level.
MSI (s) (D0:7C) [13:14:26:609]: End dialog not enabled
MSI (s) (D0:7C) [13:14:26:609]: Original package ==>
c:\d772db47e9d1d0e0f12c5d04ab0205dd\msxml.msi
MSI (s) (D0:7C) [13:14:26:609]: Package we're running from ==>
c:\WINDOWS\Installer\fe0033.msi
MSI (s) (D0:7C) [13:14:26:718]: APPCOMPAT: looking for appcompat database entry with
ProductCode '{37477865-A3F1-4772-AD43-AAFC68CFF99F}'.
MSI (s) (D0:7C) [13:14:26:718]: APPCOMPAT: no matching ProductCode found in
database.
MSI (s) (D0:7C) [13:14:26:750]: MSCOREE already loaded, using loaded copy
MSI (s) (D0:7C) [13:14:26:781]: Machine policy value 'TransformsSecure' is 0
MSI (s) (D0:7C) [13:14:26:781]: User policy value 'TransformsAtSource' is 0
MSI (s) (D0:7C) [13:14:26:781]: Machine policy value 'DisablePatch' is 0
MSI (s) (D0:7C) [13:14:26:781]: Machine policy value 'AllowLockdownPatch' is 0
MSI (s) (D0:7C) [13:14:26:781]: Machine policy value 'DisableLUAPatching' is 0
MSI (s) (D0:7C) [13:14:26:781]: Machine policy value 'DisableFlyWeightPatching' is 0
MSI (s) (D0:7C) [13:14:26:781]: APPCOMPAT: looking for appcompat database entry with
ProductCode '{37477865-A3F1-4772-AD43-AAFC68CFF99F}'.
MSI (s) (D0:7C) [13:14:26:781]: APPCOMPAT: no matching ProductCode found in
database.
MSI (s) (D0:7C) [13:14:26:781]: Transforms are not secure.
MSI (s) (D0:7C) [13:14:26:796]: Command Line: REBOOT=ReallySuppress
CURRENTDIRECTORY=c:\d772db47e9d1d0e0f12c5d04ab0205dd CLIENTUILEVEL=3
CLIENTPROCESSID=2692
MSI (s) (D0:7C) [13:14:26:812]: PROPERTY CHANGE: Adding PackageCode property. Its
value is '{2827DCD9-53FA-4885-B6CD-698623819F4C}'.
MSI (s) (D0:7C) [13:14:26:812]: Product Code passed to Engine.Initialize:
''
MSI (s) (D0:7C) [13:14:26:812]: Product Code from property table before transforms:
'{37477865-A3F1-4772-AD43-AAFC68CFF99F}'
MSI (s) (D0:7C) [13:14:26:812]: Product Code from property table after transforms:
                               Page 1
```

```
                          msxml4-KB8927978-enu.log
Property(S): OutOfDiskSpace = 0
Property(S): OutOfNoRbDiskSpace = 0
Property(S): PrimaryVolumeSpaceAvailable = 0
Property(S): PrimaryVolumeSpaceRequired = 0
Property(S): PrimaryVolumeSpaceRemaining = 0
Property(S): SOURCEDIR = c:\d772db47e9d1d0e0f12c5d04ab0205dd\
Property(S): SourcedirProduct = {37477865-A3F1-4772-AD43-AAFC68CFF99F}
Property(S): ProductToBeRegistered = 1
Property(S): ReplacedInUseFiles = 1
MSI (s) (D0:7C) [13:14:57:953]: Note: 1: 1707
MSI (s) (D0:7C) [13:14:57:953]: Product: MSXML 4.0 SP2 (KB927978) -- Installation
completed successfully.

MSI (s) (D0:7C) [13:14:57:953]: The Windows Installer initiated a system restart to
complete or continue the configuration of 'MSXML 4.0 SP2 (KB927978)'.

MSI (s) (D0:7C) [13:14:57:984]: Cleaning up uninstalled install packages, if any
exist
MSI (s) (D0:7C) [13:14:57:984]: MainEngineThread is returning 3010
MSI (s) (D0:70) [13:14:58:093]: Destroying RemoteAPI object.
MSI (s) (D0:20) [13:14:58:109]: Custom Action Manager thread ending.
=== Logging stopped: 1/30/2007  13:14:57 ===
MSI (c) (84:F8) [13:14:58:109]: Decrementing counter to disable shutdown. If counter
>= 0, shutdown will be denied.  Counter after decrement: -1
MSI (c) (84:F8) [13:14:58:109]: MainEngineThread is returning 3010
=== Verbose logging stopped: 1/30/2007  13:14:58 ===
```

IMAGE 32
CLAY IMAGE OF BUZZARD 36 FT. BELOW GROUND

IMAGE 33
THE TREASURE CAVERN – 36 FT. BELOW GROUND

IMAGE 34
THE 20 FOOT-LONG PLASTIC PIPE

IMAGE 35
MARKING THE HOLE FOR THE WELL DRILLERS

IMAGE 36
THE DRILLING CREW IN ACTION

IMAGE 37
LOOKING UP THROUGH ARCH AT BOTTOM OF THE PIPE

IMAGE 38
THE GOLD-COVERED ROCK

IMAGE 39
THE GIANT EMERALD

IMAGE 40
EXCAVATION DESTROYED OVERNIGHT BY HEAVY RAIN

IMAGE 41
ROBERT POWER REALIZED THE REAL PLATE
WAS STOLEN AND REPLACED WITH AN REPLICA

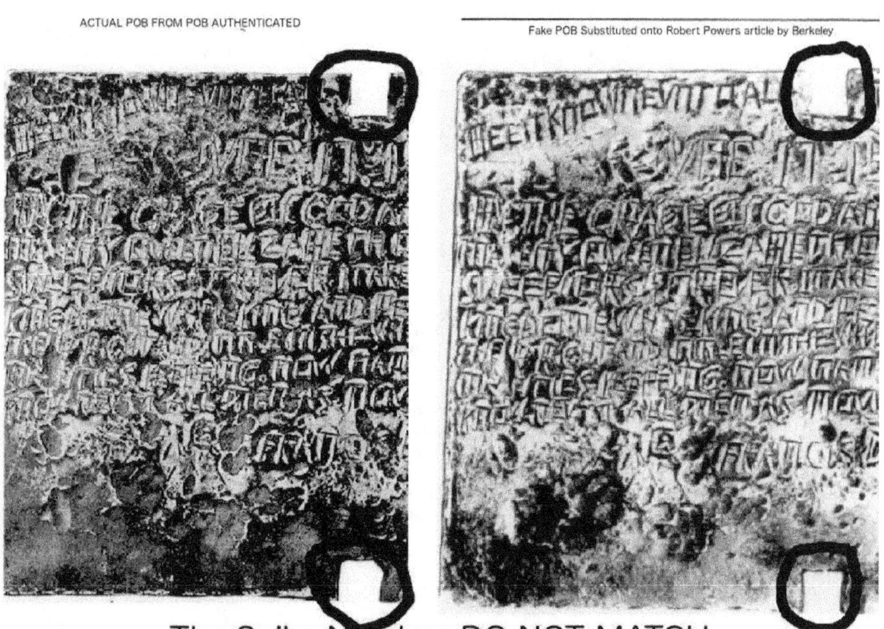

The Spike Notches DO NOT MATCH

IMAGE 42
ROBERT POWERS WRITES OF DIFFERENCES NOTED

```
                    WHO LOST THE
                        "N"
                   IN "VNTO" ON THE
                 DRAKE PLATE OF BRASS?


     In 1937, the California Historical Society stated in The
Plate of Brass that it was presenting to the University of Cali-
fornia at Berkeley a manuscript in old brass which in part read:


               NOW NAMED BY ME AN TO BEE
          KNOWNE VNTO ALL MEN AS NOVA ALBION.

                     C  FRANCIS DRAKE.


     In 1976, the Lawrence Radiation Laboratory at Berkeley made a
positive print of a radiograph of the Drake Plate of Brass which
revealed that the "N" in "V[N]TO" is missing.  If the Stanford
Indian took this letter from the Plate of Brass as he tradition-
ally takes back his axe, then the Plate of Brass is a clever XX
century hoax.  However, if Francis Drake's engraver was the re-
sponsible party, then it is a clumsy XVI century manuscript.

     If one ponders B, P, R and D in Elizabethan black letter,
writes B, P, R and D in Nova Albion brass letter, he may be
able to tell the work of a clumsy Elizabethan knave from that
of a clever Stanford brave.
                              Robert H. Power
                              September 20, 1977
```

IMAGE 43
ROBERT POWER CONTINUES TRYING TO IMPLICATE BANCROFT

Robert H. Power * Nut Tree, Ca. 95688 * U.S.A.

                    Director   May 11/79
The Bancroft Library
University of California
Berkeley, California   94720

Dear   ,

     I appreciated receiving A Supplement 1979
which allowed that "By Me C G Francis Drake" was
a "scholarly investigation."   I still find it a
most intriguing contradiction that an inscription
with the traits of the 16th century is inscribed
on a piece of brass with traits similar to those
found in twentieth century brass. This contradiction, of course, is precisely the basis of the
exchange of correspondence between Dr. .   and
myself in September-November, 1977. I shared this
correspondence with Professor Smith who likewise
reflected a similar theme in his letter to you
(April 1, 1979).

     In late March while in England, I talked
briefly to Dr.   and was disappointed to
learn that Oxford had not been requested to do
any further investigations on the Plate even
though Dr.   had personally suggested a
test to determine if the patina had been formed
at high or low temperatures, and he further mentioned a recommendation that the lead isotopes
be studied to determine if possible the origin
of zinc component in the Plate.

IMAGE 44
ROBERT POWER DEATH CERTIFICATE

STATE OF CALIFORNIA
CERTIFICATION OF VITAL RECORD

COUNTY of SOLANO

CERTIFICATE OF DEATH
STATE OF CALIFORNIA
USE BLACK INK ONLY

39148   000804

DECEDENT PERSONAL DATA

Name: Robert Harbison Power
Sex: M
Date of Death: May 13, 1991, 1840 hours
Race: White
Date of Birth: April 19, 1926
Age: 65
State of Birth: CA
Citizen: U.S.A.
Full Name of Father: Edward Power — CA
Full Maiden Name of Mother: Helen Harbison — CA
Military Service: 1944 to 1945
Social Security No.: 569-36-8806
Marital Status: Married
Name of Surviving Spouse: Margaret Casey
Usual Occupation: Chairman-Manager
Kind of Business or Industry: Food Industry
Name of Employer: The Nut Tree
Years in Occupation: 43 Yrs.
Education — Years Completed: 14 Yrs.

USUAL RESIDENCE
Street and Number or Location: Off Monte Vista Ave.
City: Nut Tree
Zip Code: 95696
County: Solano
Years in This County: 55 Yrs.
State or Foreign Country: Ca.
Name, Relationship, Mailing Address and Zip Code of Informant: Margaret Power-Wife, P.O. Box 106, Nut Tree, Ca. 95696

PLACE OF DEATH
Place of Death: Residence
County: Solano
Street Address: Off Monte Vista Ave.
City: Nut Tree

CAUSE OF DEATH
Immediate Cause: Respiratory Failure — 2 hrs.
Due to: Pulmonary Metastases — 3 mos.
Due to: Metastatic Gastroesophageal Carcinoma — 5 mos.
Other Significant Conditions Contributing to Death: Disseminated Intravascular Coagulation
Operation performed: Esophagoscopy: 1-7-91

PHYSICIAN'S CERTIFICATION
Attended since: 6-5-72
Last seen alive: 5-3-91
Physician's License Number: A21739
Date: 5-15-91
Physician's Name and Address: Ronald S. Rushford, M.D., 601 Buck Ave., Vacaville, California 95688

FUNERAL DIRECTOR AND LOCAL REGISTRAR
Disposition: Burial
Place of Disposition: Vacaville-Elmira Cemetery, Vacaville, Ca.
Date: 5-17-1991
Signature of Embalmer: Laura J. Armitage
License Number: #4443
Name of Funeral Director: McCune Garden Chapel
Funeral License No.: FD 388
Signature of Local Registrar: Thomas Cavanaugh
Registration Date: May 15, 1991

005280803

IMAGE 45
CONGLOMERATE STONE TOOL WITH INCA MARKING

IMAGE 46
EARRING OF INCA QUEEN MATCHES GLYPH FROM NAZCA PLAINS

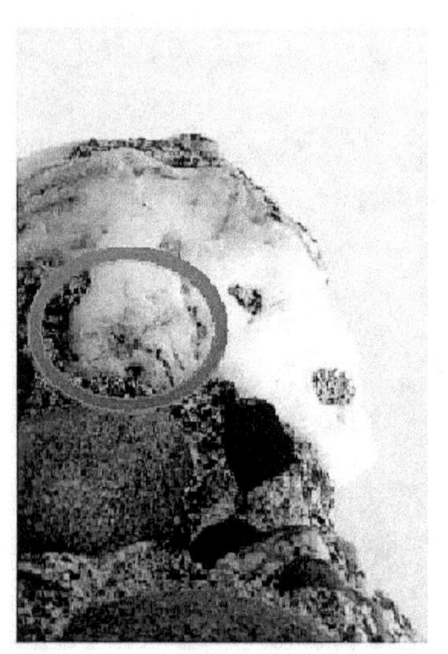

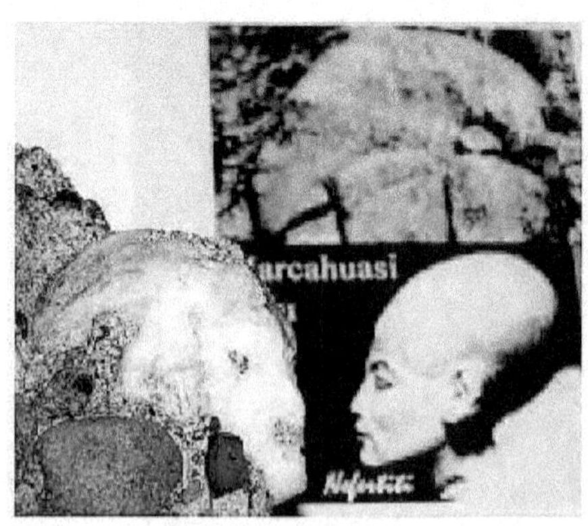

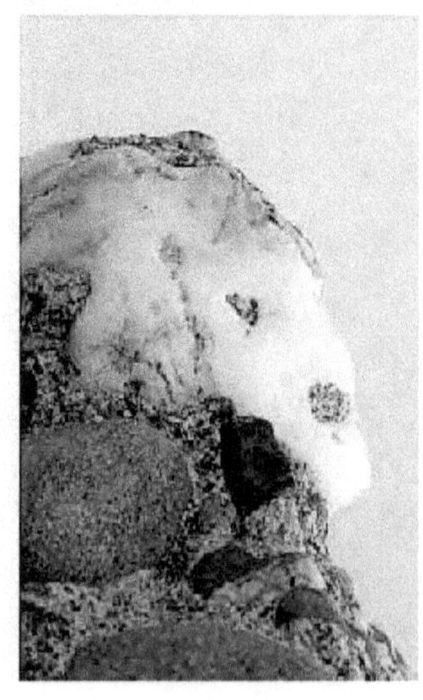

IMAGE 47
THE CEILING OF THE FRONT CAVERN LOOKED LIKE THE HEAVENS

IMAGE 48
DRAKE MODELED NOVA ALBION CRYPTS AFTER A CELTIC BURIAL MOUND IN IRELAND

Plan of the passage at Newgrange, showing the path of the beam of sunlight which enters the roofbox above the entrance at sunrise on the Winter Solstice, penetrating the passage all the way to the backstone at the rear chamber.

IMAGE 49
272 LB. STONE WITH IMAGE OF MAYAN WARRIOR

IMAGE 50
IMAGE ON STONE COMPARED TO MAYAN TEMPLE

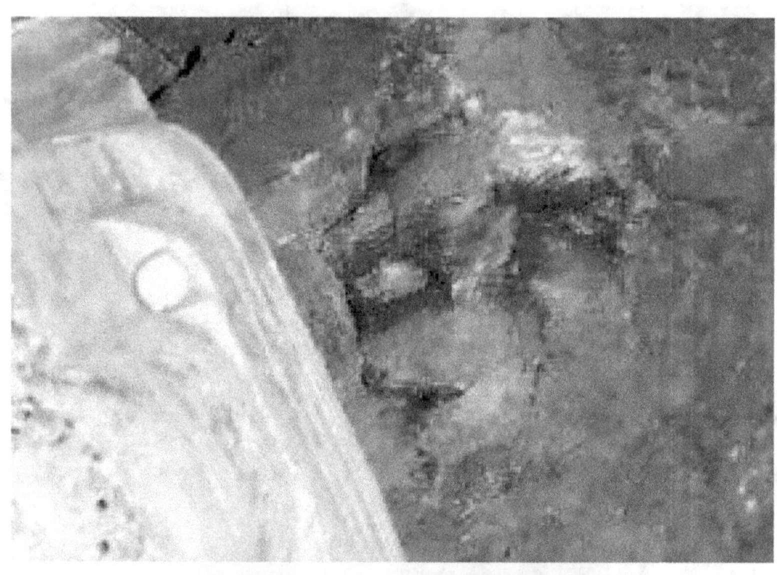

IMAGE 51
FRONT YARD COVERED IN PLASTIC SHEETING

IMAGE 52
COLLAPSE OF THE FRONT YARD

IMAGE 53
CERTIFICATION OF DIAMOND

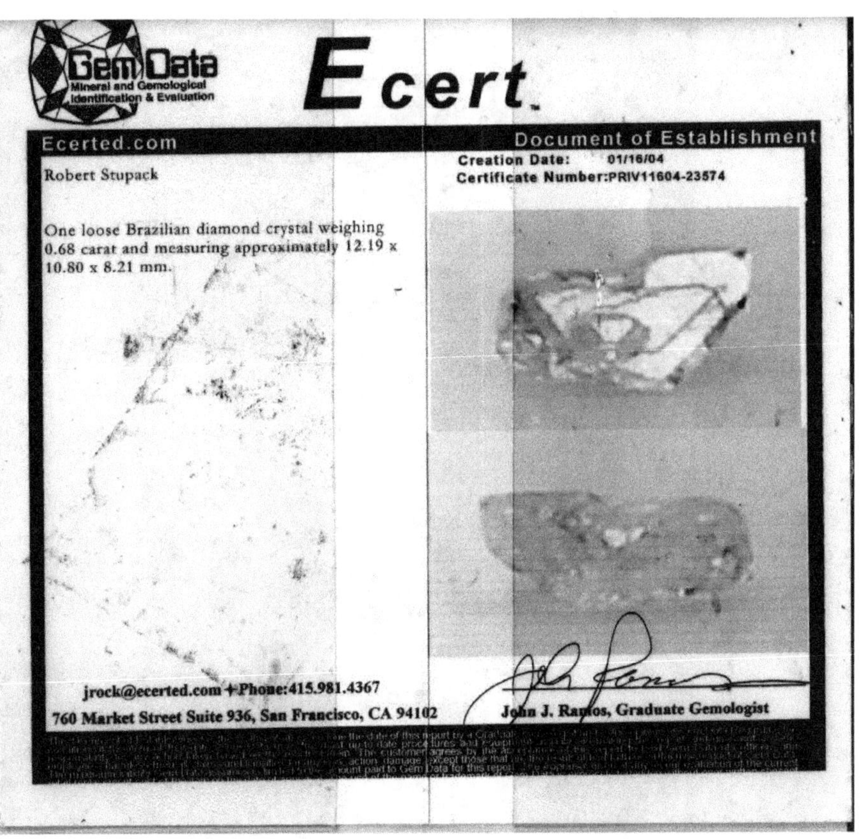

IMAGE 54
CUPELLATION HEARTH FOUND ON GREENBRAE RIDGE

IMAGE 55
CLOISONNE WRITING INSTRUMENT
AND MING CHARM

5   6   7   8

IMAGE 56
LOCATION OF "THE LOST HARBOR"

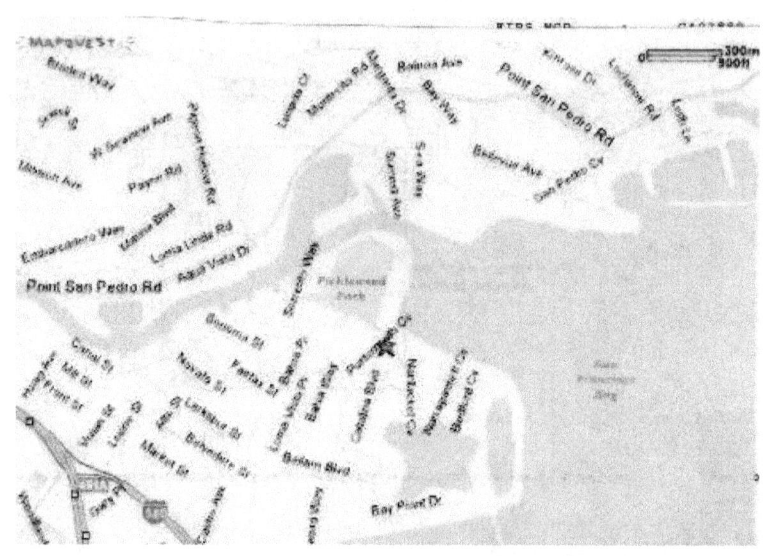

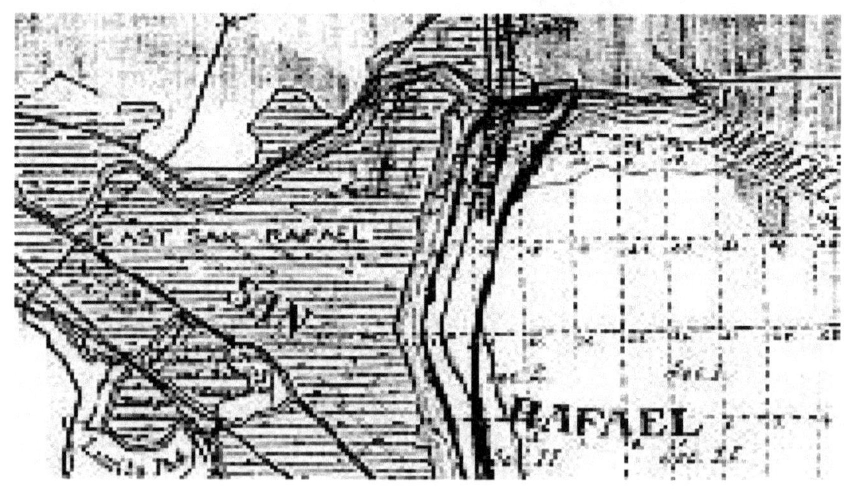

38.3 degrees - .72 degrees= 37.58 degrees
Today, it's Pickleweed Park

IMAGE 57
GALLEON AND CARAVEL DECKING NAILS

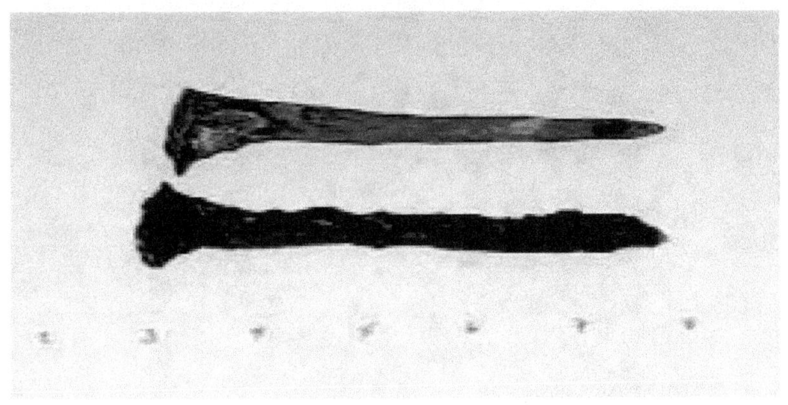

SPANISH GALLEON NAILS (ABOVE)

PORTUGUESE CARAVEL (BELOW)

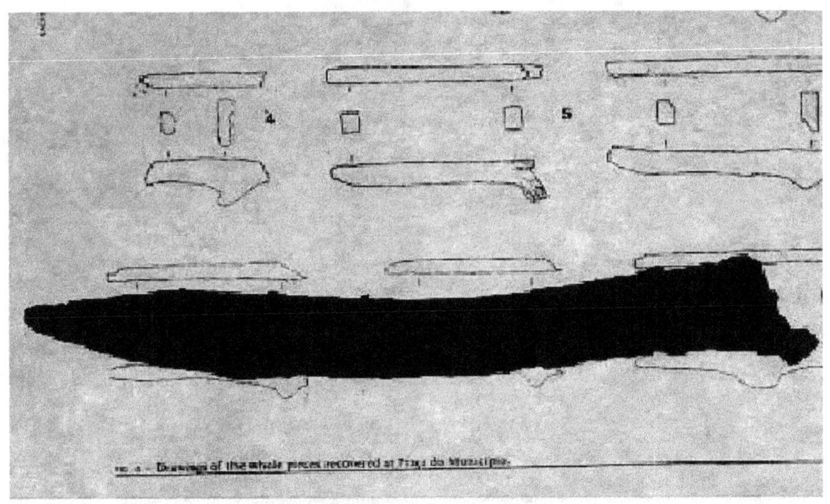

IMAGE 58
GUNPOWDER LADLE FROM SPANISH GALLEON

IMAGE 59
RUDDER SYSTEM PINTLE FROM SPANISH GALLEON

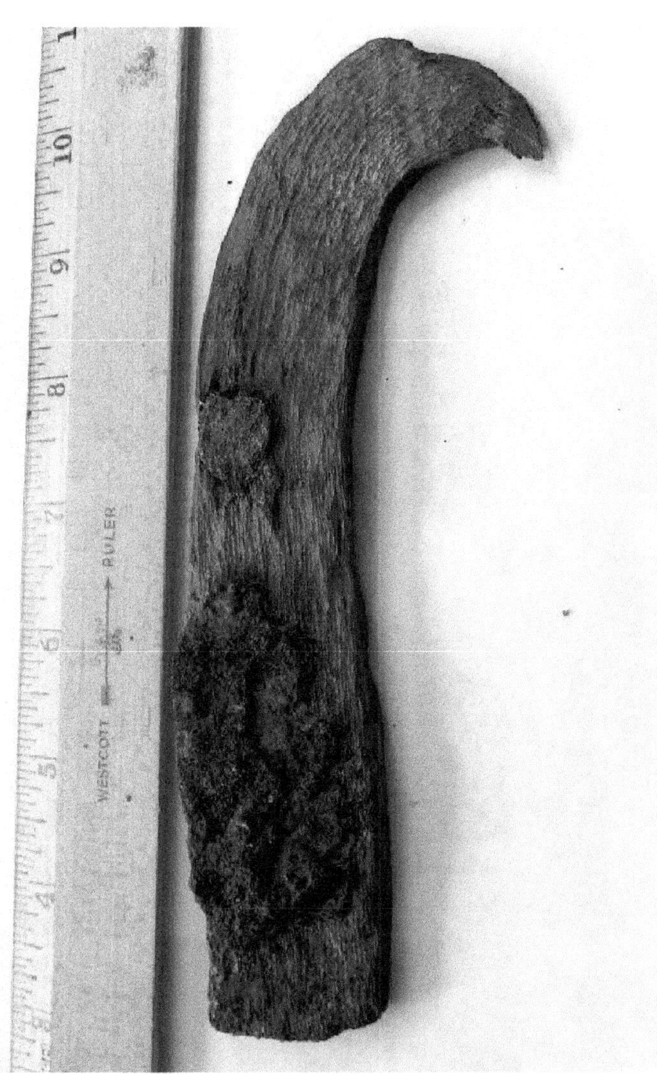

IMAGE 60
FEATURES OF THE ROD MEASURED BY ENGINEERING COMPANY

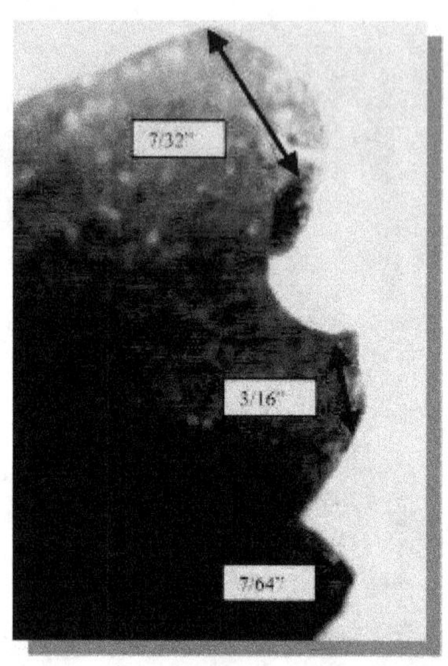

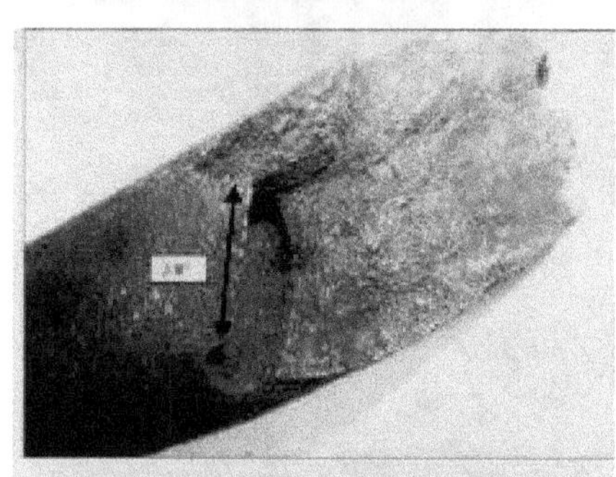

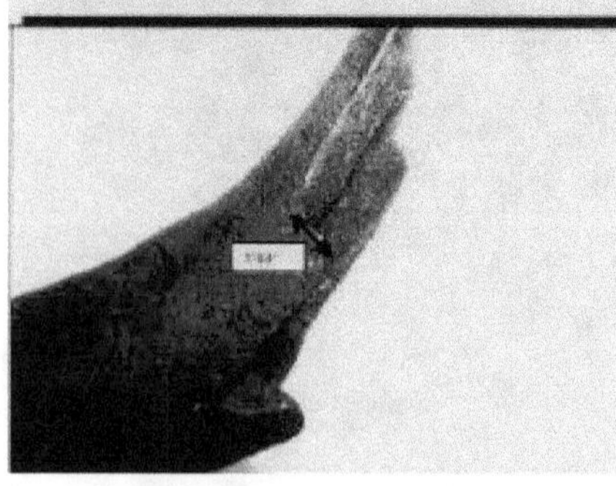

IMAGE 61
METAL FLAWS ON SET OF TOOLS MATCH
REAL PLATE OF BRASS

IMAGE 62
CEILING OF CAVEN MODIFIED BY ADDING SHARP ROCKS AND SECTION CUT-OUT

IMAGE 63
THE SMILING GHOST/FROWNING GHOST

THIS IS THE SAME PICTURE UPSIDE DOWN

IMAGE 64
THE HISTORICAL SKETCH OF THE TALLOWING SITE

IMAGE 65
GIANT ARROW ON THE MARSH

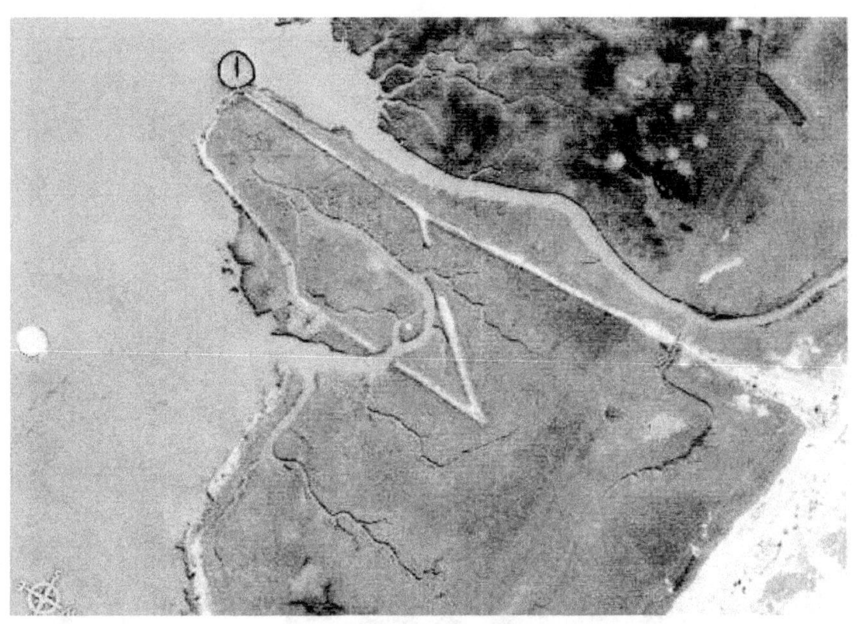

IMAGE 66
MOVING THE STONES TO STORAGE

IMAGE 67
565,000 LBS. OF STONES IN 10 STORAGE UNITS

IMAGE 68
WASH PLANT AND SORTED PILES AT MINING COMPANY

IMAGE 69
BEAUTIFUL BUT OPAQUE STONES OF THE TREASURE

IMAGE 70
THE IRON FASTENER USED TO MAKE THE MOLD FOR THE PLATE OF BRASS

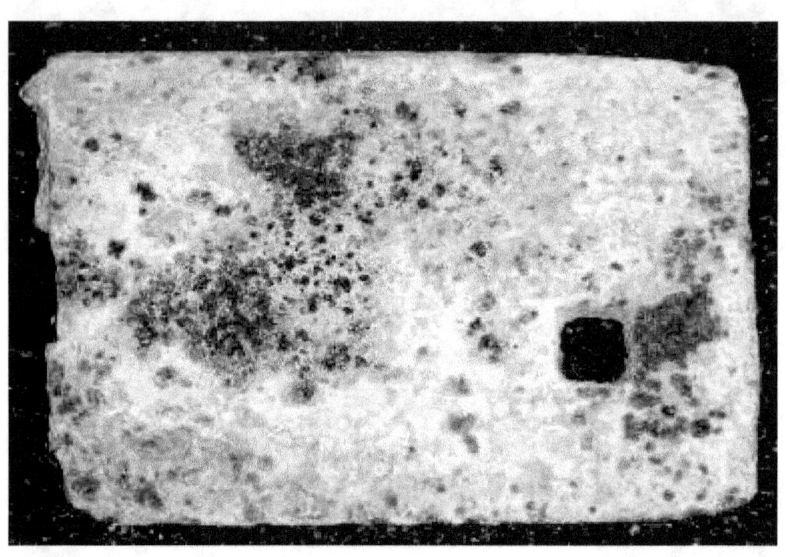

IMAGE 71
THE ROULETTES MADE THE PATTERN FOR THE INSCRIPTION

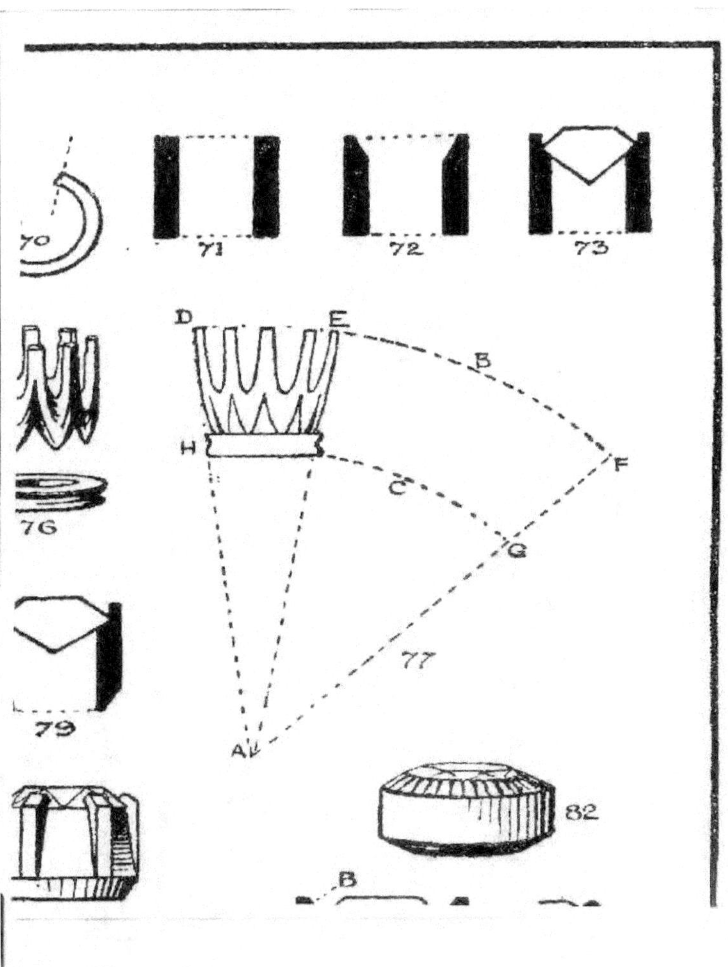

IMAGE 72
THE TRACER FUNCTION OF THE ROD

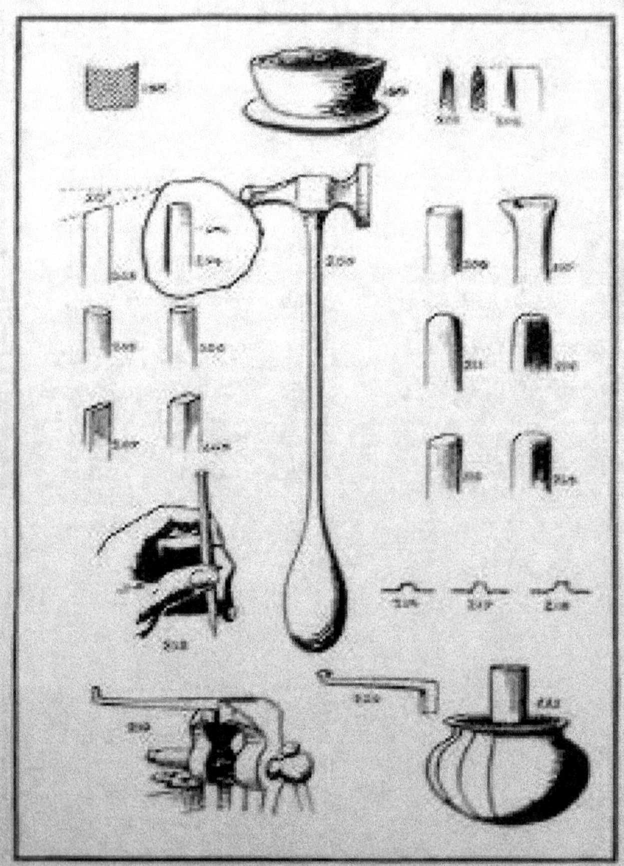

IMAGE 73
THE SCORPER FUNCTION OF THE ROD

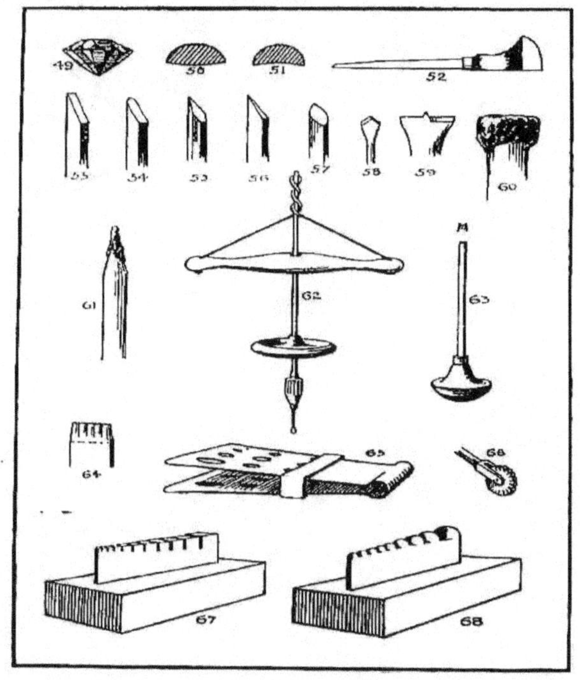

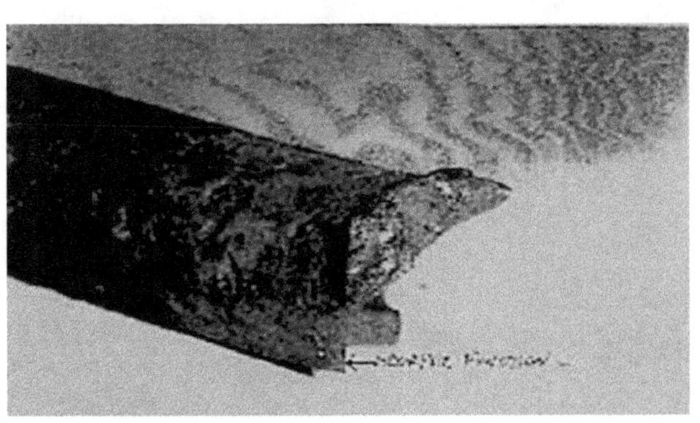

IMAGE 74
THE V-SHAPED CHISEL FUNCTION OF THE ROD

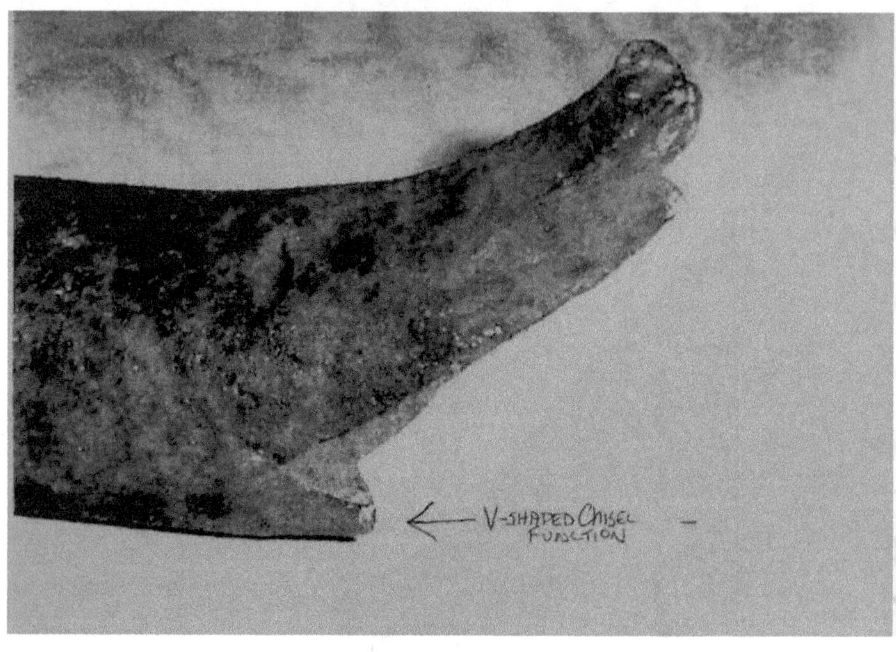

IMAGE 75
THE HOOKED K-TOOL AND SPINNING FEATURES OF THE ROD

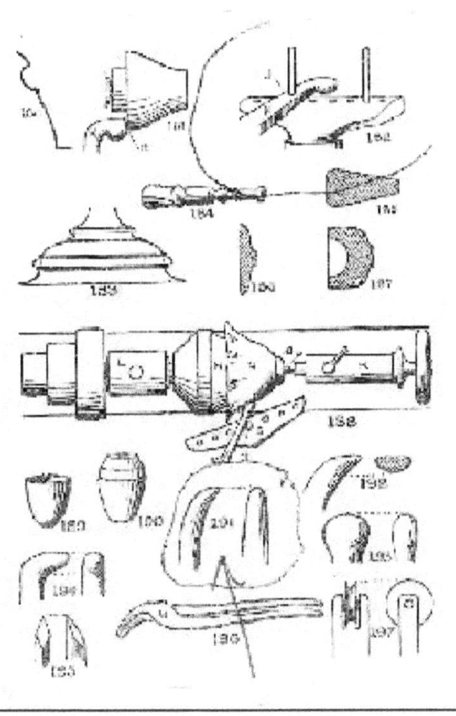

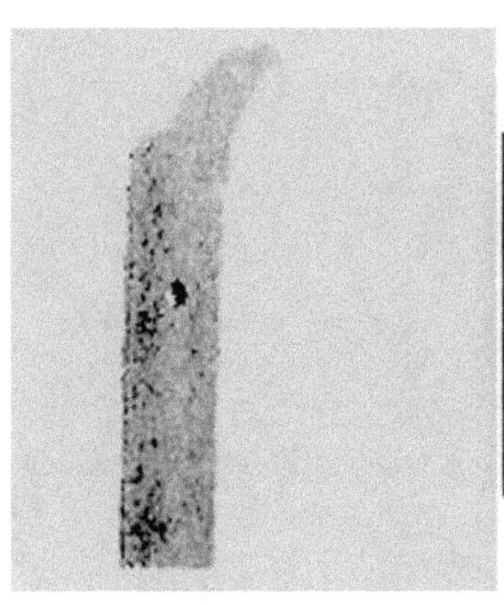

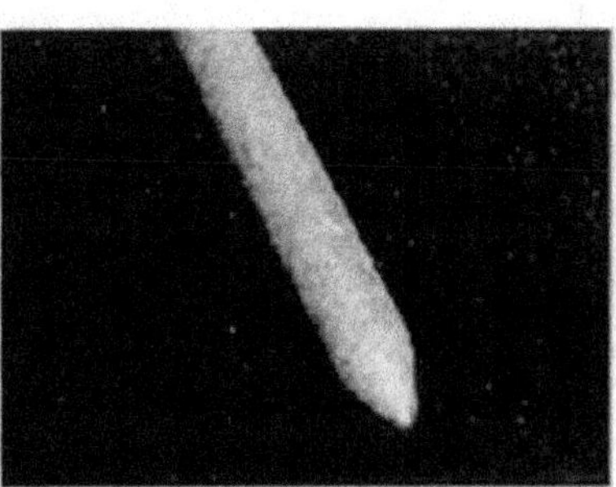

IMAGE 76
THE END OF THE ROD USED TO MAKE
THE "C" ON THE PLATE

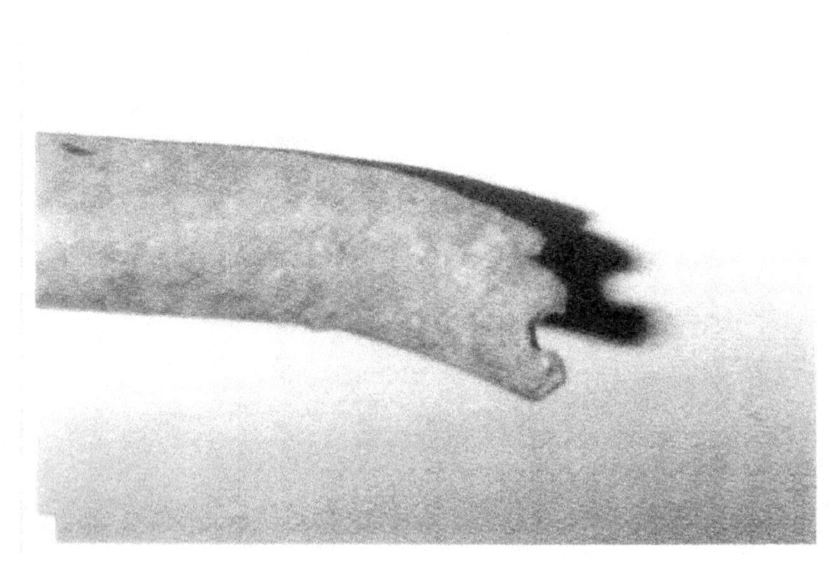

IMAGE 77
THE " GREAT POSTE " TO WHICH THE PLATE
OF BRASS WAS NAILED

WHEN LINES FILLED IN SPELLS FRANCIS
DRAKE AND JUNE 17, 1579

IMAGE 78
ALCHEMY SYMBOLS ON THE GREAT POSTE

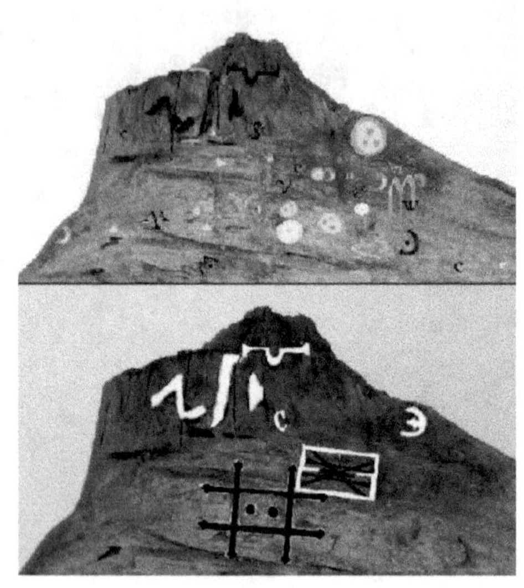

IMAGE 79
FINGER INGOT COMPARED TO HISTORICAL IMAGE

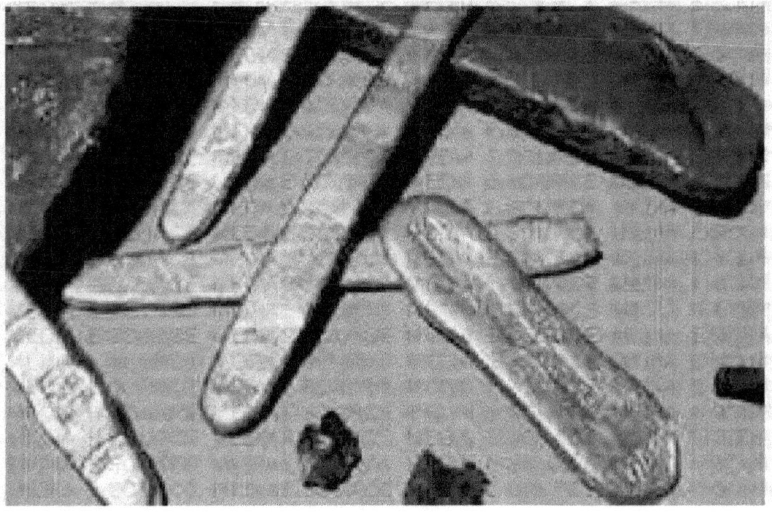

IMAGE 80
THE CALDERA AT SAN QUENTIN

IMAGE 81
DISCOVERY OF DRAKES MOORING SITE
AT SAN QUENTIN

IMAGE 82
LARGE MAP ROCK SHOWING LAND
BEFORE (L) AND AFTER BURIAL (R)

IMAGE 83
PHOTOGRAPH OF THE PLATE OF BRASS

The Plate of Brass
reproduced full size

IMAGE 84
USE OF THE ROD TO RE-CREATE THE INSCRIPTION ON CLAY

IMAGE 85
THE FOLDED IMAGE SHOWING
THE GOLDEN HIND SAILING AWAY

IMAGE 86
THE NORTH (N) AND SOUTH (S) MARKINGS
IN THE CAVERN WALL

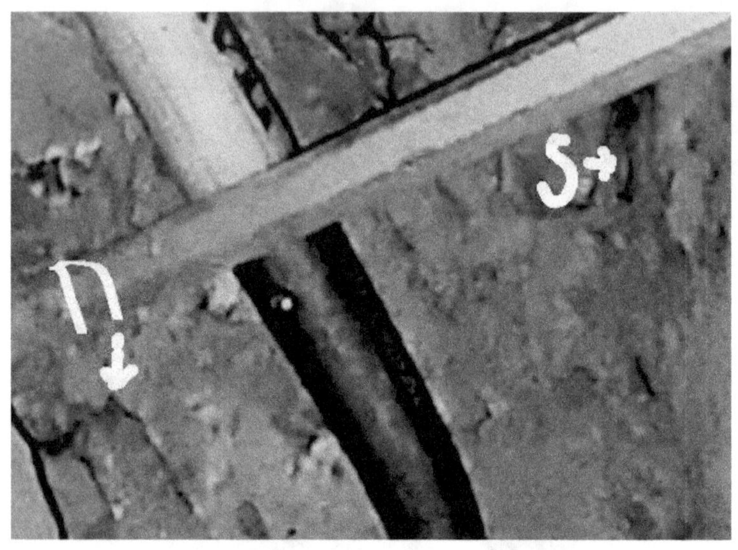

IMAGE 87
NUMBERS IN CAVERN WALL

IMAGE OF BEAR IN CAVERN WALL

IMAGE 88
THE SYMBOL SIGNIFYING THE TREASURE ENTRANCE COMPARED TO THE SYMBOL AS SHOWN ON THE HONDIUS MAP

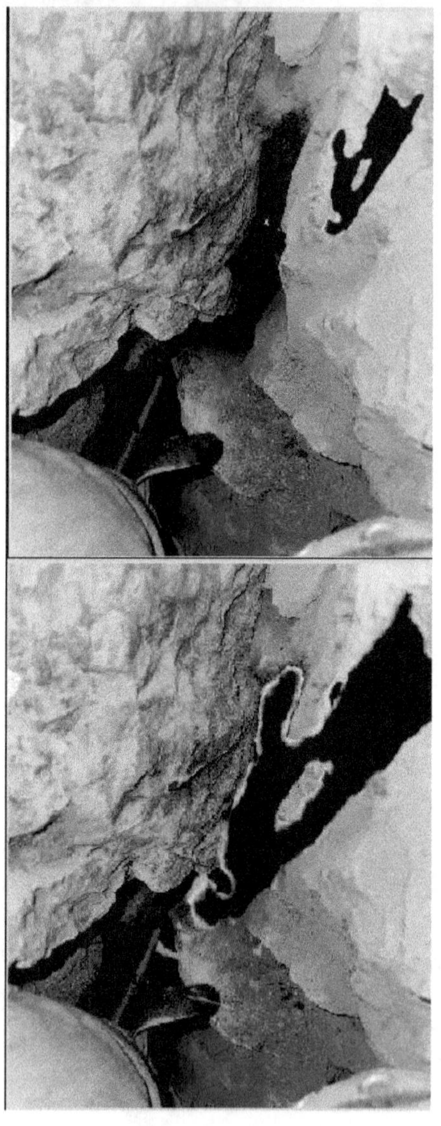

IMAGE 89
DRAKE'S NAME EMBEDDED
IN THE CAVERN WALL

CHAPTER 12

The Wizard of Oz

Suddenly, everything about the Plate of Brass began mysteriously disappearing from the Internet. <u>First, the University of Massachusetts radiograph of the Plate vanished</u>, then information regarding Dr. Napoli's tests on the nineteenth-century replica of the Plate. Eventually, all the personal and biographical information related to the people involved with the Plate during the 1970s was gone. Within a month, there were no traces left. It was as though the Plate and its history never existed.

When I realized what was happening, I began printing out whatever was not removed from the Internet before it was too late. I also searched for any information about Kenneth Wagner. I read that he worked closely with the previous Director of the Bancroft, Dr James D Hart and in the 1970, his title was Digital and Online Manager for Bancroft Library. Dr. Hessen was a major figure in the Plate of Brass controversy. This information made me wonder how Kenneth Wagner worked his way up to his current level of authority.

Wagner joined Bancroft in the '60s as a research assistant, gaining access to over 60 million manuscript items, 600,000 books, 2.8 million photographs and 43,000 microfilms, all of which he was currently digitizing. Without a doubt, he was a very smart and well-educated man, though for some reason he did not have a PhD. although he did have a master's degree. Then I saw something else that sent shivers down my spine. Wagner was the President of the International Wizard of Oz Society. For me, one of the most famous scenes from the Wizard of Oz takes place when Dorothy is ready to go back to Kansas and pays a visit to the Wizard. She expects him to be larger than life, but when she arrives unannounced, she finds a little man who runs into a projection booth and booms in an amplified voice, "PAY NO ATTENTION TO THE MAN BEHIND THE CURTAIN."

As I reflected on this, I happened to be watching the evening news on TV, and suddenly Wagner's connection to the Wizard of Oz Society hit me like a brick. The newscaster announced that UC Berkeley was the first major American university to use monitoring software to catch students who were illegally downloading music from the internet via Napster. The students had no idea that everything they were doing on their computers was being watched around the clock by none other than the man behind the curtain, Kenneth Wagner.

It was no longer a mystery why information related to the Plate of Brass was disappearing from the Internet. Clearly Mr. Wagner, Mr. Rosenthal and possibly Dr. Napoli were—and had been all along—involved with Dr. Hessen before his death in 1990 in a plot to cover-up the theft of the Plate. Now, with me on their tracks, Wagner needed to be more aggressive in preventing the discovery of any information tying them to that crime. But why did these men go to so much trouble to steal the real Plate in the first place?

My research indicated that there was widespread speculation that the Plate of Brass contained a secret code. If the secret code could be deciphered it would reveal the location of Drake's buried treasure. All these highly educated men were familiar with Mercator maps, and without a doubt knew that during the sixteenth century all maps were drawn "flat."

Mercator's work was no exception. In 1569, he set the gold standard for navigational maps, creating a flat map that could be rolled into a cylinder to create a "Mercator Projection." Numerous historical references state that Drake met with Mercator in London before his 1577 circumnavigation voyage and learned about the mathematical principles involved in this method of map creation so that during his voyage, he could prepare accurate maps for future expeditions.

I have no doubt that Hessen, Wagner, and Rosenthal knew of the Drake/Mercator connection and the principals involved in sixteenth-century map-making. Quite simply, the Earth's circumference is divided into 360 degrees, each represented by an imaginary line running either East-West or North-South on the surface of the Earth. When such a flat-drawn map is rolled properly it forms a perfect image of the Earth. If the Plate of Brass is a Mercator map, its 360 vertical lines would require it to be cut or bent to turn it into an accurate "Mercator Projection" showing the location of the treasure.

Rosenthal may have originated the idea to steal the Plate prior to 1970 and along with Hessen, persuaded the young research assistant, Wagner to join their team. Together, they concocted a plan to decipher the Plate's secret code, recover the treasure and share the spoils amongst themselves. But this plot required the theft and destruction of a priceless artifact for their own personal gain. How could men in their position of power and prestige stoop to such a level or be willing to take such a risk?

If I was correct, they must have removed the "real" Plate of Brass shortly after the 1976 press conference and replaced it with an impostor. All of Rosenthal's public claims regarding Drake's Bay as the landing site were nothing more than a smokescreen to hide his knowledge that Drake's true landing site was exactly where I posited it was. If he could succeed in this sleight of hand, all eyes would be off the correct landing site and the real Plate, making it smooth and easy for them to succeed it their ploy. Dr. Hessen's distortions of Dr. Smith's opinion served a similar purpose, discrediting the real Plate as a fake, then engineering a confirmation of the lie during the 1977 re-examination because those tests were not run on the real Plate, but on the fake nineteenth-century one that had been substituted. That's where Dr. Napoli came in, as he was the one who examined that nineteenth-century replica.

Once all of this became clear to me, I wrote a letter to Wagner at the Bancroft and sent a copy to the Chancellor of the University of California. I offered $25,000 (accounting for inflation, the exact amount paid to Beryl Shinn in 1937) to purchase the "fake"

Plate of Brass, but my offer was rejected. No surprise. My goal in making this offer was to show Wagner and his cronies that I was onto them regarding their theft of the Plate and the lengths to which they'd gone to conceal it.

Once I played that hand, I had no idea what more I could do. I knew that if I tried on my own to mount a legal case against those powerful men, I'd land back in the psych ward, this time for good. So I decided to just wait and watch, hoping that an opportunity to reveal the truth would emerge. But even though I backed off, Wagner didn't.

In the United States, computer "hacking" is a criminal offense that can be classified as either a misdemeanor or a felony, depending on the severity of the offense. However, Mr. Wagner, AKA "the man behind the curtain," was exempt. The same software he helped create and was using to catch students illegally downloading music was modified and now being used by the US Government to monitor the computers of people that they suspected of being terrorists! I made a very serious enemy by letting Mr. Wagner know that I was onto him, and willing to raise suspicions about his involvement in the "cold case" of the stolen Plate of Brass. Was I scared? Yes! But I was also angry and determined.

The same day the test results from the metallurgist were reported to Mr. Wagner without my permission, I became the victim of computer hacking. I quickly realized that every email I sent or received was being read, and many even modified before they were received. Unfortunately, the intrusion did not stop with my computer. Before long I could tell that every form of electronic communication including my telephone, my fax machine and even my Fast Trak were all being monitored.

At the time, I wasn't the only person who realized their communications were being monitored. This was the period when "Big Brother" was testing and refining the ability to inhibit subversive activities by intrusive snooping. There were many nights when David Letterman would complain about the invasion of his privacy during his monologue. Mr. Wagner was instrumental in creating a monster that was now being turned loose on the American public.

Armed with reams of evidence of criminal activity related to the Plate of Brass and computer intrusion, I prepared a binder with enough information to arouse the federal government's interest in Mr. Wagner and delivered it to the FBI agent stationed at their office in San Rafael. Then I waited, hoping to read about Wagner's arrest in my morning paper. But there was nothing. I guess his pivotal role in the development of the Monitoring Software used by the U.S. government to spy on its citizens made him "untouchable." The FBI agent did absolutely nothing with the information I gave him. After six months I contacted him again and took back my binder, hoping someone else might be more receptive.

I soon realized that since Wagner was controlling the monitoring software, and it would be impossible to contact anyone without his detection. He could easily prevent me from authenticating my artifacts and prevent me from trying to undermine the conspiracy. All he needed to do was phone or email who ever I was contacting and request that they not assist me.

To protect myself, I began changing the settings of my PC hoping that would stop the monitoring, but it only killed my hard drive and made my computer worthless. I tried buying a Mac because they were reputed to be less susceptible to viruses. But no luck. After a few months, I noticed the same symptoms of monitoring and when I again began changing the settings, my Mac's hard drive also failed. In total, five computers suffered the same fate, one after the other.

Then one morning, <u>I noticed Wagner upped the ante by downloading a program to my computer during the night. I isolated the data and printed it out, all forty-four pages of it</u>. However, it was heavily encrypted and appeared to be nothing more than random code. But in a way, it felt like good news, as the attack was too blatant to attribute to anything random. It gave me a chance to once and for all prove that my communications were being monitored, but only if I cracked the encryption code. So, for nearly a month, I sat at the computer trying to determine which language was the encryption key. Somehow, at the end of that long and frustrating exercise, I tried Japanese punctuation marks to decrypt the information and in the blink of an eye the data was displayed in a readable format. The name of the hacker was not shown, but the initials KW and the words, UC Berkeley, were clearly identified.

Everybody who reads this book can experiment to verify that this is how encryption is accomplished. Simply go to the Fonts menu of any PC and you'll see that there are close to 100 different ones available. Almost no one uses them all, but try to delete the fonts for obscure languages, especially ones that don't use the Roman alphabet and Anglo-European diacritical marks, and you can't do it. The computer won't let you remove them. To take control of any computer, a hacker need only input several lines of computer code containing the foreign alphanumeric characters and punctuation marks. From that point on, the target computer becomes a robotically controlled slave that relays all activity to its master. This allows the hacker complete access to anything on the computer, at any time, night, or day. The scary things about this invasion of privacy are that it occurs at the speed of light, it's impossible to prevent, and often impossible to detect. In the blink of an eye "Big Brother" can begin keeping an eye on you 24/7, all the while whispering, "Pay no attention to the man behind the curtain! Wagner could pretty much get away with whatever he wanted.

At this point, rather than continuing to bash my head against the brick wall he built, I decided to set aside all the intrigue and focus my attention on something over which I did have some control: my excavation under the arch.

CHAPTER 13

Drake's Constant - 72

As my excavation continued, I applied Drake's use of the number 72 to all my calculations.

The tunnel was now twelve feet long, a multiple of 72, so I decided to heed the markings on the walls that suggested I should reverse course to excavate the next leg of the tunnel. If I continued this way, zigging and zagging downward, I anticipated reaching the treasure in six twelve-foot lengths. So, I began digging in the opposite direction, passing below the first leg. The most challenging part about this phase of the work was getting the full buckets of dirt up and out of the tunnel, as each one weighed close to sixty pounds, and the tunnel was too tight for me to stand up.

By the end of July, I finished two 12-foot tunnel lengths. I was working on the third, about thirty feet below ground, feeling excited that the next leg would take me where I wanted to go, to the thirty-six-foot level.

Shortly after I started digging the next day, I found a huge stone directly in my path. It was likely another potentially deadly trick, but I knew it could be one of the map rocks. I perused it carefully with the work light. I tried to assess whether the marks on it were intended to help me find the treasure or were part of a ruse to protect the treasure from me. The images on it showed a cavern and tunnels but no directional information. Just in case it was a booby trap, rather than dig underneath it and risk having it fall on me, I began digging around it. This took several days of work, but I felt safe enough to sit and rest for a few minutes when I reached the other side. I always protected myself with a dust mask, hat, and gloves. Still, I only wore a T-shirt and jeans because it was blisteringly hot and humid, even with the fans running. As I sat and rested, I thought about what I could wear that wouldn't restrict my movements or be ridiculously hot but could protect my skin. Those thoughts were suddenly interrupted by a rumbling sound, and I knew it was time to get back to the surface ASAP!

That evening, I told my new girlfriend, Jennifer, about the rumbling sound and my eagerness to see what would happen overnight. The following day, I was blown away to see that the space where I was working was now filled with a slurry-like quicksand. When I stepped into it to check it out, it nearly trapped me, and I realized that if I hadn't heard the rumbling and gotten out, I could have fallen prey to the deadly trick.

When I returned to digging, a rush of excitement ran through me because the hollow sound now seemed to originate from an area behind the large rock that set the quicksand trick in motion.

Later that afternoon, I began feeling so nauseous

and achy that I could barely stand up. Jennifer drove me to see my doctor the following day when I felt even worse. This time, he made me do a 24-hour urine test, carrying around a plastic gallon-sized jug and collecting urine every time I needed to pee. There are so few cases of toxic metal poisoning in the continental U.S. that my urine was sent to Puerto Rico for analysis. This time, the results revealed high levels of both arsenic and selenium in my system. From that point forward, in addition to a mask, hat, and gloves, I never went underground without two layers of clothing so that when I sweated, the dust and dirt would get on the outside layer and not contact my damp skin directly.

The effects of this new round of poisoning were miserable. Still, they didn't stop me from working, although I struggled to find enough energy to remove the buckets of quicksand and haul them to the surface. Hard as that was, I knew it was essential because I couldn't risk getting stuck in that muck while moving full buckets of dirt out from the next section of the tunnel. Once I managed to get rid of the slurry, with my escape route clear, I proceeded to make a U-turn around the massive rock. Then, again guided by the markings on the wall, I started to dig horizontally. At last, I finally arrived at the thirty-six foot level.

Two more days of hard labor resulted in twelve more feet of forward progress, at which point I noticed two bright blue markings on the tunnel wall. The first one to my left looked like a stone. The other one <u>directly in front of me was an image of a blue buzzard</u>. Clearly, it meant something, but what? I took a picture of the buzzard but decided to remove the smaller blue stone because that wall sounded hollow. Within a minute after I did so, water began to trickle out of the hole it left. Within another minute, the trickle turned into a steady stream that scared the crap out of me because there was no way to tell how much water was behind that wall or how much pressure was building up. I knew to get the hell out of there, and fast, so I started scrambling backward as fast as I could, accidentally ripping the power cord right out of the jackhammer as I went. I was only able to grab a couple of tools before high tailing it back to the surface.

That night, I called Jaime and told him that I needed the entire crew to work the next day hauling buckets, and he said they'd all be ready at 8:00 AM. I drove to San Rafael to pick them up on a beautiful Saturday morning. We got to my place by 8:20, and as soon as I gave them instructions, down they went. But only a few minutes later, I was surprised to see them return to the surface. They told me they couldn't do anything because everything was severely flooded. I went down myself to look, and sure enough, the water was a good five feet deep in the cavern and filled a few of the tunnels as well. When I told the men I was sorry there'd be no work that day, they understood and appreciated my paying them for an hour before driving them back to San Rafael. I hoped it was early enough in the day for them to still pick up a job.

When I got home, I set up my pumping system to clear the water from the tunnel and cavern and I left it on for 24 hours. By the next day much of the water was gone! My pumps could move 1,200 gallons per hour, and I calculated that there was 25,000 gallons of water hidden behind the wall. The pressure of so much water trying to get out of the little hole caused the wall to disintegrate.

The flood damaged much of my equipment, so I went and purchased new extension cords and fans. I took them below ground and left them running continuously. A few days later, there was still a few inches of water, but I decided to go back to work anyway.

In the space where the wall stood, there it was, the Treasure Cavern. It was 36 feet below the surface, approximately twelve feet long and eighteen feet wide, with a cathedral ceiling that was 20 feet high. The large space for the high ceiling was the source of the hollow sound that I heard the entire time I'd been digging. I was so excited that I could barely breathe. Finally! I thought.

I expected the rest of the water to subside naturally, so I waited for a couple of days before going back down to check. Unfortunately, it didn't, and there were several tons of heavy clay to move from the wall that collapsed. The clay was too soft to hold short hooks for the electric cords so I used much longer ones. I knew that embedding them could trigger another collapse, but it was an acceptable risk because I'd be electrocuted if one of the live cords slipped into the water.

It took me five days to remove the gunk and debris, and I worked alone, because there wasn't enough space for more than one person. I wore layers of protective gear and lay on my side on several sheets of foil-covered insulation to keep my body out of the water. Using only one arm and filling only one bucket at a time, I scooped up the sludge and dragged it to the surface. When I cleared the area enough to ensure my safety, I was ready to try and cross the cavern. There was a collection of stones that I could see, neatly—and intentionally—piled at the far side.

It was a sunny Saturday morning. Jennifer was sitting on the back deck reading a magazine as I headed down below. <u>A pool of water was still sitting at the bottom of the cavern</u>, directly in the path leading to the collection of stones. The moisture rising from it was causing chunks of the ceiling to fall and splash into the pool. Some pieces weighed a couple hundred pounds. I made three attempts to wade through the water, and during each one, I barely escaped severe injury. My heart was racing after that third near miss. How frustrating it was to know the treasure was straight in front of me but I was unable to reach it, and to also know that even if I did, I'd have to make it back multiple times, carrying those heavy stones. I'd taken many risks over the past two years and avoided becoming the victim of Drake's deadly tricks. However, this time, the odds seemed insurmountable.

Working in the Securities Industry for many years taught me that there was a vast difference between gambling and investing. I didn't want to roll the dice with my life on the line this time. When I came out of the excavation, from the look on my face, Jennifer knew I was truly frightened by something. I sat down beside her. At first, she tried to get me to talk about what had happened, but I told her I needed to be still to think. I closed my eyes and turned my face up toward the sun. After sitting that way in silence for about twenty minutes, I jumped to my feet and said, "There has to be a safer way to get to the other side of the Treasure Cavern, and said I have an idea."

Rather than manually digging another hole that would open to the other side of the cavern, I decided to hire a well drilling company and purchase a three-foot diameter plastic sewer pipe to fit vertically into the hole they'd create, to prevent the hole from collapsing. After several calls, I found a company to drill it for me over the Labor Day weekend. I knew that the Twin Cities Police would be short-staffed on the holiday weekend and wouldn't hassle me. After a few more calls, I located a company that supplied the plastic pipe and placed an order for a twenty-footer. When the truck pulled up in front of my house to deliver it on Friday afternoon, I was surprised to see how large it was. I needed to remove half of my lower deck to allow access to the spot where I wanted the hole to be drilled.

On Saturday morning of Labor Day Weekend, the well drillers arrived. They maneuvered their equipment from the street, around the side of the house, and into the backyard. Then, the three-man crew began the long process of boring the hole slowly enough to prevent the drill head from breaking. When the hole reached a death of 20 feet, it hit a rock. This rock must have formed the top of the cathedral ceiling at the top of the cavern, and I knew they drilled in the right place! They inserted the 20-foot plastic pipe, and it fit perfectly into the hole. The impenetrable rock that caused the drillers to stop boring was now supporting the weight of the 20-foot pipe.

After they left, I looked down the pipe to the bottom of the hole and realized that there were two problems I needed to solve. My twenty-foot aluminum ladder didn't provide enough stability when fully extended. So, I built a sturdier one out of redwood pieces from the portion of the deck that I dismantled.

I also needed a system to move heavy buckets of dirt and stone up through the plastic pipe. After researching online, I purchased an electric hoist capable of lifting 250 lbs. Then, with Jaime's help, I secured it to the remaining part of the deck and added a hook to the end of the cable. Now, I just needed to attach the wire handle of a bucket to the hook, press a button, and the machine would do the heavy lifting. This way, the work only required two men, and Jaime helped me daily.

At the bottom of the pipe, I used a reciprocating saw to <u>cut an arch-shaped opening through</u> <u>the side of the pipe.</u> I dug straight out until I was far enough away from the stone that I could begin to create the zigzag pattern of the three twelve-foot-long tunnels I needed to get down to the thirty-six-foot level.

I only made a few feet of progress when I came upon a stone approximately the size of a football. When I picked it up, it felt different from the others of that size, so I brought it to the surface and scrubbed it off. What I found was a sure sign the hole had been drilled in the right location: <u>It was covered with gold</u>. It was like a welcome mat, just what I longed for. Jennifer and I celebrated that night by dancing till dawn, first at Club Galaxy and then at the Bottom Out.

A few mornings later, when I climbed down the ladder, at the very bottom of the hole, I saw a bag of Safeway "Treasure Chips." I started laughing hysterically, realizing that Jennifer got out of bed in the middle of the night and thrown the bag of cookies down into the hole so that I could find "treasure" first thing in the morning. We laughed so hard together that tears ran down our cheeks. After that, whenever she saw a consumer product containing the word "treasure," she bought it for me. We ended up with quite a collection.

Work continued, but forward progress was much slower than it was earlier because we needed to stop and operate the slow-moving hoist to raise the buckets of rocks and dirt up through the pipe.

A few feet beyond the gold-covered stone, I came upon a huge green one that was so big and fragile it took us over an hour to inch it through the tunnel and into the bottom of the plastic pipe. Then, with his excellent knot-tying skills, Jaime created a net to support it, and up it went. Once we washed the dirt off it, we almost couldn't believe how beautiful it was, refracting the afternoon sunlight. It glowed a deep, vibrant green. Jennifer came out to look at it, and we were all sure <u>it was a giant emerald.</u> I would have been content if there was no treasure besides this and the gold-covered stone, but I kept going.

It was the beginning of November, and I knew it could start raining at any time, so the pressure was on to move as fast as possible. Forward progress now slowed to about two feet per day, and by the time Thanksgiving rolled around, there was still about twenty feet to go. Jennifer's sister Patti and her husband Warren, who lived nearby, invited us to their place for an early Thanksgiving dinner. I worked on the excavation all morning, then took a shower, and we went to Patti and Warren's place. As soon as we finished eating, I excused myself and went back to work.

It still hadn't started to rain by the end of the first week of December, so I kept digging. Within a few days, I reached my goal of being thirty-six-feet below ground. Even though it hadn't rained in over five months, water was dripping around me as I stood there. I knew I was very close to the treasure location because I could again hear that hollow sound every time I tapped against the walls. Underground, it was impossible to determine where the "far side" of the treasure cave might be relative to my current position. I continued tunneling toward the hollow sound until once again, there was a large stone directly in my path. I knew immediately from its position that there was a trick involved. This stone's position reminded me of another scene from Raiders of the Lost Ark, the scene where Indiana Jones prepares to lift a solid gold skull from the top of a stone pedestal. When he removes it, he must simultaneously replace it with something of the same weight. The pouch he filled with dirt to use as the replacement did not weight the same as the gold skull, and the room begins to collapse. Recalling that scene, I didn't try to remove the stone. Instead, I rotated it on its pressure-sensitive pedestal until I could pass around it without dislodging the stone or triggering a deadly trick.

On December 12, light rain was in the forecast. I was still working at the 36-foot level, tapping the walls to pinpoint the spot where the hollow sound was the loudest. That day, the sound seemed to be coming from behind a rock that wasn't placed in a strange position, and I didn't suspect that removing it would cause a problem. I grabbed a crowbar, pulled the stone from the wall, and couldn't believe what I saw. A man-made secret passageway! After two years of searching for this, I knew it would lead me to the Treasure of Sir Francis Drake. I stuck my head inside and looked both ways. The passageway wasn't big enough for a man to stand up, but there seemed to be ample space for me to crawl on my hands and knees. The only thing I needed to do was make the entrance bigger. Once I did that, I could crawl in either direction.

I wanted to keep working, however, it was already

4:00 PM, and we were expected to attend the Morgan Witter Christmas party in San Francisco at 6:00 PM. I sighed with regret at not being able to explore it further and returned to the surface. After showering, we got in the car and I said to Jennifer, "I finally found the secret passageway, and tomorrow will be the big day!"

The Christmas party was help at the Olympic Club in San Francisco, and it started to rain as we arrived. By 10 PM the party was over, and it was pouring rain. Marin County always gets more rain than San Francisco, and by the time we got home, it already rained about close to three inches. As much as I wanted to go back down to check the passageway, I knew it was too dangerous in the pouring rain. As we got into bed, I told Jennifer, "I hope it stops raining soon because if it doesn't, it could be a disaster."

I tossed and turned all night, and it was raining every time I woke up. The storm produced eight inches of rain that night. In the morning, we went out to look, and <u>I was dismayed to see that the first four feet of dirt surrounding the pipe washed away and the pipe itself was filled with 20 feet of water.</u>

My heart sank! I realized it would take a miracle to get back to the passageway. After pumping the water out of the plastic pipe there were several feet of mud covering the arch I cut at the bottom of the tube. At that moment, I knew that everything below collapsed.

You can't imagine the despair and frustration that came over me. Two years of working nearly 24/7 to find the secret passageway, and in less than twelve hours, all that work was destroyed by Mother Nature!

CHAPTER 14

The Only Other Man Who Knew the Truth

In a 1976 letter to Bancroft Library, Dr. Cyril Stanley Smith recommended that additional tests be performed to determine the authenticity of the Plate of Brass. According to that letter, it was then decided that another examination of the Plate was needed, and be known as, "The Plate of Brass Re-examination, 1977." Bancroft Library Director Douglas Hessen publicly announced this next round of testing and hand-picked scientists that would do the work. He insisted that all testing be conducted at UC Berkeley's facilities.

On July 27, 1977, after this examination was completed, Dr. Hessen, Mr. Wagner, and Dr. Napoli, held a press conference. After the presentation, Dr. Hessen publicly stated, "The latest tests cast serious doubt about the authenticity of the Plate," and added, "The assembled evidence has turned out essentially negative." After the official conclusion of the press conference, Hessen was quoted as saying, "Guesses about a hoax and reasons for not revealing it are intriguing; however, with a definitive answer as to the Plate's authenticity still lacking, it will remain on public view at the Bancroft Library."

After reading this in the newspaper, I wondered: Why in the world would the Director of one of the world's greatest research institutions leave a questionable artifact on display? It was a rhetorical question because these statements were made to reinforce the deception Dr. Hessen, Mr. Wagner, Mr. Rosenthal, and Dr. Napoli perpetrated on the public! This was part of the requirements in The Plan to Re-Write History discussed in Chapter 9 of this book.

During the 1970s, the Plate of Brass was generally assumed to contain a secret code that, if deciphered, would reveal the location of the buried treasure. I contend that Hessen, Wagner, Rosenthal, and other possible accomplices stole the actual Plate of Brass and used it for personal gain. After the first round of testing, they made the switch. They then publicly called for a second round of testing but on the nineteenth-century replica, not the actual Plate. Of course, since the re-examination was conducted on the fake, the results would confirm that the proving that the Plate was...a fake!

There was, however, one man who knew the truth! His name was Robert H. Power, and during the 1970s, he was the President of the California Historical Society (CHS). As noted earlier, in 1937, the California Historical Society purchased the Plate from Beryl Shinn and presented it to UC Berkeley. When the Bancroft Library started raising questions about the Plate's authenticity, Mr. Power became suspicious!

In addition to his role with the CHS, Mr. Power was

a well-educated and highly respected businessman who owned the Nut-Tree Restaurant on US 80, and he authored several books about the Plate of Brass and Sir Francis Drake's visit to Marin County in 1579. He was the foremost expert on the Coast Miwok Indians. He visited Greenbrae Ridge often and made numerous discoveries around the area.

Before the United States was drawn into World War II, Robert Power and the California Historical Society planned to have Greenbrae Ridge and the surrounding land designated as a State Park. Like most men his age, Mr. Power and his supporters joined the army and went overseas. When the war ended, he returned to California to find that all of Greenbrae was sold to developers, and his dream of a historical designation was quashed.

But that was not the only thing that upset Mr. Power. One didn't have to be a trained metallurgist to notice the differences between the 1936 and 1977 Plates of Brass. Mr. Power noticed the differences and he spoke and wrote about them numerous times determined to prove that Hessen, Wagner, and Rosenthal had substituted a "worthless fake" for the "true artifact." It is obvious that the shapes of the "coin holder" are not the same! Power had the proof and wanted to bring this crime to the public's attention. However, at the time of his death in 1991, he failed in making the public aware of this crime because the conspirators prevented him from doing so.

Per his Will, Power's personal notes and files were given to the Special Collections Library at UC Davis. After arranging to see those files, I visited the campus and reviewed everything he left to the University. Numerous letters showed that he contacted several prominent scientists trying to engage their help in exposing what happened to the actual Plate of Brass.

<u>In one letter to Cyril Stanley Smith, dated August 22, 1977, he referred to a recent conversation with Mr. Rosenthal, whose responses prompted him to consider the possibility that the Plate subjected to testing in 1977 was not the Plate discovered by Beryl Shinn in 1936.</u> He asked Dr. Smith to make further recommendations about suitable tests to examine the method of engraving used to produce the Plate. That same day, he also wrote a letter to Dr. C. R. Bridges of Oxford University, in which he raised questions regarding the rest of the Plate's testing at Oxford.

As part of the same letter noted above, Power inquired about the necessary procedures to make a cast of the Plate's inscription. He was fully aware that the report by the Berkeley scientists erroneously stated that the letters of the inscription were "chiseled." This was in direct contrast to Dr. Smith's letter of April 27, 1976, which stated that "the letters were traced (impressed) not engraved or cut."

One month later, on September 27, 1977, Mr. Power observed that the wording on a positive print from a radiograph of the Plate made by Lawrence Radiation Laboratory at Berkeley in 1976 did not match the wording of the Plate presented to the University of California in 1937.

On November 7, 1977, he wrote another letter to Dr. Smith, which began with his expression of appreciation for the "opportunity to verbally relate my own opinions that I have concerning the Plate of Brass at Bancroft Library." The letter continued with an outline of the additional scientific procedures to which the Plate could be subjected. The fourth test on his list was "take a cast in plastic FBI ballistics-test-style to ascertain the form of the tools used to make the Plate of Brass inscription." Dr. Smith wrote back to Mr. Power on December 28, 1977, thanking him for an article Power sent him and expressing his willingness "to abandon my earlier position if I could have a few quiet hours with the Plate." Dr. Hessen received a carbon copy of this letter.

The files at UC Davis also contained a 1978 article that Mr. Power published in the California Historical Society magazine. This gave specific details of the differences between the Plate of Brass discovered in 1936 and "a plate of brass" which was the subject of the 1977 re-examination conducted by The Bancroft Library. Mr. Power wrote: "Also unnoticed by the Re-Examination 1977 was that the Plate had a mistake in the final line of text. <u>The original inscription read 'KNOWNE TO ALL MEN' but this was changed to read 'KNOWNE UTO ALL MEN' with the N in UNTO never struck.</u>" Furthermore, there were several other differences between the 1936 Plate and the one examined in 1977. Power's article openly challenged Director Hessen.

Another letter in the file, dated January 22, 1979, was written by Donald Cummings, Head of the Department of Special Collections of UC Davis. Mr. Cummings's letter referred to various luncheons that Mr. Power, Dr. Hessen, Mr. Rosenthal, and Mr. Wagner attended recently and fourteen more events that these men would attend between April and June of 1979.

On May 11, 1979, Mr. Power informed Dr. Hessen that he corresponded with Dr. Smith and Dr. Bridges about the "contradictions" arising from the 1977 re-examination. Mr. Power also expressed his "disappointment to learn that Oxford University was not asked to do any further investigation on the Plate even though Dr. Bridges personally suggested a test to determine if the patina was formed at high or low temperatures." Dr. Bridges also recommended, "that the lead isotopes be studied to determine the possible origins of the zinc component of the Plate."

<u>Mr. Power's unrelenting questions about the outcome of the 1977 Re-examination made him an undeniable threat to the men trying to cover up their theft of the Plate of Brass!</u>

Eleven years later, in 1990, Dr. Hessen passed away, and Kenneth Wagner was named Interim Director of the Bancroft Library.

The following year, on May 13, 1991, Robert Power died suddenly, even though he appeared to be in good health. I believe that the conspirators needed to eliminate Mr. Power because he never stopped trying to bring their crimes to the public's attention.

To validate my suspicion, <u>I ordered a copy of Mr. Power's, Death Certificate from Solano County.</u> It listed his cause of death as "respiratory failure" and the "time interval between onset and death" as two hours. This was due to "pulmonary metastases" for three months triggered by metastatic gastroesophageal carcinoma for five months. More importantly, line 25 of the certificate lists "other significant conditions contributing to death but not related to the cause given in line 21." This line contains the medical term "Disseminated Intravascular Coagulation," often called DIC.

While researching DIC, I located an Agency for Toxic Substances and Disease Registry (ASTDR) report that provided an Ah Ha moment.

This agency is part of the US Department of Health and Human Services, and the report in question is entitled "Case Studies in Environmental Medicine – Arse nic Toxic ity – Clini cal Evalua tion ."

Following is a partial list of human bodily systems that are affected by acute arsenic exposure:

1. Gastrointestinal
2. Cardiovascular and respiratory
3. Hematologic

Four disorders are listed as resulting from the effect of arsenic in the hematologic system:

1. Anemia
2. Leukopenia
3. Thrombocytopenia
4. Disseminated Intravascular Coagulation

The report goes on to say, "the onset of milder GI symptoms may be so insidious that the possibility of arsenic intoxication is overlooked."

Exposure to arsenic and its related compounds is the most frequent cause of DIC.

Chronic arsenic exposure evaluation usually reveals multi- system involvement such as some combination of anemia, leucopenia, skin diseases and/or elevated liver, kidney, bladder, and prostate problems.

"Manifestations of chronic arsenic ingestion depend on both the intensity and duration of exposure. An intense exposure of several milligrams a day results in anemia, with new properties of toxicity within a few weeks to months. Hematological and neurological signs may occur after a similar latency. Skin lesions, however, take longer to manifest (3-7 years for pigmentation changes and keratoses; up to 40 years for skin cancer) and may occur after lower doses than those causing neuropathy. Lung cancer and skin cancer or serious long-term concerns can also result from chronic arsenic exposure."

Over the years, Robert Power attended many of the same Drake-related social functions as Hessen, Wagner, and Rosenthal. It would have been easy for them to slip some arsenic into his drinks at conferences, meetings, cocktail parties, or dinners. This was a virtually undetectable way to kill an adversary because, until the late 1990s, Medical Examiners did not look for arsenic poisoning when they determined a cause of death in a routine autopsy. Given how Power consistently worked to thwart their plan and the dire consequences they would have suffered if he succeeded in discrediting them, I am convinced that Robert Power was murdered.

CHAPTER 15

Tangling with The Law

Paul Charles and his wife were an elderly couple that lived for many years at 57 Via Corona, next door to Steve Stern and his family. After Mr. Charles' 85th birthday, he held a yard sale to dispose of household items and most of the sporting equipment he accumulated over a lifetime. Walking down the street, I saw something I never noticed before: Grandma's mailbox was attached to a gnarled piece of wood that looked like part of an early sailing ship.

I purchased several things from Paul that day, the most important of which was a pair of "waders" he'd used for duck hunting and fishing. This was the perfect protective gear to prevent another round of poisoning if I ever got up the steam to try for the treasure again.

One day in early March 2003, I was searching for more Drake-related items near his landing site in Larkspur. As always, I stopped to look at anything that was oddly colored, oddly shaped, or seemed like it was out of place. Those criteria helped me find three artifacts that day: <u>The first was a conglomerate stone tool with a white stone protruding from the top</u>, partially buried in the dirt. I used a screwdriver to extract it from the ground, then picked it up to look closer. The first thing I noticed was that the creamy white stone was carved in the form of a face with an elongated head. Next, I found a brown stone carved with an image that looked like E.T., the alien. The third item was a blue-green stone carved with what seemed to be a smiley face on it.

Many of the boats that Drake captured were taken in the waters off Peru, so when I got home, I searched for information about the Incas online. The first piece looked like images I found of the Inca royalty with elongated heads. <u>When I checked this against pictures on the internet of Inca Queens...they matched. The head was wearing an earring and when I checked this against the glyphs on the Nazca plains....it matched!</u> Several articles mentioned that aliens might have visited the Incas, which was reflected in some of their artwork. To my eye, the image on the brown stone was undoubtedly the image of an alien. The blue-green stone turned out to be a jade carving, probably a ceremonial knife, and the smiley face also turned out to match to one of the glyphs on the Nazca plains.

The Inca, the Maya, and the Aztec cultures were destroyed by the Catholic Church and Spain's greed during the 1500s. Spanish settlers did not arrive in Northern California in the 1800s. Considering this timeline, only Francis Drake could have brought artifacts from these three civilizations and left them behind on the San Quentin Peninsula.

At the end of March, while mowing the front lawn

one Saturday morning, I noticed some small but very bright green stones protruding from the dirt next to one of the sprinkler heads. They made me wonder if there might be another entrance to the tunnel system from the front of my house that led to the passageway that I found in December before it flooded.

So far, all my work was in the backyard to keep the project secret. But by now, everyone on my street–– hell, lots of people in Marin County—knew what I was doing. Most of them thought I was crazy, so they just shook their heads and continued their lives. If I started a new excavation in the front yard, I was concerned about possible confrontations with the police. After talking it over with Jennifer and figuring I would deal with the consequences, I started digging one day when I got home from work. Within a few hours, I had a hole six feet deep.

To prevent any neighborhood children from falling into it, I enclosed it with sturdy wire fencing.

Immediately I began to see the familiar white lines in the dirt. I continued to dig, and within two weeks, I excavated a large room a <u>with a ceiling that looked like the heavens in the night sky with sparkling stones reflecting the light from my work lights</u>. As I stood there gazing up, I realized the surface was not far above me and wondered why this cavern was not further below ground. Later that night, I revisited the topographic map, and realized that the bulldozers removed approximately ten feet of dirt from the area to flatten it in preparation for constructing the subdivision.

"Grandma" Mary who lived a few doors away, knew I was trying to recover Drake's treasure. One afternoon, the doorbell rang, and when I answered it, she was holding a shopping bag. Mary told me there were things she wanted me to have, so I invited her in. She opened the bag and handed me an ashtray made in the 1970s. There were stories in the news so frequently that a local bank began giving out commemorative ashtrays with an image of the Plate of Brass. Her other gift was a ceramic bust of Sir Francis Drake that she had for many years. Mary told me she thought these artifacts might bring me luck. I thanked her very much and told her they were now a part of my treasure. She was the person who had remained most unconditionally supportive of my efforts from the beginning, and I was grateful.

One afternoon, not long after her visit, I went into the house, having completed my work for the day, when the doorbell rang. I opened it and was confronted by Tim Hendricks, head of the City of Larkspur Building Department. He told me that if I didn't stop digging immediately, I risked losing my property to the City, and they would auction it off. This problem hadn't occurred to me, but I didn't take kindly to his threat. The following day, I went to the Larkspur City Hall and demanded that Hendricks come out of his office and talk to me. In a few minutes, he came to the counter accompanied by Captain White of the Twin Cities Police. The three of us cordially spoke for a few minutes, and I invited them to come to my house and see what I was doing, assuring them that I had nothing to hide. I had a good relationship with Captain White and suspected that he knew Hendricks was completely wrong to threaten me.

They accepted my offer and came to the house within an hour. I walked them all over my property, explaining the details of my dig and what I discovered so far. Before they left, I told them that the best way for us all to move forward would be for me to meet with the

City's Planning Commission to present my research and the results of my excavations. They agreed and scheduled me to do so the following week. When I arrived at City Hall fully prepared, I was surprised to see that one of my ex-wife Melanie's friends, Michael Allbright, was in attendance. He worked for the City of Larkspur, though I needed to figure out in what capacity.

Nevertheless, I proceeded with my talk, prefacing it with a request that everything discussed remain confidential. All present agreed to honor that request, so in good faith, I told them about what I was doing and why. I was unsure whether they believed me when I finished. But at least I tried to open a dialogue.

A few hours later, Melanie called me, and she was furious. She thought I was over my "crazy Drake delusions." Then she repeated, almost verbatim, what I told those gathered at City Hall, ending her tirade with, "And I'm not going to let you get away with it!"

I didn't need to ask how she knew. It upset me that Allbright blatantly disregarded his promise to keep the information confidential. I returned to City Hall that same day to try to find him. Michael wasn't there, so I wrote a note demanding an apology for divulging confidential information. The next evening, he came to my door and said he was sorry, and that Melanie weaseled the info out of him. I accepted his apology, but the damage he'd done couldn't be undone. Now, Melanie had another reason to make my life miserable and further mess up my relationship with my daughter. By then, the poor kid didn't know what to think. Over the past year, whenever she visited me, Jennifer tried to help her view my treasure hunt as an exciting adventure she needed to keep secret from her mother.

Now that Melanie was back to smearing me as unstable and deranged, I wasn't surprised that she seemed nervous around me the next time I saw her. It was clear Melanie convinced her I was a lunatic.

Despite this, I continued excavating underneath my front yard with a jackhammer. After two more months, the total size of all the caverns and tunnels ballooned significantly, and this new part of my excavation contained several exciting features. The walls along both sides of the main tunnel contained numerous square spaces, each holding different types of stones. I surmised that Drake chose this layout based upon something from ancient history as he'd done with the section patterned after the Rio Tinto Mine. I was curious about what his model was this time. I embarked on more research and discovered that this area's design resembled a Celtic Burial Mound, some of which remain in England, Ireland, Scotland, and various parts of Europe. Given Drake's erudition and travels, I felt sure he'd read about them or visited them because <u>the layout of my tunnel and the squares in the walls were an exact match to the layout of the crypts in the burial mound at Newgrange, Ireland</u>.

Each crypt in that mound would have been occupied by human remains. In my tunnel, each one contained a different set of stones, another mystery for me to solve. Eventually, it became clear. Drake filled each crypt with the stones taken from a particular town or port he visited along the route to Nova Albion. The more I learned, the more dazzled I was by this man with whom I seemed to have such an uncanny connection.

By June 30, work was progressing smoothly, and I was once again confident that the treasure would be mine before long. I believed that soon I would find a buyer for the tools used to create Drake's Plate. I estimated the price tag for those tools to be one million dollars or more, and I began to think of it as money in the bank.

The next day I made a big decision based on the value of the tools. I went to my office in San Francisco, sat at my desk, wrote my letter of resignation from Morgan Witter, and made an appointment to meet with Ben Catalanatti. That afternoon, we sat down in his office, and I thanked him for all his support and for giving me the freedom to pursue my quest and take as much time off as I did over the past two years. I explained that my reason for resigning was not job dissatisfaction. I truly believed the value of the items I already recovered was as good as winning "Lotto," and I wanted to spend 100% of my time on this project. Ben understood and sincerely wished me well.

When we finished our talk, I went back downstairs, cleaned out my office, loaded my car, and drove home a "free" man.

With no daytime job, I decided it was better to remove the filled buckets from underneath the front yard at night. That would hide the scale of my excavation from the watchful eyes of anyone who might impede my progress. I continued digging daily and accumulated buckets of dirt and debris inside the tunnels. Then, at night, Jaime and his friends would come over. I passed the buckets up to them, and they would carry them to the backyard.

One day while I was working below ground in the front yard cavern, I heard a man's baritone voice singing. This was the third time I heard voices. Jennifer and my cousin were sitting on my back deck when I walked through the house to tell them, for some crazy reason, the song "The Rock of My Soul is the Bosom of Abraham" was stuck in my head. I found this odd, not being a religious man or an Elvis fan. Helen and Jennifer got a good laugh over it, but I suspected there was some deeper meaning. So I went to the computer and searched for the words in the title.

Most results related to Elvis, Louis Armstrong, or several black Southern preachers. But one of the results identified these words as a phrase describing how ancient Hebrews ate their meals in a reclining position, with the most honored guest reclining near or "in the bosom of" the host. The article also showed an image of this reclining position. It showed the same uncomfortable position I was in all that day, working in the confined space with my mini jackhammer. Why did I hear that song? Perhaps one of Drake's men sang it when he became trapped below ground, and he died before the rest of the crew could rescue him.

While, digging directly beneath the concrete walkway leading to my front door, <u>I came across a massive stone weighing 272 lbs.</u> Given my prior experiences, I was cautiously clearing the dirt away from it when I noticed an unusual image of a man's face on its surface. I got my camera and took a picture of it, then showed it to Jaime and asked him what he thought.

Although he had no formal education, Jaime was wise in many ways. As soon as he looked at the photograph, he said, "I know what this is. It's a Mayan Warrior." We were inside the house when this conversation happened, so I went to my computer and searched. There it was; <u>the image on the stone exactly matched a picture of a Mayan Warrior carved in stone</u>

<u>on a Mayan Temple in Guatemala</u>.

The stone was only four or five feet below the surface, and we were able to move it to the opening; however, it was too heavy for two of us to lift. At that time, I owned an aging Infiniti Q45 that was not in good condition, so I was willing to try something I would not have done with a better car. Jaime used his knot tying expertise and created a large, strong basket for the stone. We tied the other end of the rope to the back of my car. But, when I started driving forward, instead of the stone coming out of the ground, the trunk ripped off the back of the car, making a horrendous sound!

Oh, well, I thought, it was probably time for a new car anyway. The most important thing was getting the stone up and out of the hole, and later that day, we were able to do so with the help of a third man. I was excited to show Jennifer the Mayan Warrior emblazoned on it, but she was not impressed.

When my daughter visited me, she glared at the massive rock by my front door and asked, "Are you feeling alright, Daddy?" I knew this question resulted from Melanie's ongoing bad-mouthing of my quest. I tried explaining the importance of this discovery to Susan, but she kept rolling her eyes and frowning at me with the same look of disdain as her mother.

Another week passed and on Friday night, I called Jaime because I needed his help the following day, but when he didn't answer the phone, I left him a message. Saturday morning Jaime returned my call and said, "I can't work today because I'm in jail."

"You're what?" I was shocked to hear this because he was a religious and law-abiding man who would never do anything serious enough to land him in jail. When I asked him what happened, he told me while walking around his neighborhood in the Canal area of San Rafael, a cop mistook him for a criminal they were searching for. Apparently, Jaime was wearing the same color coat as the criminal. When the police realized he wasn't the suspect; they turned him over to the INS because he had no papers. Now he was in jail awaiting deportation.

I assured him that I would do everything I could to help him. He told me there would be a hearing in a few days. This gave me some time to do a bit of research about the deportation process.

On the day of the hearing, I sat in the Hearing Room and watched the Hearing Officer. His role was like a Judge in a Courtroom. I sat and listened as ordered the deportation of one person after another. When Jaime shuffled into the room with several other men, I approached the bench. I told the Hearing Officer that Jaime was helping me on a unique project and I needed him to remain in the country until it was completed.

The Hearing Officer was shocked because nobody ever came to the defense of these illegals. He immediately granted Jaime the right to stay in the States for several more months. I went to a different floor and posted his $5,000 bail, and Jaime was released. We both breathed a big sigh of relief on the drive back to San Rafael.

This situation presented Jaime with two options:

1. If he left the country voluntarily by the date ordered by the Hearing Officer, he could return when he had a proper green card.

2. If he didn't leave and choose to stay in the country illegally, and was caught again, he would never be allowed back into the U.S.A.

We continued working together until a week before his required "departure" date. Then, I made him an offer I hoped he wouldn't refuse. I would buy him a one-way ticket to Guatemala at my expense. Then, if he wanted to return to the US, he only needed the proper paperwork. To sweeten the deal, when the INS refunded the $5,000 bail, I would take that money, subtract the cost of the one-way airline ticket, and open a bank account for him in Guatemala so he would have money when he got home.

His eyes grew wide with surprise. "You'd really do that for me, Roberto?" I told him, "Of course, because you've been such a good worker and friend." He said, "Okay."

It took some running around and a few calls to Guatemala, but everything went according to plan. We continued working until the day I drove him to SFO to board his flight home.

Jaime still calls me a few times each year to see how I'm doing, and he always offers me a place to stay if I visit Guatemala. Sadly, he's never returned to the States, and I missed his company.

On July 2, I was digging underground, when I heard loud banging on the piece of wood I placed over the entrance to the front cavern. I made my way up to the surface and found it was Tim Hendricks, the Larkspur Building Inspector, along with a lot of police cars, uniformed officers, and official "suits" standing in the street in front of my house.

I walked toward them, covered with dirt, and Tim thrust a "Cease and Desist Order" at me, saying that my house was now "Red Tagged," and telling me I needed to appear in Court. I asked how my house could be red tagged since it was obviously habitable.

He sneered at my excavation site and shook his head, refusing to say anything more. Then I turned and said, "Hold on just a moment." I took the paperwork, entered the house, washed my hands, grabbed my video camera, returned outside, and started filming. Everyone scattered like flies, hiding their faces from my camera. Clearly, they'd only come hoping to see how I would react when I was served. Instead of getting riled and acting like a madman, I turned the tables on them. But inside, I was seething.

The next day, I emailed the following letter to Captain White of the Twin Cities Police Department:

To preserve the peace in the City of Larkspur and my immediate neighborhood, you need to know that I am no longer looking for the treasure of Sir Francis Drake. I have found it and have partially completed the recovery process. The actions taken by the Larkspur Building Department have jeopardized my plans for a public announcement that will undoubtedly draw worldwide media coverage. I hoped to tell the media that the treasure had been recovered and nothing remained on or my property for the curious to see or criminals to steal.

Yesterday's action with its circus-like atmosphere has made my planned announcement impossible. In addition, it has severely damaged the peace, quiet and security of my community. When I report the destructive interference of your men and the Building Inspector, I expect the media will have a field day at your expense.

Yesterday's unnecessary "show of force" against me and my project was conducted by Tim Hendricks who was completely unaware of the Building Department's own regulations regarding permitting requirements. There is a specific exemption afforded to hand-dug excavations of less than 25 cubic yards.

I trust that you and I can work together to determine what security measures need to be in place in advance of the press conference. If the Building Department persists in their effort to stop me from completing this project, I cannot assure that you'll have adequate time to prepare your department for my press conference, as I may need to inform the media sooner than I would have preferred.

I have scheduled a meeting with R L. Stanton of the Building Department for 11:30 AM Monday. Ahead of that meeting, you may want to discuss the information contained herein with various City officials. I give you my permission to do so at your discretion.

Furthermore, I need to have the "red tag" removed from my home immediately, and I must be allowed to complete my work without further interference! You and I have had an open and honest relationship and I look forward to working with you.

Feel free to call me with any questions.

The City of Larkspur had one trick that blindsided me. The reason I received the Summons to appear in Court was that I violated an arcane Larkspur regulation that must have been on the books since the City was founded in the nineteenth century.

A City Permit was required if one excavated more than 20 cubic yards of dirt. As noted earlier, the excavation was approximately 1,400 square feet, which, if I factored in the height of each tunnel and Cavern, equaled some 7000 cubic feet. So, there was no way out of this situation. The wording on the face of the Summons said, "Must Appear," and the following week, I went to Court and discovered that this was an Arraignment, during which I was charged with a

Misdemeanor for which the City of Larkspur wanted to put me in jail!

Jennifer's ex-husband, Mark Anderson, worked as a city planner at some point in his life, and he worked with the man who was now the Attorney for the City of Larkspur. Mark liked me, and I was able to recruit him to advocate on my behalf. My next Court date was not scheduled until December. Over the next few months, Mark met with the Larkspur Attorney several times and was able to mediate a settlement before the case went to trial.

Meanwhile, I continued to feel the urgency of moving forward with my project, all the time knowing that the rainy season would soon begin.

Mother Nature defeated me in my backyard, and I would not sit back and let the same thing happen to the Cavern in my front yard!

To prevent a repeat of prior years' disasters, I ordered a fiberglass spraying machine, a 55-gallon drum of resin and a roll of fiberglass cloth. My plan was to fiberglass the cavern's walls, ceiling, and floor and make it watertight. My calculations indicated that if applied thick enough, the strength of the fiberglass would keep the water out and preserve the excavation for all time.

A week later, I received notification from a warehouse in Oakland that my machine arrived! Driving a rented pick-up truck, I made my way to the warehouse, where a forklift placed the massive box containing the device into the truck.

When I got home and opened the box, there were complex assembly instructions and hundreds of parts. Every day for the next two weeks was spent following every step of the instructions, and in the end, I did things correctly because there were no parts left over.

After I ordered the machine, I learned that air quality regulations require a permit to operate this type of machine in the Bay Area. Not wanting to derail the deal that Mark worked out with the City of Larkspur, it seemed best to avoid applying for the permit. I had no intention of going to jail, so the machine sat in my backyard, fully assembled and ready to operate.

As the rainy season drew closer<u>, I decided to cover my entire front yard with plastic sheeting to prevent the rain from penetrating the ground and collapsing the Cavern.</u> Until this point everyone except Rod and one neighbor down the street were supportive of my efforts since the beginning, perhaps because they all knew and respected Grandma Mary, who'd been my champion since day one.

Two weeks after I laid down the plastic, my neighbor across the street, Kay Parsons came over to talk to me while I was out in front of my house. Up to this point, the Parsons had been supporters of my endeavor. Mr. Parsons even went below ground once to see what I was doing. However, this time, Kay complained that I was bringing down property values on our street and insisted that I remove the plastic sheets as soon as possible.

I was tired of fighting and realized that Kay didn't understand what would happen as soon as it rained if the sheeting was not in place. Nevertheless, I complied because I wanted to keep peace in the neighborhood.

<u>During the second day of rain, the entire front yard collapsed, leaving a vast, gaping hole</u>. In a way, it struck me as funny. Kay complained that the plastic sheeting damaged property values. What about a water-filled chasm?

When I returned to Court in December, Mark arranged a deal with the City Attorney that required me to pay for a professional property survey. I pleaded "No Contest" to the charges against me. I was sentenced to eighteen months' probation, with the understanding that I would fill-in the entire excavation with clean, County-approved dirt and fill the plastic sewer pipe in the backyard with cement. There would be no fine if I satisfied these conditions.

I accepted my punishment and complied with the Court Order.

CHAPTER 16

The Fax, The Farm, The Experts

The probation period began in January 2004 and was in effect until the end of June 2005. During this time, I satisfied the requirements of getting a survey and filling in the excavations. While dutifully meeting these demands, I spent time tracking down people who might be willing and able to authenticate the set of tools I found. I knew that once the tools were proven to be authentic, I could start looking for a buyer—perhaps a museum, university, or wealthy individual somewhere——who'd be willing to pay a significant sum for these important pieces of history.

I made several calls to people in the metallurgy field and was eventually referred to Edwin Warner in Pleasanton, a world- class metallurgist with a wide variety of interests. I sent him an email providing a little background and a request to talk to him about the Plate of Brass.

He responded by phone, furious that I contacted him. "How did you get my name?" he yelled so I told him. Then he asked an odd question: "Do you believe the Plate was made in a mold or by hammering?" Before I could answer he snapped, "You should know whom you're going to talk to before you contact them," and he hung up. His response was so strange and intense that by dumb luck, I stumbled across yet another participant in the conspiracy to steal the Plate of Brass.

My probation also provided me with time to expand my scientific studies, satisfying the deep craving I shared with Sir Francis to know and understand everything I could. I did more research into the long-term implications of exposure to toxic elements. Although it was three years since I'd been diagnosed with Boron poisoning and well over a year since my arsenic and selenium poisoning, I continued to have bouts of lethargy whenever the temperature rose above 85 degrees. I found a report on the Internet entitled "The 1996 World Symposium on Boron." This 100+ page document contained everything known about Boron's effects. I read it thoroughly. The biggest potential problem it cited was the effect of ingesting Boron, for example, via drinking water.

Once each year, along with the monthly water bill, Marin County Municipal Water District (MMWD) includes a brochure detailing the composition of the district's drinking water and the sources for various compounds detected in the drinking water. Since I saved all my old bills for tax purposes, I had the brochures from several prior years in addition to the current one.

Reviewing them all, I realized that although MMWD

acknowledged Boron's presence, they didn't list its source.

I called Scott Steiner, an MMWD employee I met through my daughter, to tell him I believed the source of the Boron was in my backyard. He listened to what I said but did nothing with the information. I wasn't sure why.

When the following year's brochure came out, I noticed Boron's source was still not listed. Now, Vanadium has disappeared from the list of toxins in our water. I called Steve to discuss this with him, but he wouldn't take my call. I didn't focus much energy on his reasons because, throughout this time, my philosophy was that when one door closed, another one would open! There was too much to do to get hung up on any one roadblock.

I focused my energy on determining the nature and source of some unusual rocks I found. I visited the US Geological Survey in Menlo Park, thinking they might be interested in a large piece of granite I found. I showed it to Dr. Hayden Palmer, who'd done extensive research on the geology of Marin County. He said he'd come across small pieces of granite in Marin but never such a large piece. He also said that all the granite that did turn up here most likely originated in or around Point Reyes as part of a tectonic plate that moved northward millions of years ago. At that time, what is now the California coastline was deep underwater.

Although this piece of granite didn't have anything to do with Drake, I still found it fascinating.

During the winter months, I spent whole days testing the various stones I excavated by measuring their specific gravity, a test first employed by the Greek Archimedes. I placed a rock on a scale and weighed it.

Next, I weighed a glass of water. Finally, I attached the stone to a thin wire and suspend it in the water without letting it touch the sides or the bottom. Then, I would weigh it. A few calculations were needed, resulting in the stone's specific gravity. I was looking for stones with specific gravities corresponding to Emeralds and Sapphires.

I worked at home almost every day and conducted as many specific gravity tests as possible. On a sheet of paper, I drew a grid and then placed each stone into one square. After I tested each one, I put it back on its box and wrote down its specific gravity. I repeated this thousands of times. If the result matched what I was looking for, it went into a container with other stones of the same specific gravity. The stones that didn't meet my criteria were thrown back into a bucket that was marked accordingly.

In addition to my specific gravity testing, I spent some time each week smashing the white stones stored in buckets in my garage. One afternoon, I noticed that one piece contained clearly defined triangles on its face. Research indicated that it might be a diamond, so I took it to San Francisco to have it examined by an expert. Martin Garcia, Gemologist, and his colleague both confirmed that it was an authentic uncut diamond.

<u>Martin prepared a written certification, which read, "One loose Brazilian diamond crystal weighing .68 carats and measuring approximately 12.19 x 10.80 x 8.21 mm."</u> I couldn't have been happier. I knew Drake spent time along the coast of Brazil, so this made sense.

Wondering how many more diamonds I might have, I decided to stop smashing the white stones and purchased a hand-held diamond tester like the ones used by many jewelers. I was excited when many set off the tester, indicating they were diamonds. All the white stones were alluvial in nature (they came out of a river). If they were diamonds, their distinctive triangular features were worn down by the river water passing over them. This made me think of a line from a Steely Dan song... "You wouldn't know a diamond if you held it in your hand...the things you think are precious, I can't understand." The tester worked great, but Brazilian diamonds came in a full spectrum of colors, and the colored diamonds were more valuable than the clear or white diamonds! By now, I had millions of stones and wondered if there might be some easy way to identify them by sight. I went online and purchased several out-of-print books with pictures of rough diamonds. Unfortunately, the books didn't give me the information I needed. Maybe this is what it meant when I heard, "All white stones are good"?

After a little research, I learned that before South Africa became the diamond capital of the world, Brazil held that title and that the largest Brazilian diamond ever discovered was found in 1867 and named "The Star of the South." That stone was sent to Amsterdam, where it was cut by the Royal Van Fleer Diamond Company. The company was still in business and was now run by two great-grandsons of its founder, Jacob Van Fleer. I had no doubt that those two men would recognize a rough Brazilian diamond when they saw one.

When I told Jennifer I needed to go to Amsterdam and asked if she wanted to go with me, she responded, "You're crazy! No, I don't want to go!" I needed their expertise in identifying a rough diamond by sight and to have them evaluate the quality of the diamonds I found.

During the last week of April, I sent a fax to the Van Fleers informing them that I would come to their office in Amsterdam at 8:00 AM on May 6 to meet with them. I immediately purchased an airline ticket and waited for their reply. Several days passed without a word from them, and I began to get a bit nervous. Still, I told Jennifer in the spirit of "whatever it takes," I'm getting on that plane and going to Amsterdam regardless of whether they responded or not. If they did not see me, there were plenty of other diamond experts in Amsterdam who would spend a few minutes looking at some of my stones.

Shortly after I purchased my airline ticket, my next-door neighbor at 39 Via Corona informed me that she and her husband decided to move and sell their house. Without hesitation, I told her I wanted to buy it and asked them not to list it with an agent because they would save over $50,000 in commissions if we could arrange a private sale. Unfortunately, they nixed that idea and hired an Agent. The reason for my wanting their house was to ensure my privacy because my other next-door neighbor, Rod, recently built a large deck in his backyard, and now he could see directly into my yard. Jennifer prepared and delivered my offer to the seller's Agent. The agent told Jennifer they were expecting multiple offers, and it would be a few days before we found out who would get the property.

As women so often do, Jennifer suddenly changed her mind about going with me to Amsterdam, so I purchased a ticket for her.

Eight bids were opened the day before our flight and I turned out to be the highest bidder, so Jennifer began negotiating the terms of the sale with the Agent.

The following day, we drove to the airport even

though I still hadn't heard from the Van Fleers. But, by then, the excitement of the adventure had taken over. We arrived at Schiphol Airport in Amsterdam on the morning of May 5 and, from there, took a taxi to our hotel. Neither of us slept much during the flight.

Throughout the day, Jennifer called California, relentlessly working on the house deal. When she wasn't busy on the phone, we were walking around the city, admiring its canals, checking out nearby bars, and restaurants and discovering that Amsterdam's open drug culture and permissiveness was not exaggerated.

After a full first day and an excellent dinner, we went to bed exhausted.

The morning of May 6, I got up early so I could be at the Van Fleers' shop at 8:00, as promised. I took public transit and arrived at 7:55. At 8:00 sharp, I knocked on the door, and Max Van Fleer opened it in less than a minute. I introduced myself and asked if he received my fax. His English was excellent, and he apologized, telling me that he did, but didn't have a chance to respond.

He invited me to come into his office where I gave him a brief synopsis of the Sir Francis Drake story. I added that I wanted to meet with them because of their great-grandfather's work on "The Star of the South" and thought I might have found some uncut Brazilian diamonds during my Drake research. I told him I could think of no one better in the world to evaluate my stones.

I was fortunate that Max was willing to look at what I brought, as he was the science side of the Van Fleers' business. He took the bag of stones, sat at his workbench, and examined twenty. When he finished, he said, "Yes, you have some diamonds here."

His brother Hans entered the room as soon as he finished that sentence. The two brothers were complete opposites; Hans was all business. Once again, I introduced myself and told him why I was there. Then Hans called Max aside, and they briefly held a discussion in Flemish. When they finished, Hans turned and asked me in English, "Do you have the proper paperwork?"

I replied, "No, but these diamonds come from California and not from Africa."

Hans was obviously disturbed and said sternly, "You do not have anything here, and don't tell anybody you've been here." I stood up and said, "Thank you very much; I appreciate your time, and the next time you hear from me, I'll have the proper paperwork." I wished them a good day, and they saw me out the door.

I knew that "blood diamonds" from the Congo and other parts of Africa was a hot topic in the news. There were lots of black-market diamonds being introduced to the market by unscrupulous profiteers, so I fully understood why the Van Fleers were hesitant to have any discussion with me without the proper paperwork proving the stones' provenance. If I was working for law enforcement, they could have lost their business license or even been sent to prison for dealing in illegal diamonds. But I knew from Max's response that the stones I found were diamonds regardless of whether I possessed a Kimberly Process Certificate. I walked out of there, a very happy man!

I called Jennifer, told her what happened and asked her to meet me outside the showroom of a different diamond-cutting company. When she arrived, we took a tour to see how diamonds were cut, and afterward, we again strolled through the streets of Amsterdam looking for antiquarian bookshops since I thought they might have some old books on diamonds. We visited many booksellers but only found one book with enough pictures of rough diamonds to help me assess all the different stones in my garage.

That evening, we went to a nightclub we noticed earlier that day. Just our luck, it was one of the most popular spots in Amsterdam. It was crowded when we arrived, and as I looked around, it quickly became apparent that everybody in the club, except us, was high on Ecstasy. We weren't there more than fifteen minutes when a Dutchman a few years younger than us came to our table and asked if we wanted some. We said, "Sure," and he gave us each a hit. Then he sat and talked with us for a while, saying he was there with his boyfriend who happened to be a famous hairstylist for Vidal Sassoon in Amsterdam. His English was perfect, and as the conversation progressed, we discovered that this fellow was known around town as the Merv Griffin of Amsterdam because he was the producer of every game show taped in Flemish.

He invited us to join him and his boyfriend. The four of us laughed and partied until the club closed. Then Merv invited us to check out his floating boat home, a short distance away. It was a sailboat moored in a canal. We were there for a few minutes when he said, "I want to take you somewhere you'll love—The Farm."

I heard about "The Farm" because it was as famous a sex club like Plato's Retreat in NYC was in the late '70s and early '80s when I lived in Manhattan. The Farm was located about thirty miles outside Amsterdam, so we piled into Merv's car and drove for 40 minutes until we pulled off the highway and parked at a farm.

We went inside a huge barn, and as a first-time male visitor, I was required to wear a ridiculous clown outfit to mark me as a newbie. Women weren't required to wear special rookie attire. Perhaps thirty minutes after we'd arrived, the guys asked Jennifer to go upstairs with them, and off they went. Meanwhile, I stayed downstairs, trying to flirt, but my "first-timer" outfit made each woman I approached giggle and turn away. When Jennifer and the guys came downstairs, it was about eight in the morning, and the sun shone brightly. I put my street clothes back on, and we all climbed back into Merv's car. We were driving back toward Amsterdam when the guys asked if we'd like to go to the beach that day. By this time, Jennifer was passed out, so I said, "We'll have to take a rain check."

They dropped us off at our hotel, where I thanked them for everything, they'd done to make it an unforgettable night. We exchanged phone numbers, but that was the last time we saw or heard from them.

We were in Amsterdam for five days. Jennifer and I saw several "coffee houses" where it was legal to smoke pot and Hash. During our last day in Amsterdam, Jennifer informed me she planned to buy hashish and smuggle it back to the States in her suitcase. I told her I wanted nothing to do with that, but she was determined and wasn't afraid of getting caught. I told her that if she tried to take Hash back into the US, I wanted nothing to do with it and wouldn't stand beside her in the Customs line. I didn't need any further hassles with the law.

However, Jennifer was set on doing it, and there was nothing I could say that would change her mind.

Thank God I was smart enough not to try and

smuggle anything because when we arrived at Schiphol Airport, the Customs Agents at the very first checkpoint opened my suitcase. He pulled out my bag of diamonds and, before opening it, asked, "What's this?"

"Oh, just some pieces of quartz a friend gave me."

He peered inside, but because he'd never seen alluvial diamonds before, he just shrugged and shoved the bag back into my suitcase. On the other hand, Jennifer just smiled at them and walked right through.

When the plane landed at SFO, we stood in different Customs lines. This time, she was the one who was stopped while I breezed right through. Despite her charming smile the Customs agent opened her bag and pawed through it. I looked back and saw her being escorted off the main floor and into a back room. I figured, "This is it; she's going to jail," but I decided to wait and see what happened.

Ten minutes later, she walked out smiling. Jennifer told me that the Customs Agents saw the Hash in her suitcase. They let her go without confiscating it or arresting her for smuggling. She possessed the gift of gab and the nine lives of a cat!

Soon after our return, with Jennifer's help, I closed on the property at 39 Via Corona for $1,072,000, a high price, because I needed to outbid seven other potential buyers. My bid purposely included Drake's favorite number, 72, which once again brought me good luck.

I contemplated my options for the new house. I thought about renting it out, but since I took an "owner-occupied" loan, I knew that wouldn't fly. No need to start off on the wrong foot by blatantly violating the terms of the loan agreement. I decided to move into that house but didn't want my nosy neighbors knowing what I was up to. One night after dark, I took down the fence that separated the two properties and used a hand truck to wheel my belongings across the yard and into the new house.

Altogether there were twenty houses on Via Corona, and the lot where 39 stood was where the excess material from the grading process was pushed and allowed to settle for ten years before a house could be built on the land. Because of this, I expected to find some artifacts there too.

As soon as the sellers moved out, I went next door. <u>I found several damaged two-part cupellation hearths</u> in the yard and moved them to my garage.

After moving in, I found Chinese artifacts dating from the Ming Dynasty on two different occasions while mowing the lawn in the backyard. <u>First, was a cloisonné writing instrument and then a gold charm in the shape of a Chinese Warrior</u>. These items could have been aboard the Chinese merchant ship that Drake captured on April 4, 1579.

The World Encompassed makes several references to "The Lost Harbor" and gives its location as Latitude 38.30° North. This erroneous latitude has caused much of the controversy over Drake's landing site. In my effort to resolve it, I used a combination of math and intuition. I thought that since Drake's obsession with the number 72 was a factor in many calculations, it might also be relevant for this situation. I subtracted .72 from the 38.30° North coordinate and the answer was Latitude 37.58° North. <u>When I sat down at my computer and entered the new coordinate, a computerized map pinpointed the location in San Rafael at Pickleweed Park, along the edge of San Francisco Bay.</u> I jumped into my car and, upon arrival at the park, observed what a fine location it would have been for the "Lost Harbor.". A ship moored there would be impossible to see any from any vantage point south of what is now the Richmond-San Rafael Bridge. It seemed 100% certain that after the Golden Hind was careened and repaired, the crew sailed it around the tip of San Quentin Peninsula and headed here, to "The Lost Harbor." I knew this was the answer to another of the mysteries about Drake's visit to Nova Albion.

I sat in Pickleweed Park, with my eyes closed, my face lifted to the sun, imagining Drake's men load the provisions, gold, silver, and other treasures onto the Golden Hind without being detected or disturbed as they prepared to make their voyage across the Pacific.

Then, I stood up and, as if being led by Drake himself, walked out on the marsh and identified the routes used by the carts as they moved things between The Lost Harbor, Drake's Fort, and the Treasure site. I spent many weeks walking along these routes, looking for anything of interest and found numerous decking nails that I was able to identify as belonging to the Cacafuego and a Portuguese Caravel. The most noteworthy item I recovered was an odd-shaped piece of metal that looked almost identical to the rod used in crafting the Plate of Brass, so I deduced that it might have been the "original rod." Maybe it fell off a cart and was lost in the mud? It explained why Drake needed to fabricate a new rod to because he needed the right tools to create the Plate and the inscription.

A few months after finding that intriguing item, I was walking toward the Lost Harbor when I came upon a large metal ladle with a wooden handle. I brought it home and for the first several days thought it was just some kind of serving ladle. After several attempts at searching the Internet, I saw something about a "gunpowder ladle." I clicked that link and Eureka! During the 1500s, it turned out, cannons were loaded with stone or metal cannonballs, and the "gunpowder was measured out by ladle from a large barrel and placed into the cannon."

I found additional information on the website of Mel Fisher, a world-renowned treasure hunter who'd discovered the remains of many sixteenth- and seventeenth-century ships off the Florida coast. His website was filled with historical information and photographs of items he'd recovered from these ships. There was one whole page devoted to different types of cannons and cannonballs from that era, and links to charts containing images and details about the specific gunpowder ladle that was used in conjunction with every different style of cannon. By measuring and comparing my ladle to those listed, I found it matched only one, the type carried aboard Spanish galleons! I was so excited that I emailed several pictures of it to Mr. Hopkins, Head Curator of the Mel Fisher Museum. He promptly replied, "Yes, it does indeed look like a ladle from a Spanish galleon!"

Toward the end of August 2004, I returned to The Lost Harbor at an extreme low tide. I discovered a piece of a ship's rudder system known as a Pintle. Rudder systems vary greatly but this one's pintle seemed to match what I could find regarding sixteenth-century rudder systems.

That month, I decided it was time to try a different approach for authenticating the set of tools. I called Tariq Houssein, my contact at E & M Labs, Inc. We worked out a deal that cost me $1,500. For that he would measure the lengths of the lines on the reeded edges of my disks, fully describe and <u>measure the features of the rod</u>, and compare what they found with the markings on the radiograph of the Plate of Brass.

When the results came back, the lines on the 21 disks matched the vertical lines on the Plate of Brass and the measurements and features of the rod matched the lengths of the horizontal lines on the Plate. Anybody who looked at Iron fitting could see that <u>the metal flaws on the Plate matched those on the mold.</u>

Finally, I had undeniable evidence.

But then, out of the blue, E & M Labs refused to issue a written opinion regarding the tools and their relationship to the Plate of Brass. I tried to argue with them but to no avail. I could only think that, yet again, Kenneth Wagner was the culprit.

The news that year was not all bad. In early September, I received the following letter from the City of Larkspur Attorney's Office:

This is regarding the dismissal of Marin County Superior Court case number CR131999A.

You were previously charged by the City of Larkspur with two misdemeanor violations relating to excavation activities on your property located at 35 Via Corona. As you may recall, you entered into an agreement with the City whereby one misdemeanor count was dismissed, and you entered a plea of "no contest" regarding the other count. Based upon your plea, the court imposed a conditional fine of $1000; however, imposition of that fine was suspended, conditional upon compliance with the terms and conditions of a Notice and Order from the City of Larkspur.

Under the terms of the agreement, the suspended fine would be discharged upon verification of compliance with the Notice and Order. The City of Larkspur considers your recent mediation efforts to be in substantial compliance with the terms of the Conditional Sentence and Dismissal Agreement. Therefore, we will not seek to have the suspended fine of $1000 imposed.

We appreciate your efforts in retaining the services of Jess Knight to coordinate the remediation project and Miller Pacific Engineers to provide a remediation plan and project oversight. Having received the Engineer's Report from Miller Pacific, the City now considers the matter resolved. Once again, thank you for your cooperation.

One less thing to worry about.

CHAPTER 17

It's All about Chemistry

In earlier chapters, I referred to the white patterns that guided my excavations, the parrot wearing a crown, and the blue stork. I want to make it perfectly clear that these were not delusions, illusions, figments of my imagination, or hallucinations resulting from my use of illegal drugs. Those patterns and images directly resulted from Drake's knowledge of alchemy and ancient processes. Today, we have a term for combining these two types of knowledge. The word is "Chemistry."

Certain elements and simple compounds react readily with oxygen, and each produces a specific color. The test results on the 1936 Plate of Brass reported the presence of the following elements: Barium, Magnesium, Manganese, Cobalt, and Strontium, all of which oxidize quickly.

These same elements were also detected in tests by UC Davis on samples of the dust and water from my property.

Throughout the tunnel system, within one to two minutes after I removed dirt or clay and exposed the underlying soil to air, one or more colors appeared to form the patterns and images I've described as if by magic! So, why were they there, and how did they get there?

One of the biggest challenges for Drake and his men was to hide the treasure in such a way as to make it recoverable. Drake used his ingenuity and knowledge about the reactive properties of certain elements and simple chemical compounds to accomplish this.

His 1577 voyage had two primary goals. He was to steal as much gold and silver as possible and collect minerals that were needed by mineral-poor England at the start of the Industrial Revolution. He gathered the raw materials containing the elements noted above during his voyage and, after processing, incorporated them into the cavern and tunnel system during the construction phase. When he went to recover the treasure, he knew these elements would react with oxygen when exposed to air and produce the desired patterns. These were to serve as aids to help guide his men to the treasure's underground location. He knew that a pattern would only form if the oxidizing minerals were mixed into the slurry in the right proportion.

I also discovered two other techniques that were incorporated into the design of the Hondius Map and the tunnel system to help Drake when he went back to recover the treasure. Back in 2000, when I uncovered the image of the "parrot wearing a crown," I compared its shape and position to one of the large black marks on the Hondius map inset. I noted that the overall shape of the parrot image was virtually identical in shape to the large black mark. If Drake did not have the Hondius map, the image of the parrot (and later images) could be used as a map substitute because it showed the exact shape and size of the excavation that was needed.

Two years into the project I became aware that there was a large rock every 6 or 12 feet throughout the underground system. Each time I found one of these rocks, I washed it off and compared it to the enlarged section of the inset where I worked. I soon realized that the placement of these rocks was intentional. Each rock was modified by chipping it to the desired shape and then embellishing it with chemical compounds to make the colors the desired features. Each "map rock" showed the exact shape and size of the section of the tunnel system I was about to begin excavating. At first, the idea of "map rocks" was pure conjecture. However, when I compared them to the black marks on the Hondius map, and they matched.

CHAPTER 18

The Giant Map Rock

In early 2005, I decided to revisit the location where I discovered the disks and rod that were used to make the inscription on the plate. I climbed over the retaining wall in the parking lot and noticed a rusted piece of metal about 25 yards away. I walked over and picked it up to take a closer look. It was roughly the same size as the Plate of Brass and contained a square hole on the lower right-hand side which was in the same position as the "coin-holder" of the Plate. This was how I found the Iron fastener that was crucial to the creation of the Plate of Brass.

With this, all the parts used to create Drake's, Plate of Brass were in my possession!

It was spring, and I noticed that there were workers in Rod's backyard terracing the hillside and digging holes for new fence posts. I walked outside and observed that these new holes were on the same line as the existing fence. When Rod came out to inspect the work, I told him the current fence didn't correctly reflect our shared property line, according to my court-mandated survey. The new fence needed to move three feet further into his yard. I showed him the study to prove it, and his workers re-positioned the new fence accordingly.

In the far corner of my now slightly larger backyard, there was a dense thicket of bamboo that previously was on Rod's side of the fence. When I was trimmed the bamboo, I noticed it completely obscured a huge rock that was hidden inside the thicket. I realized that it was no ordinary rock; it was a giant map rock that showed the caverns, the tunnels, and all the features of my yard as they were in 1579! It was placed there by Drake and sat there undisturbed for the last 426 years. Astounding!

It was June 30, 2005, the final day of my 1½-year probation period. This could not be a coincidence! I sat and stared at the map rock and thought that Drake must be smiling down upon me!

I visually aligned the position of the cavern on the giant map rock with the topographic features of my backyard. I saw that there was a second entrance to the cavern. I measured the map rock's features to calculate its scale relative to my yard, went to the garage, picked up a shovel, and began digging just ten feet away from my deck. Small planes and helicopters often flew overhead on a regular basis and if one passed overhead while I was working, I pretended to be planting a tree. After digging for a week, the size of my new entrance was equivalent to the large opening shown on the giant map rock. My level of excitement was at its peak, when suddenly the sound of a low-flying helicopter was directly overhead. It was so close;

I could see somebody inside it filming my activity. I used my tree-planting ruse, and they flew off.

Working out in the open so soon after my probation ended was a high-risk undertaking. I realized that I could only pretend to plant the same tree once for each observer, and the ploy was used up by now. I needed to devise a more clandestine way to get into the cavern.

I purchased two 4 x 8 sheets of plywood, placed them over the hole, and covered the wood with dirt. It was too risky to use that entrance again.

The best way to hide my activity would be to cut the floor from under one of my kitchen cabinets and pass through the cabinet into the crawlspace immediately below. Once there, I could tunnel under the foundation and emerge close to where I was working via the now abandoned entrance.

The owner-occupancy period required under the terms of the loan for 39 Via Corona was over so I decided to use that as a rental property. During the last half of July and the first half of August, I prepared for new tenants. I painted the interior, refinished the living room and dining area floors and made numerous minor small repairs.

I posted the house on Craigslist and within a week, found a qualified tenant who wanted to move in the last week of August. After moving my possessions back into 35 Via Corona and settling in, there was no time to waste. I removed the dinette set from the kitchen and sawed through the bottom of the cabinet, creating a hole large enough for me to climb in and out of without difficulty. The power cords for the lights, fans, and jackhammer passed through the opening. Then they wrapped around a water pipe in the crawlspace so they wouldn't get in my way or become disconnected as I moved in and out of the cabinet. I removed just enough dirt from below the foundation to pass beneath it.

On the other side of the foundation, there were only 2-3 feet of clearance between the soil and the ceiling, so there was not enough room to sit or kneel. I found that a regular-sized shovel was too large to maneuver in such tight confines, so I purchased a miniature shovel to get started. No soil was on the other side of the foundation, only the highly toxic multicolored clay. To make matters worse, it was intensely hot because there was no ventilation to release the heat generated by the lights and jackhammer.

I pulled the heavy buckets underneath the foundation into the crawlspace, lifted them up through the cabinet, and pushed them onto the kitchen floor. I decided that the 20-year-old linoleum kitchen floor was expendable.

The pair of waders I purchased from Paul Charles two years earlier was exactly what I needed to protect myself against such a toxic environment. Every time, before I went below, I put on two pairs of socks, two pairs of underwear with pants over them, and then a tee shirt covered by a long-sleeve shirt. Then I put on shoes and stepped into the waist-high waders, completing my outfit with a hat, dust mask, and latex gloves underneath rubberized work gloves.

I did not deviate from this routine.

Once every three hours, I returned to the surface, removed the entire outfit, and started again. This created a lot of laundry, but it was much better than getting sick again. Unfortunately, washing machines don't last long when subjected to nearly insoluble clay and small stones passing through the drainage holes at the bottom of the drum. Mine never survived more than a year before they had to be replaced.

During September and October in Marin County, daytime temperatures exceeded 85 degrees every day, so the work was hot and sweaty as autumn progressed.

The first time I passed under the foundation, I expected to be right below the original cement patio that was now hidden below a wooden deck. What I saw was entirely different!

It was the roof of the ancient natural cavern depicted on the giant map rock. This was the cavern that served as the source of water for the Miwok during the summer months. About twelve feet from my entrance point, I saw an oddly shaped metal piece attached to the cavern ceiling that was a marker of some sort. <u>The top of the cavern had been modified by Drake and his men. They created a cement and added a layer of very sharp, pointed rocks along the ceiling.</u> The slightest bump against them drew blood and hurt like hell, even with my protective clothing.

As work progressed, I connected the new entrance to the now abandoned one out in the yard. Once completed, the area became much more comfortable as enough air could seep in for the fans to do their job.

My daily goal was to fill at least twenty buckets and move them into the kitchen. About twelve feet from the foundation, I noticed that a large section was cut-out from the cavern's roof and then replaced with such precision that it did not appear disturbed.

Fortunately, 426 years of small earthquakes caused that section to shift just enough for me to see the cut marks that identified it as another deadly trick. If I was working underneath, and removed the wrong stone, the cut-out ceiling would fall, and crush me.

Little by little, I worked my way completely around that section. I was jackhammering to remove just enough clay to keep me out of harm's way when I noticed yet another large image on the wall, this one creepy looking, frowning ghost. I got my camera and took a picture of it then stopped to study it more intently, realizing its role in this latest deadly trick: <u>from one direction it appeared to be smiling and from one direction it appeared to be smiling and pointing one way, but from the direction I came, it was frowning and pointing the opposite way.</u>

If I worked my way into the cavern from the backyard entrance and seen the smiling ghost, I would have continued to dig in the direction it was pointing. That would have led me right below the deadly section of ceiling and killed me. This bizarre trick refreshed my memory, so I remained vigilant for signs of any other tricks.

After connecting the foundation entrance to the yard entrance, I turned my attention to the other end of the cavern near 39 Via Corona. This would be an escape route if anything happened and provide the cross-ventilation I desperately needed during the heat of Indian summer. To access the cavern from that end, I had to dig through a dense jumble of rocks. As soon as the hole was large enough for me to crawl through, fine-grained sand came from behind the jumble of rocks and poured in. In a few minutes, the entrance hole was blocked by sand, so I shoveled it out, but more sand kept coming! I repeated this process several times, and eventually, the sand stopped. This trick was designed to catch unsuspecting treasure hunters who entered the cavern from that end. Once inside, they would be trapped by the sand. The seemingly endless sand would pour right back in when they attempted to dig their way out, making escape impossible. It wouldn't take long before the unsuccessful raiders would suffocate due to a lack of oxygen. They would become the skeletons of dead men trying to recover the treasure.

Fresh air now circulated through the cavern. It was already November, and with the rain in the forecast, I was unwilling to risk another costly fiasco and removed all my equipment. Within a few days, the rain began, and the cavern filled with over 20,000 gallons of water.

Now, I would have to wait until spring before continuing.

CHAPTER 19

Hell's Half-Acre

As 2005 ended, I reflected on everything that occurred in the prior twelve months, and what I wanted to accomplish in the upcoming year. The treasure hunt was moving slower and costing more than I anticipated. Dark clouds were gathering on my financial horizon. I was not bringing home a regular paycheck. I needed to sell large blocks of stock from my portfolio to cover my cost of living and investigation. If I didn't take action to reduce my expenses, I would run out of money within 2-3 years. The tools used to create the Plate of Brass were the only thing I found that might be convertible into cash!

The rent being paid by my tenants in 39 Via Corona covered the mortgage but not the $18,000 per year in property taxes or the insurance on the house.

I thought that I'd be rolling in dough from selling the tools, but every attempt must have been blocked by Kenneth Wagner.

I received some sad but timely news just over a week into the new year. My grandmother passed away at the age of 97. I flew to New York, attended her funeral, and met with her attorneys. I was shocked when they informed me that my grandmother left me $250,000 in her will. Sadness gave way to a renewed spirit of anticipation when, during the return flight to San Francisco, I decided to use my inheritance money to continue my search for the treasure.

During the rainy season, I continued my intensive research. I found another historical drawing that could help prove the location of Drake's landing site. <u>It showed the Golden Hind completely out of the water and lying on its side while being careened at the edge of a marsh</u>. From the shape and distance of the land formations in the background of the drawing, I knew where the work was performed.

A few days before my grandmother passed, I met an adventurous woman named Sarah Tompkins, who didn't have (or need) a job. She found my Drake project intriguing and wanted to join me in the next step of my investigation. I told her that would be a trek to the furthest point of the Corte Madera marsh, where it met the bay. This location matched the sixteenth century drawing of the careening. My mission was to take pictures from that location and collect any physical evidence to confirm this as the location shown in the historical sketch.

One dark and misty Sunday afternoon, we went into action. I drove to a small strip mall in Corte Madera and parked in an out-of-the-way lot behind the buildings. From there, we pulled a hand truck, fully loaded with supplies packed in plastic storage containers. We hauled everything for 1 ½ miles along a dirt path to the marsh's edge. This part of the marsh was divided into sections, each separated by a small channel filled with brackish water as the tide came in. When we arrived, it was after sunset, and it was raining heavily, so we stashed everything in the tall marsh grass, thoroughly hidden from view.

We agreed to return on the first sunny day and attempt to cross the marsh.

On Wednesday, the weather was perfect, so we walked back to where we'd stored the ladder, prepared for a challenge. Using the ladder as a bridge, we were able to pass over the mud in the various channels without any problems. It was extremely low tide when we arrived at our destination...so low that I was able to walk far out on the bay floor and retrieve several metal spikes that matched those shown in the historical sketch of the careened Golden Hind. When I looked back to the marsh, I saw part of an old ship half-buried in mud. I wondered if it could have been a piece of the Golden Hind removed during the careening. I wanted to get closer to it to confirm my suspicion and perhaps take a piece of for carbon-dating, but the tide started coming in, so I snapped several pictures and hightailed it back to where Sarah was waiting. While we were out there, we noticed something important that did not appear in the historical sketch. The marsh was altered and there was a line of dirt that rose two or three feet above the rest of the marsh.

On the way back to my car I foolishly attempted to leap across one of the channels rather than use the ladder but came up short and sank knee-deep into the stinky mud. Even with Sarah's help to try and get me out, I couldn't free myself and ended up having to leave one of my boots in the muck and walk back to the car with only a sock on that foot. Sarah found my hobbling gait thoroughly amusing and imitated me all the way.

I got some great pictures that day, and when I compared them to the land formations in the background of the historical sketch, I saw they matched. I used Google Earth to see what the line of dirt we noticed, looked like from above. As I zoomed in, it was apparent that <u>Drake created a massive arrow on the marsh that pointed in the direction of Greenbrae Ridge and could be used to confirm that they were close to the location where he'd buried the treasure.</u>

At the end of every working day, I power-washed the stones I found and then put them into five-gallon buckets purchased at Home Depot in San Rafael. In the beginning, I stored them in my garage, but when that was full, I decided to move them into a storage unit so that I could put my car in the garage. As the project continued, <u>I bought 50 buckets at a time and kept them in my backyard until there were enough to justify renting a truck and moving them to storage</u>. Eventually, I became the largest customer for orange "Homers" in the United States. If San Rafael was out of them, I'd go across the bridge to the Home Depot in El Cerrito to make my purchase. Over a five-year period, I purchased 4,000 buckets and nearly 1,000 thirty- gallon storage containers with lids! This cost me approximately $25,000.

By the end of 2005, I was the largest customer of Costless Storage in Richmond, CA. and had nine large (10 x 20) storage units filled with neatly stacked buckets and storage containers filled with stones.

To avoid squandering my inheritance and to avert the financial crisis that I envisioned, I needed to cut costs, and the easiest way for me to do that was to eliminate the storage units.

Sarah grew up in Nevada City, California, a small town near the Gold Country. She knew the owner of the famous Sixteen to One Mine. This gold mining company operated continuously since 1869. Sarah made the arrangements for me to meet the owner and after I explained my predicament, he agreed to process the stones using his mining equipment. Every few weeks I loaded up my car with buckets and storage containers filled with stones and drove three hours up to the mine.

I became friends with Stan, the fellow who ran the operation day-to-day. One day I went with Stan and his wife to have a drink at a bar in the little town of Allegheny. As it turned out—because there are no accidents in life—this was the birthplace of "E Clampus Vitus," or as the locals called them, the "Clampers." This was the fraternal organization was rumored to have made the fake Plate of Brass to prank Dr. Bolton. This rumor was an integral part of the plan to steal the actual Plate of Brass. I told the bartender part of my Drake story, and before we left the bar, he gave me a baseball cap with the Clampers' insignia on it: a red skull and cross bones, known as a "Jolly Roger,"

Taking a carful of stones from my storage units every couple of weeks barely made a dent in what I needed to take to the Sixteen to One. I needed to bite the bullet and remove them to stop paying for storage. I hired a trucking company to haul everything up to the Mine. To give you an idea of the scale of this project, <u>the State of California weigh stations recorded the total weight of all eight trucks at just below 565,000 pounds.</u>

After the eight trucks dumped their loads at the Mine. I removed and disposed of all the plastic containers. That is another story in itself!

Stan and I put all the stones through a "wash plant" that cleaned the dirt from them and sorted them according to size. <u>We ended up with three huge piles of small, medium, and large stones. During the washing and sorting, there were a lot of problems because the Mine's machinery was so old it kept breaking down.</u> We could only finish about half of the stones before the winter snows started in the Sierra. By mid-In November, half a foot of snow was on the ground, which stopped the processing.

After the snow melted in spring, I worked alongside Stan to process the rest of the stones. Then, I still needed to figure out what to do with them. <u>They didn't have any gemological value because all the stones were opaque!</u>

Stan suggested I buy 55-gallon drums from a local company and use them to store the stones somewhere. Even with the dirt and clay removed, it required 100 drums to hold everything. Stan and I drove them to "Hell's Half-Acre," a little place in the middle of nowhere and left the drums in a field. It took at least a dozen trips to move them all, and after the last load, my personal financial situation looked a little brighter.

CHAPTER 20

The "Bible" of Metallurgy

When Francis Drake landed on a small island in what is today called Drake's Passage, far south of Tierra del Fuego, he left a small stone plaque stating the date he was there and claiming the land for Queen Elizabeth. He also wanted to claim Nova Albion in much the same way, except this time, he wanted to create a more permanent record using metal rather than stone. I sought the most reputable source to fully understand how he made this metal marker.

The "Bible" of metalworking techniques is "Metalwork and Enameling" by Herbert Maryon was first published in 1912 and reissued in 1971. I purchased a copy and found everything I needed to support my claim that the tools in my possession were indeed the ones used to produce the lettering on Drake's Plate of Brass.

The Plate itself was formed using the "lost wax" process. This method of casting metals has been used since the third millennium BC and is still used today. In this procedure, molten metal is poured into a mold created utilizing a wax model inside a plaster shell. The liquid metal melted away the wax and filled the space it left behind. Once cooled, the metal object is removed from the plaster.

The model used to create the mold for the Plate of Brass was a broken iron fastener that came from one of the dismantled ships.

According to Maryon, the "disks" I found were properly known as "roulettes." they were traditionally used by goldsmiths to create ornamentation on rings, and the pattern of thin metal bands (the bezel) that hold the stone setting in place. To make the Plate of Brass, they were rolled across the surface of the mold, creating the a pattern for the vertical lines of the inscription. The "rod" contained all the other features that were necessary to produce the Inscription's horizontal lines and to impress the thin lines guided by the pattern made by the roulettes. The "rod" contained the following ancient metalworking features: a tracer, a scorper, V-shaped chisel, a forming stake, a punch, a hooked k-tool, and a spinning tool. The end of the rod was used to impress the "C" before the name Francis Drake.

When the Plate cooled and was removed from its shell, the Plate was given a patina by applying hot or cold oxides to the surface of the metal, creating a thin veneer of corrosion. The patina not only protected the surface but also gave it color. This slightly brown, green, or blue layer enlivens the brass's surface. Some patinas form naturally over time and are affected by the chemical composition of the medium in which the brass is kept.

As I reviewed every step of the process, I wanted to determine that this was the complete set of tools. Where else to find all the information needed but in Maryon's book? Using it as my guide, I sought to determine how many tracing tools the Plate's creator used by examining the height of each letter and the length of each line of the Inscription. I noted that only two lines required the use of a single tracing tool, one containing the date "June 17, 1579," and the one having Francis Drake's name.

Then, I recorded the Circumference of each tracing tool, noting that the total Circumference of all 21 equaled 99 inches. I also carefully measured the length of each line of the Inscription. The length of the Inscription = 59.625 inches.

The question I then needed to answer was: Could the 59.625-inch inscription be produced using 21 tracing tools with a total Circumference of 99 inches if two tracing tools were required to produce 5.25 inches of that Inscription, and 19 more were available for the remaining 54.375 inches?

~ Total Length of the Inscription required for completion = 54.375 inches (59.625 inches - 5.25 inches)

~ Excess Length available = .002 inches (54.377-54.375)

The answer was precisely what I hoped for: The entire inscription on the "Plate of Brass" required 21 tracing tools to produce. The total space available on the Circumference of the 21 tracing tools was 2/1000 of an inch greater than the space needed for the Inscription.

CHAPTER 21

Finger Ingots

As an additional cost-cutting measure, I decided to find a couple of roommates to share my house so I could increase my cash flow and continue my treasure hunt. When I interviewed interested people, I explained what I was doing and quickly eliminated those who were hesitant. I finally found two people I could live with who were both okay with my excavation activities and could afford the rent. One was a woman named Kate who worked in the cosmetics department at one of the department stores in a nearby mall. The other was a guy named Pete who worked at a boatyard in Sausalito. They were okay with my excavation work; Pete even helped occasionally, and we shared my house harmoniously.

Finally, my finances were under control, and there was still $200,000 remaining from my inheritance.

In the spring of 2007, my neighbor Paul Charles passed away, and his widow decided to move from 57

Via Corona into a rest home. She could no longer manage the house by herself. Mrs. Charles was holding a garage sale one Saturday morning, so I walked down the street to see if there was anything of interest. I also thought I might find a way to eventually, purchase the Charles' house and two other properties on Via Corona.

Much to my surprise, there was a vintage automobile parked in the Charles' garage that belonged to my neighbors, Donald, and Kay Parsons. They moved to Via Corona the same year as I did, and we had a neighborly relationship for over twenty years. Aside from the plastic sheeting fiasco, they were very supportive of my Sir Francis Drake work, so I asked Donald why his car was parked in Charles' garage. He told me he purchased the house from Mrs. Charles via a private real estate deal. Immediately, I asked Don if he wanted to flip it and sell it to me! He thought for a minute and said that he wanted to talk it over with Kay and he'd get back to me.

Two weeks later, I was gardening at 39 Via Corona when Don called me over and asked if I still wanted to buy 57 Via Corona?

My response was, "Absolutely," so we all sat at the Parsons' kitchen table later that week to discuss the idea. Don explained that because they were getting up in years and Kay was undergoing chemotherapy, they thought it might be better to sell their large house and downsize into the smaller one-story place that would be easier to manage. I explained that I was interested because my goal was to acquire all five houses that comprised "Greenbrae Ridge" and ultimately donate the properties to the State or Federal Government with the stipulation that it be named a Historic Site in

Drake's honor. If they would sell it to me, I'd begin renovation immediately and find tenants to lease it as soon as the renovation was complete.

In retrospect, what seemed craziest about this plan was that I was already up to my eyeballs in debt.

Nevertheless, in May 2007, I took out a second mortgage on 35 Via Corona and bought the Charles' house from the Parsons. I spent the next three months working 24/7 doing all the sorely needed renovations to clean up decades' worth of filth, dog urine, fleas, and neglect. The supplies and materials for that job cost $40,000, but the house looked great in the end! I found good tenants who signed a one-year lease and moved in on September 1. The rent covered the monthly mortgage payment and the taxes on that property.

When I needed to take a break during the renovation work, I searched the grounds for anything related to Drake. I noticed a large piece of wood alongside the driveway that was sitting there for years. At first, I thought it was just a stump that Mr. Charles used as a border for a flowerbed. But upon closer investigation, I saw markings scratched into it that looked like this: VI-XVII-MDLXXIX. As I studied it, I realized they were Roman numerals that spelled out 6-17-1579, the date that Drake claimed Nova Albion for England. It struck me that this was the "Great Poste." to which the Plate of Brass was nailed. I carted it down the street and displayed it proudly in my front yard. Several years later, using my computer, I filled in all the lines. In addition to June 17, 1579, Francis Drake is there in the same style as is shown on the Plate of Brass. The Great Poste also contains many Alchemy symbols. When I deciphered them, it gave the chemicals and elements he used in the smelting

<u>process.</u>

Not long afterward, while mowing the grass in the backyard of that house, I heard a loud noise that I thought must have been the mower hitting a rock. I looked around until I found what it was and saw a piece of metal about the shape and size of a human finger. My earlier research into the cargo carried by <u>Spanish galleons stated that the Spanish transported their gold and silver from South and Central America back to Spain as "finger ingots"</u> as well as standard-sized ingots. I tested the specific gravity of the piece. I determined it was silver, so I returned to the spot where I hit it and began to dig. Within ten minutes, I found four more silver finger ingots. Given my current finances, these, and the others I soon found were a godsend.

The rainy season lasted well into April, and there were several times during those long months when I'd look down through the hole under the kitchen cabinet and see water that filled the tunnels and cavern lapping at my foundation. I estimated its volume at some 20,000 gallons. Once the rain stopped, it took over a week to pump it all out.

It was still very muddy at the beginning of May, but I returned to work anyway. Rather than moving the buckets up through the kitchen cabinet, I took them out through the entrance at the cavern's end near 39 Via Corona. Less than a week after starting up, a big rainstorm filled the cavern with another 20,000 gallons of water. When it finally stopped, I set the pumps to work and, a week later, could start one more time. Fortunately, Pete and Kate were very tolerant housemates.

Then, quite suddenly, I was so weak that I could barely get out of bed. I reached a point where I just had enough: enough mud in my house, filthy, poisonous muck on my clothes, and enough discouragement, harassment, and ridicule. My financial position was in a downward spiral again. After renovating 57 Via Corona, it was re-appraised at a significantly higher value, so I took a $150,000 second mortgage against the property. The rental income did cover the mortgage and taxes. However, I used the positive cash flow on that house to offset the negative cash flow on 39 Via Corona. The financial meltdown alarm was ringing! I attempted to collect Unemployment Insurance but was unsuccessful because back in 2003, I voluntarily left my job as a broker.

The entire country was suffering through the Real Estate crisis. Since I fully leveraged my holdings, I could only sell something by taking a significant loss. I was teetering on the edge of financial disaster and knew I might lose everything if I did not act quickly.

Hard as it was, I accepted that I would never get around the Wizard of Oz. The set of tools, the rough diamonds, the Emerald Goddess, and other gemstones, could not be converted into cash to pull me out of the financial grave I dug for myself. Moreover, it felt like Drake's spirit gave up too. There was only one way to avoid bankruptcy. I told my roommates that we all needed to move out because I planned to lease the house to somebody willing to pay a premium to be in the Bacich School District.

After that, I restored the property at 35 Via Corona, filled all my excavations, re-leveled, and planted the front and back yards, and replaced the kitchen cabinets and the damaged kitchen floor. I disassembled the fiberglass spraying machine as methodically as I put it together and built a large crate to hold all the parts.

After a few days on eBay, I found a buyer in Russia. I contacted an overseas freight hauler who picked up the crate! I was determined to leave no trace of what happened, just as Drake did when he left Nova Albion. I was so thorough that it looked like nothing ever happened.

Few people were moving during the economic slump that paralyzed the country at the end of 2008, but fortunately, I found a tenant in January 2009.

CHAPTER 22

Nobody is above the Law!

I figured out how Hessen, Wagner, and Rosenthal executed their plan to rewrite history, as shown in Chapter 9. Here are the actions they undertook to satisfy the requirements of each step in their scheme to steal the Plate of Brass, substitute a fake in its place with impunity, and make the public believe that the actual Plate was never a real artifact:

Step 1. Take something regarded by the public as historical truth: From 1937 until 1970, the world accepted as truth that Drake's Plate of Brass was genuine and had been discovered near his landing site at San Quentin.

Step 2. Create credible doubt about the truth by publicly quoting contradictory statements associated with someone regarded as authoritative: The conspirators created credible doubt about Drake's landing site by repeatedly referencing the Plate of Brass found by William Caldera near Drake's Bay in 1935. Because Caldera was chauffeuring the Chairman of the Board of Bank of America (regarded as credible), the conspirators were able to plant doubt about the site where Drake really landed and, therefore, about the authenticity of the Plate found by Beryl Shinn in 1936.

Step 3. Create a credible alternative to the historical truth by publicly quoting statements by an expert in the field: Edward Von der Porten's 1970 presentation portrayed the Plate as part of a hoax perpetrated by E. Clampus Vitus against Dr. Herbert Bolton. Rosenthal was considered an expert because of his position in Drake's Navigators Guild, even though there was no evidence to support this claim or corroboration of his story by E. Clampus Vitas. The public accepted this as a credible alternative to the historical truth.

Step 4. Publicly reaffirm the credible alternative whenever evidence is presented to further undermine the historical truth: In 1976, when Mr. Wagner publicly misrepresented Dr. Smith's opinion and the press disseminated the falsehood, it undermined the historical truth. At the end of the 1977 re-examination, Dr. Hessen seized the opportunity to publicly reaffirm the credible alternative when he was quoted as saying, "Guesses about a hoax and reasons for not revealing it are intriguing. With a definitive answer to the plate authenticity still lacking, it will remain on public view at Bancroft Library."

Step 5. Repeat step four above until all individuals who know the historical truth have died or are incapacitated: Placing the "fake" Plate on public display and having numerous articles published about the "fake" Plate satisfies the ongoing requirement of repeating all the steps. After Donald Hessen died in 1990, Robert Power in 1991, Ralph Napoli in 2014, and Edward Von der Porten in 2018, all the men with knowledge of the historical truth died except for Kenneth Wagner. However, someone still knows the historical truth and can prove it. Me! I have the tools that created the Plate. I have shared verifiable knowledge of the historical truth with my readers to try and counteract this step in their plan.

Step 6. Make a final public statement affirming the credible possibility. With nobody remaining alive to dispute it, history can be rewritten with impunity: In 2011, while I was away from the Bay Area on vacation, I turned on the national news one evening and was shocked to see Edward Von der Porten standing at Drake's Bay, once again touting it as Drake's "real" landing site. But it didn't stop there. The perpetrators took the effort to hide their crimes to the next level. Rosenthal succeeding in having the Federal Government name Drake's Bay as the official landing site.

My goal throughout this project was to correct History!

Dr. Martin Luther King, Jr. pointed out, "The arc of history is long, but it does tend toward justice." Oh, how I look forward to seeing justice served on this culprit!

CHAPTER 23

Kaboom!

Over the years, I've thought about the forces that motivated my search for treasure, the fulfillment I felt with each small victory, and the excitement that filled me when I learned some new piece of information.

Earlier, I discussed the high percentage of silver in the heavy clay I encountered at several locations around my yard. Eventually, I realized that the distribution of the clay was not random; it was in a pattern identical to the lines that made up the edges of the "fireplace" and the smoke rising from it as depicted on the Hondius Map inset.

When Drake first visited Greenbrae Ridge, he found two seasonally dry arroyos and a small year-round creek. All three were fed by the natural spring at the top of the hill above Rod's yard, where the water tank now stands. At the turn of the 20th Century, the City of San Rafael diverted the spring to provide water for their growing population. There is still a visible depression in the ground that marked the sides of the creek before the water was diverted.

The arroyos were formed by thousands of years of rainwater flowing downhill during winter storms. Before Drake's arrival, some of the water flowed down the steep hillside and discharged into the bay at Larkspur Landing. The rest of the water traveled down through Rod's yard and split into two branches as it approached my yard. One branch ran off the hillside and down to the bay, and the other branch continued along Greenbrae Ridge for several hundred feet. When it reached the far end of what is now 57 Via Corona, it also ran downhill to the bay. It must have seemed like a brilliant idea when Drake ordered his men to fill these natural channels with the clay slurry containing the silver. Remember the old tag line, "It's not nice to fool Mother Nature?"

The historical sketch by Montanus, "The Crowning of Drake," shows many Miwok coming from behind a rock promontory to attend the ceremony. That outcropping is the only thing missing from the San Quentin peninsula that was shown in the drawing, and I wondered what might have happened to it. During the second year of my investigation, I was working below ground in the backyard when I smelled hydrogen sulfide. This is a strong rotten egg smell often emitted by oil refineries and sewage treatment plants. I was alarmed, so I called Dr. Palmer at USGS who told me he wasn't surprised, as the San Quentin Peninsula was the southern tip of a chain of geological formations that produced geothermal steam. The other end of the chain was 50 miles northeast in Geyserville, one of the most active geothermal sites in the country, rivaling Yellowstone for its geysers and other hot spring phenomena. In Geyserville, the steam from these naturally occurring vents is used to produce energy at the Calpine Power Plant.

Years later, I realized that my discussion at USGS that day provided me with the information needed to resolve one of the last unanswered questions about Nova Albion. Sir Francis Drake was in control of his men and everything they did while they were at Nova Albion. The one thing he couldn't control was "Mother Nature."

Many residents of Marin County know that that the average annual rainfall is approximately three feet. The winter of 1580 must have been one of those "wet" years when rainfall can be far more than the average. The volume of runoff was far more than what Drake anticipated when he put together his plan to bury the treasure. That winter, the normally porous silver-slurry became fully saturated, and prevented the rainfall runoff from passing through it. Without a natural course to flow downhill, the runoff began to pour into the natural steam vents of the geothermal chain. When the water reached the bottom of the vent, it landed on super- heated rocks that converted it into steam. This process continued and the pressure from the steam rose until the rock promontory (representing the southernmost point of the geothermal chain), could no longer contain the pressure. The result was an enormous explosion that blew apart the rock promontory, sending huge boulders flying into the air and crashing down over a wide area.

Google Earth shows that a caldera from the explosion now exits where the rock promontory once stood.

CHAPTER 24

The Indian by the Fireplace

There's a wide disparity between the historical accounts of Drake's departure from Nova Albion and the truth. Historical reports state that the Miwok wept inconsolably when he left and set fires as their way of saying goodbye as the Golden Hind sailed out of the bay. The truth is much more disturbing. By the time the Golden Hind was ready to leave, the 25,000 Miwok that lived in every village between the bay and the ocean (along what is now known as Sir Francis Drake Boulevard) died at the hands of their captors. The image on the Hondius Broadside Map of the Indian standing next to the fireplace represents the men, women, and children who perished because Drake needed the zinc in their bones to purify his looted gold and silver in the 1000-degree smelter. This is why there haven't been any discoveries of Miwok burial sites close to the Sir Francis Drake Boulevard corridor. In the end, only a handful of Miwok were left alive to place marker rocks in critical locations and to haul the last provisions across the marsh in the carts to the Golden Hind. The fires discussed in historical accounts of his departure resulted from Drake and his men burning their fort, anything that remained of the ships dismantled in the marsh, and the grass that covered the hillsides. Drake planned to leave no trace of his visit or indication that he ever made landfall along the San Quentin Peninsula. The only way the Spanish could ever identify this location as Nova Albion was if they climbed up Greenbrae Ridge and found the Plate of Brass. His plan was a complete success because it would be another 357 years until Beryl Shinn came along.

When he left Nova Albion, Drake aimed to return home quickly and safely. However, once he'd crossed the Pacific and sailed through the Philippines to the Moluccas, he decided to take the opportunity to initiate a trade agreement for England with the Sultan of Ternate, who controlled most of the World's spices. The result of his meeting with the Sultan was a mutually beneficial arrangement, whereby in exchange for English protection at sea, the clove trade would be taken from the Dutch and given exclusively to the English. After closing the deal, Drake sailed southward and was circling the island of Celebes when the Golden Hind became lodged on a reef. The wind was blowing so fiercely that they couldn't free the ship. Their survival demanded they lighten the heavy load by dumping a large part of their cargo. They jettisoned most of their precious cloves, the heavy cannons, and a lot of ammunition, but not the gold and silver ballast stones or the precious gems.

The significantly lighter ship freed itself, and all the men aboard breathed a sigh of relief. Francis Fletcher came to the deck and led the men in prayer before the crew took Communion below deck. This was followed by a sermon during which Fletcher suggested that the extreme and life-threatening challenges endured during the expedition were God's way of punishing all of them, especially the captain, for the great crimes committed during the voyage. He specifically mentioned Thomas Doughty's execution. Fletcher's comments were not well received by Drake, especially since Fletcher signed his name to most of the counts in the indictment against Doughty.

Drake was so enraged that he summoned the crew to the main deck. Fletcher was brought out in leg irons and was shackled to the base of one of the ship's masts. Drake called for a pen and paper and wrote, "Francis Fletcher, I hereby excommunicate thee out of the Church of God and from all the benefits and graces thereof, and I denounce thee to the Devil and all his angels."

Drake attached a metal band to Fletcher's arm that read, "Francis Fletcher, The Falsest Knave that Liveth," and warned that if anyone removed it, they would be hanged.

Popular history claims that on September 26, 1580, the Golden Hind sailed into Plymouth, England, after three years of global adventures. The cargo hold was filled with gold, silver, pearls, and precious stones. He was greeted with almost universal acclaim in England because he circumnavigated the globe and was the first Englishman to accomplish this feat. The Queen ordered the Golden Hind to be brought to Deptford on the Thames so that all of London could see the ship, upon which Drake hosted a banquet for the Queen. Six months later, in April 1581, she knighted him on the Golden Hind deck, making him the mayor of Plymouth. The Queen had good reason to be grateful to Drake since for each pound she'd invested in his journey, she earned 47, not to mention the wealth that would accrue to England from the spice trade agreement Drake negotiated.

He certainly deserved the honors bestowed on him. According to the economist J. M. Keynes, the English foreign debt was paid off from the Queen's share of the proceeds from that journey. There was enough left over for her to capitalize on a new venture, the Levant Company, that would be essential in developing British foreign trade in the eastern Mediterranean.

The Queen demanded that Drake turn over his Captain's log of the voyage and gave strict orders that, under penalty of death, no crew member could reveal the route the Golden Hind traveled. Her last order was to keep the total value of the treasure he brought home a secret. The plunder was split between the Queen and the voyage's other private investors. With his share of the proceeds, Drake purchased Buckland Abbey, a manor house in Devon, not far from Plymouth.

As ordered, all details of the voyage were kept secret for more than a decade. When the first account of it was printed, it was anonymous and undated. It appeared merely as an addendum to a newly published book titled Maritime History of England. Although this account is considered one of the two or three authoritative records of the circumnavigation, it was not based on Drake's log (which was turned over to the Queen). It was riddled with errors, exaggerations, and more than a few deliberate deceptions. Even the so-called "accepted truths" about Drake's life and voyages are full of misinformation! All history books claim that he landed at Nova Albion on June 17, 1579, and departed on July 23. After eight years of extensive research and investigation, I believe he left Nova Albion on or about July 23, 1580.

Drake's return voyage dates are erroneous because it would have been physically impossible to unload the treasure, smelt the gold and silver into an unrecognizable form, repair his ship, and bury part of the treasure in five or six weeks! According to my calculations, once his smelting operation got up and running (probably about 30 days), the smelter needed to operate constantly for one year to smelt 26 tons of silver. If 4,000 pounds of silver were smelted each month, the zinc contained in one human body every twenty minutes would be required to keep the smelter operating. My estimate for the number of Miwok who perished is based on this one year. One body every twenty minutes equates to 26,308 Miwok.

The World Encompassed states that the voyage across the Pacific to Palau took 86 days, meaning he arrived in Palau on October 17, 1580. As Palau is 6,600 miles from San Francisco, they would have traveled an average of 76.7 miles daily. Using that same average, it would have taken another 101 days to reach the tip of Africa and another six to seven weeks to arrive in Plymouth. By adding the number of days for each leg of the voyage, he probably arrived on or about March 25, 1581. This would have been a few days before he shared a banquet with the Queen and 10 days before he was knighted. This makes much more sense if one considers Drake's striking accomplishments. Why would the Queen wait over a year to knight him?

Throughout his career, Drake's successes relied upon his mastery of deception. During the 1577 voyage, he claimed to hold a royal commission, giving him absolute authority over the fleet's men and ships and the authority to attack and seize Spanish ships and ports. There may have been no such commission because he refused to show any proof to support this claim to his own men. Queen Elizabeth was also highly skilled in this area. For her, rumors, deception, and secrecy were crucial elements needed to best Spain and gain mastery of all the earth's oceans. By working together, they could keep the location of Nova Albion a mystery for over 400 years!

CHAPTER 25

Round and Round He Goes

The information you are about to read will differ from all other accounts of Drake's life.

After completing the 1577-1580 circumnavigation, Drake made two more undisclosed and secret circumnavigations. These were undertaken to observe and take measurements of total solar eclipses. Geometric principles were applied to the data he gathered. This enabled Drake to make Nova Albion's location disappear from all maps. Unfortunately, this feat of geometrical genius generated a problem in calculating time that has never been corrected. Here is some vital background information:

In 1582, after consulting with his science advisor, Pope Gregory decided that the Julian calendar did not reflect time correctly, so he changed the number of days in a year from 362.25 to 365.25 and established the Gregorian calendar, which is still used today. Drake realized this change was a mistake because it assumed the Earth was round. He also knew that Gregory's decision moved the astronomical correlation between time and distance in the wrong direction. The Gregorian calendar would not be accepted in Great Britain until 1752; however, at the time of the Pope's proclamation, the Catholic countries adopted it immediately and did so in a way that led Drake and Queen Elizabeth to assume that accepting it would become inevitable even for those countries well outside of Rome's control.

When Pope Gregory initiated this change, Drake already spent over twenty years conducting scientific and geometric research into the necessity for "leap periods." in calendaring systems. Leap periods were based upon the false assumption that the Earth was a perfect sphere. The preliminary results of his research indicated that the Earth was not perfectly round and that a calendar system that eliminated leap periods could reflect time more accurately. He needed to take additional measurements during five total solar eclipses during the next eleven years to prove his theory according to geometric principles. Sailing to these sites at just the right moment posed significant challenges, but since his ideas and the research supporting them contradicted someone as powerful as Pope Gregory, his project needed to be conducted in secret. So, while history tells us Drake was quietly living in his Devon manor house and serving as the Mayor of Plymouth, he was continuing his adventurous life on the high seas.

Drake devoted his life to the Queen. When she took his Captain's log and personal diary away at the end of the 1577-1580 voyage, he was disgruntled because it contained the notes, measurements, and calculations he made for his scientific endeavors. Long before he met privately with Elizabeth, he knew she would jump at the opportunity to hide the location of Nova Albion. Drake was a fair and just man who believed he'd been mistreated! What better way to even the score than to have Elizabeth cover the cost of the two additional circumnavigations he wanted to make, so he could replace the data that Elizabeth wrongfully took from him?

In preparation, he met privately with the Queen. He provided her with a detailed explanation of the error in the Pope's new calendar. He then explained how he could also use the results of his observations to England's advantage. His mastery of geometry would allow him to make a small and undetectable change to the Earth's longitude and latitude grid system. The result of this change would cause the location of Nova Albion to disappear from all future maps. Elizabeth listened attentively and agreed that the site needed to remain hidden. The Queen would provide Drake with the ships, crew, and time he needed. Drake immediately began planning the two voyages that would put him in the right places at the precise times to observe the five total solar eclipses. Verification of his measurements demanded that he return to each of those positions precisely one year after the eclipse date. This would be an incredible feat to accomplish on a sailing ship.

Drake recorded the preliminary measurements while voyaging to Africa and the West Indies. Off the coast of Africa at Longitude 22.7° South, he measured the eclipses of May 15, 1565, January 15, 1572, and May 20, 1574. He also took measurements at Longitude 19.86° North in the Atlantic between Africa and South America during the total eclipse of January 25, 1571.

Drake's crews on these clandestine voyages were never told what he was doing. Queen Elizabeth was the only person besides Drake who knew the reason for these voyages. Even if he succeeded in accomplishing this tremendous nautical feat, it would not be reflected in the records of the English Monarchy. This assured Queen Elizabeth that if Drake did not recover the treasure he buried at Nova Albion, only she and her successors would know where it was located!

Drake's second circumnavigation voyage began in February 1582.

For this voyage, he passed through the Strait of Magellan during the autumn in South America. He visited the same ports and cities along South and Central American coasts that he raided during his first circumnavigation. He stole additional precious metals and gems along the route. For the total eclipse of July 20, 1582, he took measurements at Longitude 27.789° South. This was the first of three total eclipses that would occur off the coast of Chile. From there, he sailed northward and returned to Nova Albion, where he planned to recover the buried treasure and process the gold and silver acquired during this voyage. On the way north, he captured a Chinese trading ship and took the vessel with him.

Drake sailed into San Francisco Bay with the trading ship. He would use it to carry the buried treasure back to England. As Drake's boat approached the landing site at Nova Albion, the topography changed. The rock promontory, representing the first of several identifiable markers to guide him, was nowhere to be seen. Instead, huge boulders were strewn all along the shoreline of the San Quentin Peninsula. He set anchor and took a small party of men ashore. He was shocked to see steam rising from the super-heated ground through gaping fissures. He had no idea that the silver clay slurry he buried in the arroyos would cause a massive eruption and prevent him from recovering the treasure.

He was visibly shaken as he returned to his ship, saying to Edward Fenton, his second in command, "I know what we can do!"

They sailed seven miles north to an area near the mouth of Gallinas Creek. There, they set up camp and, to a lesser degree, repeated what they did at the previous site. They captured as many natives as they needed to do the heavy labor. Once again, the indigenous people were sacrificed to provide the zinc required for smelting. As before, the smelted gold and silver were formed into ballast stones. This time, they did not have to leave any treasure behind and loaded everything onto one ship. Instead of burning or dismantling the Chinese Trading ship, they simply abandoned it in a tidal marsh. This entire operation was completed in less than two months because Drake needed to hurry back to the coast of Chile to take his verification measurements on July 20, 1583.

Today, in the town of Lucas Valley, there are streets named Nova Albion, Drake's Passage, and a host of other Drake-related names. In the late 1800s, early settlers discovered the remains of the Chinese ship that Drake abandoned there. They mistook it for a vessel from his initial visit, adding to the confusion surrounding the 1579 arrival at Nova Albion.

After the verification measurements near Chile, he crossed the Pacific, stopping a second time at the

Spice Islands. He would need to spend nearly a year in the region to be correctly positioned for the total eclipse of October 22, 1585. The path of this total eclipse stretched from Chile to Australia! However, before he returned to England, there were two more measurements that he needed to make.

Drake's timing was perfect! After rounding the southern tip of Africa, he sailed northward. He moved into position to measure the total eclipse at 19.86 North Longitude on October 12, 1586. He now had ten days to turn around and sail almost due South to be in the correct place to make the verification measurement related to the 10/22/1585 eclipse.

He returned to England for several months, analyzed the data he collected, and began his adjustments to the Apogee and Perigee charts that would be needed to hide the location of Nova Albion. He was called into action by the Queen. After he raided Cadiz, Spain, in April of 1587, he returned to the proper location to make verification measurements for the October 12, 1586, eclipse.

After a disastrous campaign in Portugal ended in June 1589, Drake prepared to set off on his final circumnavigation. This would be the most time-sensitive of all. He set sail from England at the beginning of August 1589 and again passed around the tip of South America during the summer when the seas were calmer. He traveled up the coast to Chile in time for the eclipse of February 4, 1590. He waited until February 1591 to verify his work. He needed to remain in this area for over a year. He careened his ship and raided all the same ports a third time. On June 9, 1592, he took measurements of the fifth total solar eclipse from a position far out in the Pacific Ocean. The verification measurement was not crucial because the previous four verifications were sufficient to confirm his theory, so Drake returned to England.

CHAPTER 26

Drake's Scientific Discoveries

The depth of my research on Sir Francis Drake took me well beyond all common knowledge about him and deep into the arcane studies that preoccupied him for much of his life. Although he had no formal schooling, he became an avid reader and thinker and pursued many avenues of scientific inquiry. With wealthy aristocratic friends who maintained extensive libraries, he could access to every book extant at the time.

A lifelong quest for Drake was to determine and geometrically verify the actual shape of the Earth and its magnetic field. He believed that neither was spherical. This belief was based on the work of Pythagoras, who postulated that the shape of the Galaxy was a three-dimensional, twelve-sided polyhedron known as a dodecahedron. Drake believed the Earth's magnetic field shared the same properties. It would affect many geometric formulas related to time and space if he could prove this theory. In our own time, the genius neo-futurist Buckminster Fuller came to some similar conclusions, as did geniuses of the past, such as Kepler and Da Vinci, who both subscribed to theories of "Divine Geometries" that proposed the dodecahedron as the shape representing the idealized form of the Universe.

The renowned Greek astronomer Ptolemy asserted that each planet revolved uniformly around the Earth. That geocentric model held sway for centuries, as it seemed to support prevailing religious beliefs that God ordained Earth as the center of the cosmos. Early in Drake's own century, Copernicus shook things up when he speculated that the planets—all six known by then—traveled around the Sun. Religiously devout as he was, Drake had no trouble accepting the heliocentric model. His contention was that its actual motion patterns could be represented by choosing the proper diameters and speeds for the two circular motions ascribed to each celestial body (the revolutions and the orbit). He also knew that, in some cases, a third circular motion was required to make such a calculation. He knew that by taking measurements of the Sun, Moon, and Saturn (the most distant known planet then), he could determine the angles at which energy (sunlight) entered the Earth's magnetic field, and this would enable him to determine the actual shape of the magnetic field.

To make the measurements, Drake used an instrument known as an astrolabe and a technique called triangulation to create the astronomical charts, maps, and the data he needed for his calculations. He considered the direct correlation between time and distance. He made his calculations based on the core of the celestial bodies rather than their surface.

Another of Drake's personal scientific goals was to determine why eclipses occurred. During the Middle Ages, total solar eclipses caused rioting by the uneducated masses because they were seen as a sign that the world was coming to an end. This was absurd because 5,000 years earlier, the Babylonians studied eclipses and coined the term "Saros Cycle" to explain the cyclical and serial nature of solar and lunar eclipses. The Babylonians knew that the position of each successive eclipse in a "Saros series" shifted to the west a little more than one-third of the way around the globe. They also knew that each "Saros series" in the entire "Saros cycle" was separated by 18 years and 111/3 months. The Babylonians knew everything about eclipses...except what caused them to occur!

What intrigued Drake was the difference of .46 days between time measured by the Saros cycle and time measured by an astronomical standard known as the Metonic cycle, named for Meton, a Greek fifth-century BC astronomer. Drake theorized that his total solar eclipse observations would also answer this centuries-old mystery. He guessed it might be related to a "reversal" factor if astronomical time was measured correctly.

His initial observations (1565-1574) of total solar eclipses were the basis for many of his beliefs. This included his idea that the total amount of light reaching the Earth was a combination of light received directly from the Sun and sunlight reflected by the Moon. The only way he could prove the actual shape of the earth's magnetic field according to geometric principals was to take precise measurements of the angles of the Sun, Moon, and Saturn during total solar eclipses, as only then would the measurements not be distorted by sunlight reflected off the Moon.

The voyages cited in the previous chapter were timed to coincide with the total solar eclipses. The measurements gave Drake the data he needed to calculate the exact angles at which sunlight passed through space and entered our atmosphere. The results of this work showed that Pythagoras was correct.

The Cause of Leap Periods in Calendars

These measurements also confirmed that Earth's magnetic field was in the shape of a Dodecahedron. However, the form was not that of a true dodecahedron; instead, it was a Rhombic Dodecahedron. This was a significant discovery because Time and Distance were always calculated assuming the spherical magnetic field. He discovered a small but significant difference between them by applying standard geometric calculations to compare a sphere to a dodecahedron. This difference exists because a conically shaped area lies between each pair of vertices of the dodecahedron that does not exist in a sphere. When Drake applied this information to geometric calculations related to the Earth's surface area, he determined that the area under the cone (the space between each pair of vertices) was 56.52 miles and the volume of the cone to be 43.48 miles.

By analyzing all his accumulated data, Drake concluded that a "leap period" occurred because there were 361° in Earth's Longitude and not 360°. The area under the cone equaled the 1-degree difference in Longitude that could not have been determined if the measurements were taken at any time other than during a total solar eclipse and compared to those taken one year later. Drake discovered that the area represented by the leap period (time) was equivalent to the area under the cone (distance).

His determination of the angles at which light enters the atmosphere through the magnetic field and his calculation of the area under the cone resulted in another discovery. Total solar eclipses occur when sunlight passes directly through the vertices (the small space between the edges where the sides meet) of the plates forming the magnetic field. Partial solar eclipses occur when light passes partially through the vertices, and most of the time, light enters the Earth's magnetic field at angles that do not give rise to solar eclipses.

He also discovered that the .46-day difference between time as measured by the Saros cycle and the Metonic cycle was directly related to changes in the level of energy that passes through the rhombic dodecahedron's angles. When the total amount of energy reaching the Earth's surface from the Sun and Moon is at its maximum or minimum stage, magnetic north, and magnetic south begin their periodic reversals. Such reversals are physical confirmation that "time" reverses itself in astronomical terms.

I have not been able to locate anything to indicate that scientists have ever figured out what Drake knew more than 400 years ago. An internet search about eclipses will show that a solar eclipse occurs when Earth passes through the shadow of the Moon. This merely answers the question of how an eclipse occurs; it does not address why it occurs! Drake's work in these areas demonstrates brilliance that is not included in traditional depictions of him. Most authorities see him as bold, daring, cunning, quick-thinking, and rash; they ignore some of the aspects of him that I have come to know and feel compelled to share with the world.

The Effect of Drake's Adjustments

To make the location of Nova Albion disappear from all future maps, Drake made a net adjustment of .446 to the Apogee and Perigee Charts of the Moon. The repercussions continue to plague astronomers today, and "Astronomical constants" have been determined and accepted in the scientific world to offset most of Drake's changes. Unfortunately, these constants don't account for the dodecahedral nature of the magnetic field, the shape of the Universe, the reversal of time (as evidenced by magnetic pole reversal), and the 1-degree Drake discovered that should be added to Longitude (361° versus 360°).

For example, NASA records indicate that they encountered this error in 1968 when an Apollo space capsule landed 13 km or 7.222 miles from where the computer determined it would land. No documentation shows that NASA investigated the reason for this error. Drake's work proves that the Earth's grid system of Longitude and latitude is inaccurate.

All data derived from maps based on longitude and latitude lines must be corrected. New mapping technology and GPS have yet to correct the problem but simply spread that one-degree difference evenly among the other 360 degrees. The one-degree difference is too small to affect how the coordinates appear numerically or how a location appears visually. Nevertheless, in astronomical terms, this is an enormous problem.

The Astronomical Reversal of Time

The discovery of the difference between the Saros Cycle and the Metonic cycle involved several different but related measurements and calculations. His calculations identified a perfectly predictable and repetitive cycle in the years it takes for astronomical time to reverse itself. He also identified a small but significant difference within each cycle affected by the forward or backward movement of time after the current cycle. Although these reversals are imperceptible within the context of our daily lives on Earth, they are nevertheless real.

Drake was interested in such things because Pythagoras believed that escaping from our gravitational/magnetic field and traveling great distances in space was possible. Correcting the measurement of time is crucial to the future of space exploration. Unless the constant forward and backward movements of time are considered in astronomical calculations, it will be impossible to return to Earth. When the computer is given a set of coordinates, our planet will be in a different location than the computer thinks it should be. Under our current system of time measurement, time does not equal distance.

Geophysicists and those in related fields will be particularly interested in Drake's work because it provides a definite time frame for the phenomenon of Magnetic Pole Reversal. The magnetic field is generated from deep within our planet's iron core. The reversal process is continuous and ongoing as the Earth is pulled by the Sun, and the entire world rotates over time. The easiest way to envision this is to imagine the North Pole slowly inching its way southward until it is located where the South Pole was at the beginning of the cycle. This process occurs very slowly, with each leg of the reversal (North to South or South to North) taking 5,700 years. The most recent reversal happened 12,000 years ago. Drake's studies on this topic posit a specific, predictable pattern for these reversals that interestingly coincides with the Mayan calendar. Geophysicists have proven polarity reversals by measuring the polarity of the ground where the Earth's crustal plates are constantly moving. This movement is known as "seafloor spreading" and falls under the branch of Plate Tectonics. The Mayan Long Count Calendar also reflects the Magnetic Pole Reversal, as is evidenced by their calendar's supposed end date of December 21, 2012.

Reviewing all of Drake's studies in these fields, I became even more in awe of the man. There is no question that his thinking was hundreds of years before his time. In some ways, by keeping the depth and complexity of his interests hidden, Queen Elizabeth did a great disservice to generations of researchers who followed Drake. As I understood this more clearly, I became even more motivated to set the record straight on everything that intersected his life and accomplishments, which became gradually far more interesting to me than his buried treasure.

Why His Great Discoveries Were Never Revealed

Drake never made public the maps, charts, and measurements he'd been working on for over twenty years before Pope Gregory changed the calendar.

None of his results were considered in the Pope's decision. Given the enmity between Rome and Protestant England, they most likely wouldn't have been anyway. However, with the blessing of the Queen, Drake adjusted the Apogee and Perigee Charts of the Moon for many of the years, starting in 1541 and ending in 1595. He did this to reflect time and distance as if calculated on the dodecahedral basis. The effect of these changes was virtually identical to the changes created by the Pope's conversion from the Julian to the Gregorian calendar, and they were so obscure that nobody would even realize adjustments were made. These adjustments included those to reflect the "area under the cone" for the leap periods, the 360° to 361° difference and the "reversal of time factor" for the difference between the Saros and Metonic cycles.

CHAPTER 27

The Lead Coffin

The catalyst that finally prompted me to write this book occurred in October 2011. It was eleven years after my investigation started, and shortly after I went bankrupt and lost my houses on Greenbrae Ridge. I was having breakfast one Sunday morning in my favorite Sausalito Cafe when the owner said, "This should interest you," and handed me an article about a team of marine archaeologists who were on a research vessel not far off the coast of Portobello, Panama, searching for the ship Sir Francis Drake was sailing at the time of his death.

As Charles Pollock, the leader of the team, was talking with Jim Huber of the research vessel, a diver surfaced and gave a thumbs-up. Directly below them on the seafloor he'd spotted the remains of the Elizabeth and the Delight, two ships from Drake's fleet on that fateful day in 1595. The men were ecstatic about their find and hoped they'd soon locate the lead coffin that contained the body of Britain's great Admiral.

Drake was in his mid-50s at the time of his last voyage. During an unsuccessful attempt to capture the Harbor of San Juan de Ulloa, Mexico, the Spanish shot a cannonball through the cabin of his flagship, injuring him. He was also weakened by a bad case of dysentery. Nevertheless, he remained in command and ordered his crew to sail westward toward Nombre de Dios, on the Isthmus of Panama in pursuit of several Spanish treasure ships that fled from the San Juan harbor.

After reading about the research team's discovery of Drake's ships, I again slipped into the kind of trance state I experienced during the eight years when my whole life revolved around him. I felt myself on the Elizabeth with Drake ailing in his cabin. He knew that his end was near as he was now delirious from his wound and high fever. His first mate reported that he kept repeating, "I will be back; I will be back."

Drake was the first Captain to complete a circumnavigation. Magellan is often credited with this feat, but he died during the 1519-1521 voyage and a different Captain finished the journey. Without any public disclosure of his secret circumnavigations or the scientific discoveries he made; he is one of the greatest names in world history.

Drake knew more about solar and lunar eclipses than any other man on the face of the Earth in the sixteenth century. As he lay succumbing to his illness and wounds, on October 18, 1595, he knew there would be a total lunar eclipse that day. Just after 9:00 AM, he gave his final order. The first and second mates were to dress him in full military uniform and place him inside the lead casket placed alongside his bed. They were to carry the casket to the deck. As instructed, at exactly 10:48 AM, the lid was sealed, and the casket pushed overboard toward its final resting place on the seafloor.

During his life Drake was a deeply religious man who believed in the afterlife and is said to have spent countless hours contemplating applications of Pythagoras' theories regarding the transmigration of souls. Like Pythagoras, Drake believed that human energy did not die when the body lost its life but rose from the lifeless body and traveled to the heavens as the first step in its journey. In my trance state, I knew that as Drake's casket entered the water and began to drift downward, even as his life was slipping from him, his spirit began to rise and out of his body to begin the long voyage through both time and space that would eventually lead him back to Earth again.

As his life ebbed away, he thought back to his childhood, even to his birth during the total lunar eclipse of September 5, 1541. Then, after one last shudder, his body became still, and his soul escaped from the lead coffin and rose upward. He knew that if Pythagoras was correct, it would take 360 years for his life energy to complete all the phases of its journey back to the Earth, at which time he would be reborn to complete any unfinished business from the life that just ended.

The 2011 archaeological expedition never did find Drake's lead coffin, and I knew that no one ever would.

CHAPTER 28

Not Really the End

The financial meltdown and resulting real estate crisis dragged on well into 2011. During those years, the US economy remained weak, with few jobs to be had. While I was searching for work in 2009-2010, routine maintenance on my three houses was taking its toll on what little remained of my savings. Due to the housing downturn, Marin County lowered my property taxes. Still, despite their devaluation, for the three houses combined, I paid more than $30,000. Federal government programs to help struggling homeowners weren't available to me because all three houses were now non-owner-occupied rental properties. Eventually, the lenders initiated foreclosure proceedings and, in the end, took all three properties. Finally, there was no choice but to bite the bullet and declare bankruptcy. After doing so, I found a full-time position in, of all things, the real estate business, making a fraction of what I earned as a stockbroker.

The Golden Hind could carry 100 tons, and Drake took most of the gold and some of the silver back to England when he left Nova Albion. As described earlier, the remaining silver was mixed with clay to form the slurry that filled the arroyos and streambeds. When the land was leveled and graded as part of the residential construction in the 1950s, much of that silver slurry was bulldozed into heaps and carted off to who knows where. Some of what remained went into dumpsters when my backyard was landscaped in 1987, or up to the 16 to 1 Mine mixed in with the tons of stones in the three-thousand plastic buckets and one-thousand storage bins. Faceting of gemstones wasn't invented until after the 16th Century. By today's standards, known as the 4 C's (clarity, color, cut, and carat weight), all the precious stones left behind had no value because they were opaque.

CHAPTER 29

Portus Nova Albionis

My obsession with finding the treasure of Sir Francis Drake caused me to go bankrupt and move away from Greenbrae Ridge. So, I tried not to think about anything that happened during those years. But occasionally, I returned to locations I visited at the beginning of the adventure to see if I could find any additional proof of Drake's visit.

In 2018, I positively identified San Quentin as Drake's Landing Site. Near the Prison's West Gate, there is a short path that leads downhill to a small rocky beach. This beach is regularly used by windsurfers as a place to start and end their runs. There is a large sandstone rock formation that separates the rocky beach from the rest of the shoreline. When you view this formation from the roadway, it is apparent that the sandstone has been carved out to form a berth for the Golden Hind and a ramp to enter and exit the ship as the tide ebbs and flows. At low tide, I noticed a large rock with a hole bored through it. A few feet away, there were two large iron spikes driven into the bay floor. These spikes are only visible when it is close to low tide. These spikes were known as "mooring spikes" and were used by Drake to prevent the Golden Hind from floating away when the tide went out. Instead of using an anchor, a rope attached to the ship was passed through the hole in the rock and then wrapped around each of the mooring spikes to hold the boat in place. That day, the tide was already beginning to rise, so I returned the following day as the tide was going out. It took two hours of digging to extract one of the four-foot spikes. I left the other in place to evidence my discovery! The mooring spike is identical to those shown in the historical sketch of the careening of the Golden Hind!

There were other times that I looked at the Hondius Map for any additional clues I may have overlooked. In 2020, I saw an advertisement on Facebook for a T-shirt with words on it. When the shirt was folded in a certain way, it revealed a funny message. This gave me an idea! I cut the words Portus Nova Albionis out of the map. I placed each word above and below the others and even turned them upside down to see if that revealed anything. Then, I folded the words in half and repeated the process. I discovered that when the words were folded correctly and placed in the correct positions, a message was revealed. It was a series of numbers representing the longitude and latitude coordinates near the water tank at the top of the hill on Via Corona. After all the years I spent studying Drake's tactics, I knew that these coordinates marked the entrance to the other end of the tunnel and cavern system. However, I could not do anything about it because Rod Cooper still lived there.

Two more years passed, and I still lived in Marin County but was dating a woman whose home was in the East Bay. On nights I stayed with her, I crossed the San Rafael Bridge on the way home. I was on the bridge one Sunday in April 2022 when I had a premonition to drive to Via Corona and see if something was happening. It was nearly ten years since I lost my houses, and I was only back there one other time.

I turned onto the street and noticed that the garage door was open at the Cooper residence, and the garage was filled with boxes! Were they moving out? Perhaps Rod took a new job, and they planned to lease the house or even sell the property?

Intrigued, I went back two days later to check it out again. Now, the garage was empty, and a painting crew worked inside the house. That evening, I thought of possible sources of cash to buy the property to complete my hunt for Drake's Treasure. In the morning, I searched online to see if the house was listed for sale.

There it was! It was listed on the Multiple Listing Service (MLS) on Monday, and the asking price was $3MM. It was a "sellers' market," and properties in Greenbrae always sold quickly. Immediately, I called the listing agent to inquire about the listing but was disappointed when the agent told me that the Coopers already accepted an all-cash offer, significantly above the asking price. What a bummer!

The coordinates hidden in the words Portus Nova Albionis pinpointed the spot where I should look for another opening on Rod's property that would lead to the treasure. The labyrinth of tunnels and caverns on my property was merely a distraction and a time waster for the Spanish pursuers or anybody searching for the treasure. Since an offer was already accepted, I needed to wait until I could ask permission from the new owners to continue my quest. I asked the agent what the expected closing date was, and he told me that since it was an all-cash offer, it should close in 3-4 weeks.

That gave me an idea! The painters were almost finished, and when they did, nobody would be moving in for at least thirty to forty-five days. This was my chance! You may recall that after the backhoe incident, I never spoke to Rod again or had an opportunity to investigate the cascading boulders that started at the top of his property. Now, I could explore the property without any hassle, take pictures for further study, and look for the second entrance to the tunnel system according to the coordinates.

Two days later, the painters finished and were out of there. I parked in front of Rod's house and entered the property through an unlocked back gate.

For twenty years, the cascading boulders in that yard looked suspicious, and I wondered if the treasure might be buried beneath them. I cautiously made my way to the top of the hill, not wanting to be seen by any neighbors.

I was astonished to find all kinds of Sir Francis Drake markings at the top of the hill. The most incredible discovery was another large map rock depicting the area from the water tank down to the large map rock concealed by the bamboo thicket at one corner of 35 Via Corona. One side of this map rock showed the terrain when Sir Francis Drake arrived, and the other showed what it looks like today after Drake buried the treasure! I took pictures of the map rock and several boulders near it that could have been placed by Drake to conceal the second entrance to the system!

The next day, I returned with a crowbar to remove suspicious-looking boulders. I used the coordinates and the map rock to align myself with two promising boulders. The first boulder I pried off revealed nothing. However, upon closer inspection, I was pleasantly surprised that the boulder was not even a natural rock! It was composed of the same cement-type mixture that Drake used in other places I excavated.

I pried off the second boulder. Underneath it, there was not an opening to a cavern but another rock with the exact images shown on the large map rock. Years of experience told me this map rock marked the beginning of a tunnel section and was the spot to begin my new excavation! I took a picture and left the property to study the photo to figure out what direction to dig. I planned to return the following day with the equipment I needed.

I realized that I couldn't continue accessing the site through the unlocked gate to the backyard because one of the neighbors would see me, and I'd be in big trouble.

The same day I saw the garage filled with boxes; I drove around the neighborhood to see if there were any other changes in the area. I noticed a house on Via Colon directly below the water tank that appeared to be abandoned. The weeds in the front yard were four feet tall, the garage door was broken, and the gate to the backyard was knocked down. I figured a squatter must be living there.

I drove back to the abandoned property to check out the situation further. I entered the backyard and noticed a back door to the house that was ajar, and a light was on inside. The backyard was overgrown, like the front of the house. If I passed through that backyard, it would take me to the top of the hill next to the water tank and just feet away from Rod's fence.

It would be a challenging climb. First, there was a very tall, rickety deck with broken stairs and missing boards. After that, it was uphill through tall grass leading to the fence of the property line. That fence was broken down by earlier trespassers. Beyond that lay a thicket of overgrown shrubs, which ended at the steepest part of the climb. Somebody wrapped a thick metal cable around a tree so that you could pull yourself up that part of the hill to the water tank. From there, it was slightly downhill to the fence around Rod's backyard. I found a spot where I could pass under Rod's fence to enter and exit the site. The spot was hidden by surrounding bushes and not visible to utility workers or anybody who happened to be looking at the view from the top of the hill.

Access via the abandoned house was difficult, but after hauling my equipment, I was soaking wet from sweat and tired from the climb. I dug according to the markings on the map rock, but the ground was so hard that progress was excruciatingly slow.

I realized that a jackhammer was the only way to speed up my progress. However, that required electricity, and the only place to get it was from backyard electrical outlets at Rod's house or the abandoned house. The outlets at both places had power to them but were a long distance away from the hole. I purchased two 100ft extension cords, joined them, and plugged them into the outlet at the abandoned house. I was making great progress with the jackhammer when I decided to rest for a few minutes. I heard a noise and looked out from the hole. I saw a telephone lineman climbing a pole less than 75 feet from my excavation. I didn't make a sound or move a muscle, and after ½ hour, he was finished and left. I didn't know whether he saw me or not. Then, two days later, I heard men speaking in Spanish, and they were close to the hole. I didn't understand what they said, but they didn't stay long.

After these nerve wracking incidents, I decided it was better to work at night because nobody would be up there. I alternated my access route between Rod's backyard gate and the abandoned house. I left my house around 9:30 p.m. and worked till about 3 or 4 a.m.

The bottom of the hole was about eight feet below the ground level. I only used the jackhammer sparingly to keep the noise to a minimum. However, after several nights, I heard a neighbor yell, "What's going on up there," so I immediately stopped using the jackhammer. That night, around 2 a.m., I filled a duffel bag with most of my equipment and moved it down the steep hill, the rickety deck, and through the backyard to the front of the house. I walked down the street to my car and returned to the abandoned house. I threw the duffel bag in and breathed a sigh of relief.

The following morning, I returned to the site to collect any remaining equipment and dig a little more. At noontime, I heard the hollow sound below my feet and knew I was close to the entrance I'd been looking for. I texted my girlfriend to tell her what happened and let her know I was leaving to go home. I rested for a few hours and decided to try to get into the cavern again.

There was little doubt that the neighbor who yelled about the noise alerted the cops that something was going on up there. That night, I decided to access the site via Rod's gate, but when I tried to open the latch, it was locked! I got back into my car and drove around to the abandoned house. There, I found that the knocked-down gate was up righted, and it was locked!

CHAPTER 30

Winners Never Quit

Given my latest discoveries, nothing would stop me from continuing the quest! Once again, I needed to find a new access route. I drove around the neighborhood several times and scouted things out. I remembered that years ago, a water district easement passed alongside one house and then up the hill to the water tank. I went to the door of that house and asked the owner if I could go up to the tank via the easement. He told me it was no longer accessible from that easement because the water district fenced in the entire area. He added that now, they used a different easement up the street. I went to look, and sure enough, it was there but blocked by a locked gate and a no-trespassing sign. I checked it out thoroughly, and this route would be much easier than going through the backyard of the still abandoned house. I would only work at night and do everything with hand tools so I did not make any noise.

Since I was only working at night, during the day I contacted businesses that could clean up the Set of Tools that created the Plate of Brass. I found a Bay Area company that did electro-plating, and the owner was interested in the historical aspect of my inquiry. I delivered the tools to him and, a week later, picked them up. They successfully removed most of the rust and corrosion from the artifacts.

I took photos of the cleaned tools and enlarged the pictures. I now saw letters and numbers that were not visible before the tools were cleaned. I was sure that these marks were transferred to the Plate of Brass. When I first discovered the tools in 2002, I thought that a forensics firearm and toolmark expert should be able to match the "flaws" of the tools to the Radiograph of the Plate or a photograph of the original Plate. This expert would then be able to authenticate the set. It took several weeks of searching until I found an expert interested in working on this project.

For my own satisfaction, I repeated what I did twenty years earlier when I first found the tools. I purchased modeling clay, but this time, instead of rolling the roulettes across it, I used the ends of the Rod to reproduce the inscription on the Plate. It worked perfectly, and I sent pictures to the Firearm and Toolmark Expert. From their reaction, I could tell my work was impressive!

Next, I enlarged my copy of the photograph of the Plate of Brass to 400X magnification; I clearly saw letters, numbers, and images that could only have come from the roulettes and transferred to the Plate.

An Ah-Ha moment struck me!
The Plate of Brass served two purposes.

1. It claimed the land for England and,
2. It was a detailed map of the treasure site at the top of the hill where I was working.

The letters and numbers were Drake's code for the distances to where the treasure was buried and the type of "treasure" buried at those spots.

Before starting my new round of night work, I prepared a blank but signed the check and left it on my dining room table. This way, if I got arrested, my girlfriend could use it to bail me out!

I owned an old laptop computer bag, and every night, I loaded it with water bottles, dust masks, elbow pads, and dry shirts. The first night, I brought a small wrecking bar and rubber mallet. The rubber mallet was much quieter than a metal one. After dark, I put the bag in the car for the short ride to the site and parked near the easement. I climbed over the gate and made my way back to the site. This cavern was very narrow and filled with sharp rocks, making it challenging to move around. I collected the map rocks as I made forward progress.

I was already an expert at excavating the cavern according to the map rocks. When each section was completed, it was a work of art and looked identical to the rock.

I always believed that the image of the Golden Hind on the Hondius Map represented the layout of the treasure underground. The ship's square rigging showed the depth below ground, and the sails identified rooms where different things were buried. But how could I find the hidden entrance?

I enlarged the section of the Hondius Map with the sketch of the Golden Hind on it and cut out the picture.

I began folding and creasing it according to features that could only be seen on the magnified image of the ship. After many attempts, I got the folds right and solved this paper puzzle. As suggested by a video, the image looked like the Golden Hind from an entirely different perspective. The ship appeared as if you saw it from behind while sailing away! How appropriate!

I was working about eight feet below ground when I saw a very narrow hollow area about 15 feet long. It struck me that this space was the thin rigging that connected the ship's masts. Using this as a guide, I began excavating in the ship's shape. I used my phone camera to take pictures of my progress at the end of each night, and when I got home, I transferred the pictures to my desktop computer. Seeing the images on a large screen revealed details I did not notice while working. The walls were marked with N, S, E, and W, representing North, South, East, and West. Many numbers were embedded in the wall and arranged in the same pattern as the ones I identified on the magnified image of the Plate of Brass.

Twenty years earlier, I identified a mark on the map that represented the entrance to the tunnel system under the arch in my backyard. This symbol only appears twice on the map, and the second occurrence is part of the arm of the "man" standing next to the sketch of the Golden Hind. Every night, I kept my eye out for this marker. As my excavation progressed, I began to hear the same hollow sound in this excavation that I heard while working on my property. The entrance had to be close by!

The following night I was working in an area barely wider than my arm, when I noticed that the sun was beginning to rise in the East. I knew I needed to leave the site within a few minutes, so I stood back and looked at the excavation to assure myself that it matched the picture on the map rock I was using. There it was! The entrance marker that matched the arm of the "man" in the drawing of the Golden Hind. I gathered my equipment, hauled it back to my car, and smiled as I drove away,<u>Undoubtedly, the most impressive image was where the name Francis Drake was embedded in the rock!</u> I was in the right place.

I finally found the second entrance to the treasure!

CHAPTER 31

Drake's Toxic Legacy

During the years I lived on Greenbrae Ridge, I'd known a surprising number of people who either died from cancer or lived through the long hell of surgery, chemo, and radiation—the "slash, poison, and burn" of efforts at fighting it. My suspicion was that Drake's smelting operation was connected to these high cancer rates. This was the impetus behind my decision to have the groundwater and dust from my property on Via Corona tested. After reading that UC Davis used the most advanced scientific testing equipment available and their machine could identify trace elements that might cause cancer, I contacted Danielle Brand, the Manager of their Interdisciplinary Center for Plasma Mass Spectrometry Lab. I asked Danielle if UC Davis would perform "laser ablation" tests on my samples to see what toxic elements were present. I drove to Davis, bringing along the samples and the "Emerald Goddess," to introduce her to my theory regarding

Drake's visit. When we met the Department Head joined us. After I told them what I was doing then showed them the "Emerald Goddess," they enthusiastically agreed to perform the tests.

Back in 1937, Professor Harrison of MIT analyzed the composition of the Plate of Brass and reported the following results: Major constituents: copper and zinc; Minor constituents: magnesium, iron, and cadmium; Small amount: silver, silicon, and tin; Trace amounts: calcium, aluminum, manganese, and antimony.

The patina on the Plate of Brass included sodium, barium, boron, bismuth and strontium, all elements I suspected might be plentiful on my property and carcinogenic.

The UC Davis laser ablation test results showed extremely high concentrations of numerous toxic elements, some in groundwater, some in dust and some were in both samples. Here are the results in Parts per Million (PPM), and information regarding the natural occurrence of the compound.

ELEMENT	Water Results	Dust Results	Natural Groundwater
Boron	23700	Not Tested	< 10000
Lithium	None	7.08	
Beryllium	None	0.12	
Sodium	220	97.2	
Manganese	None	1.32	
Aluminum	None	0.41	
Calcium	2.39	156	

Potassium	22.4	0.2	
Vanadium	1110	13.2	None
Magnesium	501	90	< 100
Chromium	44.2	156	
Iron	357000	56	< 10000
Cobalt	None	9.48	
Nickel	3030	80.4	< 100
Copper	None	10.8	
Zinc	4710	40.8	None
Gallium	1020	7.56	< 1
Arsenic	1020	0.66	< 100
Selenium	None	0.2	
Rubidium	None	1.14	
Strontium	436000	32.4	< 10000
Silver	None	0.01	
Cadmium	None	0.04	
Barium	75600	74.4	< 100
Titanium	200	0.01	< 100
Lead	None	1.02	
Uranium	None	0.07	

My review and analysis of the results showed that specific elements were in disturbingly high concentrations on my property. I read research reports prepared by UC Davis and other major cancer research institutions that discussed health effects of each of the above elements. The reports also provided me with information about the levels and exposure pathways that represent the highest risks for cancer.

High cancer rates were a grave concern to the Marin County community. In 2002 the Marin Cancer Project was established to address the prevalence of Breast, Prostate, Colorectal, Bladder and Skin Cancer. The Project referred to its work as "The Search for The Cause," and has worked closely with numerous agencies across the US, focusing on the macro and community causes rather than family history and predisposition.

Among other things, the Davis Lab and Marin Cancer Project have reported that Boron concentrations in Marin groundwater are extremely high, something I already knew after my own Boron-poisoning. When I read this report, I took out the old MMWD Water Quality reports and did some calculations. My work showed that if only $^1/_{1000}$ of the concentration of Boron in the groundwater below my house made its way via natural aquifers into the drinking water reservoir less than two miles away, it represented nearly 100% of the Boron that was reported in the district's drinking water.

The results on the groundwater sample from my property indicated that the primary and secondary constituents of natural groundwater: sodium, calcium, magnesium, and potassium showed concentrations within the "normal" range. However, the same compounds were reported in extremely high concentrations in the dust.

The following chart highlights the 10 toxic elements that were found in the highest concentrations on my property, the organs/body systems affected by them and types of cancer resulting from overexposure:

Groundwater Sample	Organs / Systems Affected
Strontium	Liver, Bones
Barium	Kidney, Liver
Iron*	Kidney, Colon/Rectum, Liver, Skin
Boron	Breast, Prostate, Kidney
Zinc	Prostate, Kidney, Bladder, Colon/Rectum, Skin

*Excess Iron decreases the ability to fight all cancers.

Dust Sample	Organs / Systems Affected
Magnesium	Kidney, Liver
Calcium	Kidney, Colon/Rectum
Chromium	Prostate, Kidney, Colon/Rectum, Liver, Skin
Potassium	Prostate
Manganese	Prostate

The extremely high Strontium concentrations in local groundwater may be indicative of a more serious health issue. UC Davis reported that the kind detected in my property's dust was Strontium 88, one of four stable forms, i.e., non-radioactive. The health effects of exposure to Strontium 88 are identical to 84, 86, and 87, and include primarily problems with bone growth in children, especially if the diet is low in calcium and protein, as strontium tends to replace calcium in bone composition thereby weakening bone structure. Animal studies have shown that ingesting large amounts of any of these nonradioactive forms of strontium can be lethal, although in general that degree of exposure is unlikely. It remains to be seen what kinds of deleterious effects this exposure has on the children living on and around Greenbrae Ridge.

Next, I compared the Marin Cancer Project's map of Breast Cancer incidence to the details of where dust particles would blow if they became airborne in wind passing over Greenbrae Ridge. (Remember that Drake chose the ridge because every afternoon the wind was intense enough to enable his furnace to smelt metals.) I found that the areas with the highest cancer rates were directly in the path of that wind. Thus, hypothetically, if additional maps were prepared to show the distribution of the other four main types of cancers, I expected that those clusters would exhibit a high correlation with the same wind patterns. Construction and excavation activities associated with real estate development in the area have also stirred up and released the toxic dust, which then settled again on the surface of the surrounding land and dissolved in the water.

I have no doubt that the high concentrations of the elements listed below have played a significant role in the high rates of cancer in Marin County. The list also includes the contact medium through which Marin's cancer victims were affected, and the types of cancer in which each element is implicated:

<u>Barium:</u> Concentration in the groundwater is high. Barium affects the kidneys, colon, rectum, liver, and skin.

<u>Boron:</u> Concentration in both groundwater and dust is high. Boron affects the breast, prostate, and kidneys.

<u>Iron:</u> Concentration in both groundwater and dust is high. Iron affects the kidneys and liver; in excess, high concentrations decrease the body's ability to fight all cancers.

<u>Nickel:</u> Concentration in groundwater is high. Nickel affects the kidneys, colon, rectum, and skin. Excess nickel causes the over- synthesis of RNA & DNA and enables tumors to grow.

<u>Strontium:</u> Concentration in groundwater is high. Strontium 88 affects bone growth, especially in children.

<u>Vanadium:</u> Concentration in the groundwater is high. Vanadium affects the kidneys, bladder, colon, rectum, and liver. Excess Vanadium interferes with essential metabolic processes and enables tumors to grow.

I believe that the responsibility for the deposits of these toxic elements, rests squarely on the shoulders of Sir Francis Drake. During the smelting process immense clouds of noxious fumes and particulate matter arose from the smelter and were dispersed and then deposited over a wide area. The consequences and quantifiable impact of Drake's activities can be measured by the concentrations of primary, secondary and trace elements in Marin's air, dust and drinking water. His actions will continue to adversely affect the health of Marin's inhabitants for hundreds, if not thousands, of years to come, unless their presence on Greenbrae Ridge can be eliminated once and for all.

CHAPTER 32

There Are NO Accidents in Life!

EXCERPT FROM NASA CHART OF LUNAR SAROS
120 ECLIPSES

Date	Time	Type	Key Event
Sep 5, 1541	U4 11:47:40AM	Total	Drake's Birth
Oct 18, 1595	P4 10:48:06AM	Total	Drake's Death
May 24, 1956	P1 12:37:37PM	Partial	My Birth

*U4 is the time that the Moon's limb emerges from the Earth's shadow.

*P4 is the time at which the eclipse ends.

*P1 is the time at which the eclipse begins.

At the beginning of this book, I stated that there was a cosmic connection between Drake and myself. I will now explain what this means.

My birth was at the exact moment in astronomical time as the moment that Sir Francis Drake died. This needs some additional explanation. Here are the facts: Drake knew that Lunar calendars more accurately reflected time than the Solar calendars, and that the Julian system was more accurate than the Gregorian. The cycle of Lunar Saros 120 consists of 83 eclipses over a period of 1,478.47 years. The time in between the appearance of each eclipse in Lunar Saros series 120 is 6585.3 days. There were twenty such periods between 1595 and 1956. This constituted a total of 131,706 days.

Pope Gregory's decision to change the calendar in 1582 makes it difficult to determine actual dates occurring before September 15, 1582. NASA employs a method to convert Gregorian calendar dates into Julian calendar dates, but it is not the most accurate way to make this calculation. My own extensive research provided me with the optimal formula for making this conversion. Unless noted, this formula has been applied to all dates used in this book.

If you convert the Gregorian date October 18, 1595 (Drake's date of death) to a Julian Day Number and then add 131,706 days to it, you will arrive at the date May 24, 1956. However, according to my birth certificate, I was born on May 23, 1956, at 11:48AM. Under the Julian calendar system, the day started at 12 noon. Therefore, under the Julian system of time, I was born 49 minutes and 37 seconds before the start of the total lunar eclipse of May 24, 1956. Skeptics will say that this is just coincidence and stoics will say that the two times are not the same. Immediately following, I will show to the exact second that the time of my birth corresponds to the time of Drake's death at 10:48:06AM at the conclusion of the total lunar eclipse that occurred on October 18, 1595, off the coast of Panama.

The NASA system is based on the Gregorian calendar. This system uses 365.25 days per year, 1,440 minutes in each day and 31,557,600 seconds in a year.

Under the Julian system there are 362.25 days in a year, and 31,358,400 seconds in a year.

The difference between the NASA (Gregorian) and the Julian systems is 259,200 seconds.

This is a difference of 72.0 hours and equals the 3.0-day difference between the two systems.

Under both systems there are 4,320 minutes in 3 days

What accounts for the difference between 10:48:06 and 12:37:37?

There are two parts to the answer to this question. The first is that Drake died off the coast of Panama, which is one-time zone and one hour behind New York. Remember, time equals distance! If you add one hour to 10:48:06 you arrive at 11:48:06, which matches the 11:48 on my birth certificate. This proves my point down to 6 seconds.

In this example, I will use the end of the total eclipse on the date Drake was born. This is only 20 seconds from the rounded time of birth on my birth certificate. Eclipses have very specific measurements and NASA's chart identifies as 11:47:40 as the moment the eclipse entered the U4 stage. This is defined by NASA as the moment that the Moon's limb emerges from the Earth's shadow. The May 24 eclipse is listed as a partial eclipse, but at 96.47% it was the largest partial eclipse out of all 83 eclipses in the Saros 120. In addition, 11:47:40 falls into the range between 11:47:30 and 11:48:30. Any birth that fell within that minute could be recorded by the hospital as 11:48!

The last reason for selecting this moment is the adage, "the circle of life." Since Drake believed in the afterlife and there is a strong indication that his energy/spirit did return exactly 360 years after his death, this may lend credence to the term, "old soul" and provide a clue as to the timing of the "circle of life" on the Earth. If Drake was correct about the dodecahedral nature of the magnetic field, it would make sense that his energy would return to Earth at the exact same moment in astronomical terms as the moment of his prior birth. His energy would have completed the "circle of life" perfectly! Under this scenario, his return in 1956 needed to occur under the same conditions as his birth in 1541 and that would be when there was an inverse match in the amount of light being reflected by the moon. The most basic principle of Physics states, "Every action has an equal but opposite reaction." In 1541, Drake's birth must have occurred when the eclipse changed from total to partial as noted by the designation U4 on the NASA chart. At that moment, 3.53% of the Moon emerged from the Earth's shadow. In 1956, the opposite occurred. Within a few seconds after the eclipse began at 12:37:37 only 3.53% of the Moon was covered by the Earth's shadow. In the following calculations, I have assumed that these conditions occurred simultaneously.

The time 12:37:37 in the Gregorian system must be converted into the Julian system. Because the Julian system is 3 days shorter the adjustment must be subtracted from 12:37:37.

There are 12 minutes and 20 seconds between 11:47:40 and Noon and 37 minutes and 37 seconds between Noon and 12:37.37. This is a total of -2,997 seconds of time in both systems. Next, multiply the seconds representing the difference in time by the number of days in the Julian calendar. Then, divide the total number of seconds in Julian terms by the number of days in the Gregorian calendar:

-2,997 X 362.25 = -1,085,663.20

-1,085,663.20 ÷ 365.25 = -2,972.3838 seconds.

Next, divide the total seconds required to convert the Gregorian to the Julian system by 60 seconds per hour. This determines the number of minutes of the adjustment:

-2,972.3838/60 = 49.53973

Finally, it is necessary to convert the decimal above into seconds.

-.53973 x 60 = -32.3838 seconds

-49 minutes + -32.3838 seconds = -49:32 rounded.

12:37:37 − 00:49:32 = 11:48:05.

This still leaves 1 second difference. Light reflected off the Moon takes 1.3 seconds to reach our eyes. The Moon is 400,000 km from the Earth and the speed of light is 300,000 km/s, so the time taken is about 1.3 seconds. In Saros 120, all twenty of the eclipses beginning with 1595 and ending before 1956 were total eclipses so no adjustments were necessary, but the 1956 eclipse was a 96.47% partial eclipse. Therefore, a small amount of light was still being reflected by the

Moon requiring that it be added back to the number of minutes that converts the Gregorian to the Julian system. In this case, it is necessary to add back 1.25 seconds (1.3 seconds x .9647 = 1.25 seconds). -32.384 +1.25 = -31.134.

12:37:37 – 00:49:31 = 11:48:06. This is the exact moment of my birth and Drake's death. Simply converting the Gregorian to the Julian system accounts for the 00:49:31 difference to the second!

This is mathematical proof of my connection to Drake. Without his guidance, I wouldn't have located the tools or the treasure ... and I probably would have perished because of one of the deadly tricks! I have no doubt that Drake was trying to come back to Earth exactly 360 years after he died, and he did it! My obsession with him, my intense desire to complete his unfinished mission, my perseverance in the face of insurmountable obstacles all indicate that there is a circle of life on this planet that returns the souls of those who have passed before us, back to Earth.

For some, it may be apparent from birth. For others, it may take time to recognize. In my case, there were early indications that went unrecognized, and it took nearly forty-five years before it became clear that a part of my soul came from one of the greatest explorers and adventurers of all time...Francis Drake.

CHAPTER 33

The End

In case you're curious, let me assure you that there is nothing left to see at 35 Via Corona, or anywhere else along Greenbrae Ridge. The excavation sites have all been filled in and thoroughly cleaned up.

I wrote to the new owners several times asking permission to complete my twenty-two year project. After my third request, they tersely responding," We are not interested." I guess people who buy a house for $3.8M cash don't care about money!

Overall, I am quite content now, living in an over 55 Community less than ten miles from Greenbrae Ridge. These days, I have no need to second-guess myself about anything I did or anything that happened. I sleep well at night, knowing that no man has ever or probably ever will have the opportunity to experience this type of adventure or undertake the extreme measures and measurements that were required to put an end to all speculation regarding Sir Francis Drake's visit to Nova Albion in 1579. Nevertheless, there are still a few things

I would like to see happen to bring my efforts to full closure.

Here is my list:

1. I would like the Attorney General of the State of California to:
   - Investigate my claims regarding the theft of the Plate of Brass and bring the perpetrators to justice.
   - Exhume the body of Robert Power to determine if the cause of his death was arsenic poisoning.
2. I would like the US Secretary of the Interior to correct the National Register of Historic Places by removing Drake's Bay and replacing it with the San Quentin Peninsula as Drake's landing site.
3. I would like to return "The Emerald Goddess," a national treasure, to the people of Peru.
4. I would like to find a buyer—or an auction house willing to sell—the Set of Tools I found that were used to create Drake's, Plate of Brass.
5. I would like the scientific community to review Drake's discoveries related to:
   - The cause of "leap periods."
   - The cause of eclipses and their relationship to the dodecahedral nature of Earth's magnetic field.
   - The reversal of time for astronomical purposes.
   - Errors in the measurement of time since adoption of the Gregorian calendar.

6. I would like to be free of the ongoing surveillance by Kenneth Wagner, so I can conduct research online about whatever interests me and carry on phone conversations, etc., without feeling that at any moment, some new roadblock could be raised to impede whatever it is I am trying to investigate.

Final Advice to My Readers

The activities discussed in this book demonstrate the level of commitment it takes for any adventurer, explorer, researcher, scientist, or inventor to prove a theory or concept that seems impossible. Few discoveries and inventions come about by sheer accident. If you firmly believe that you have a great new idea or have made a discovery, do not be swayed by any negative feedback that you may receive from family, friends, colleagues, or other naysayers. Don't let roadblocks stop you, go around them! Continue forward and have no fear to take whatever actions are necessary to achieve your goal!

About the Author

Robert L. Stupack lives in Marin County, not far from his previous home on Greenbrae Ridge where much of this book takes place. He graduated from Penn State University in 1978. He received a B.S Degree in Accounting. While at Penn State he was the President of Colloquy, a student-run organization that produced Lecture series for the University community. He was a member of Delta Chi Fraternity (social) and honored to be a member of Skull and Bones and Omicron Delta Kappa. He worked as a CPA for Price Waterhouse before embarking on a career on Wall Street.

Discoveries of several Drake era artifacts motivated him to read everything he could find about Sir Francis Drake's life, his voyages and the unanswered questions surrounding his landing at a place he named, Nova Albion in 1579.

Armed with a copy of the Hondius Broadside Map of 1595, Stupack determined that Greenbrae Ridge was the site where Drake buried a massive treasure of gold, silver and gems taken from Spanish villages in South America.

Nova Albion and the Treasure of Sir Francis Drake contains almost 100 images that keep you in the action every step of the way. This is Stupack's first book.